Advance Praise for
Green Weenies and Due Diligence

"A way to laugh and learn the nuances of the business world—certainly you won't learn these in school, unless it is the school of hard knocks . . ."

DAN HANLON,
Chairman, CEO and Founder, Union Hill Ventures, Excelsior-Henderson Motorcycles

"Mandatory reading for all entrepreneurs, deal junkies, and rainmakers big and small!"

WILLIAM SANTANA LI,
Chairman and CEO, The NORTH Company

"Amazingly true-to-life. This book is a great tool for any business woman, whatever her profession."

NANCY WATKINS,
Former Mayor and NE Tarrant Chamber Board Chair

"This collection of terms cost me millions to learn over 30 years of investing, management and consulting. Sturgeon has accelerated that curve by 30 years short of a few hours. A must read for ANY business person, dealmaker, business student or investor."

GREGORY A. WINFIELD,
Greg Winfield Consulting

"Green Weenies, written by a successful self-made entrepreneur who understands the business complexities in the dialect of corporate jargon, while appreciating the humor (and sometimes absurdness) of the language we've created. An *insider's* knowledge with the refreshing perspective of an *outsider*. Entertaining, yet a valuable reference asset."

KEVIN R. SMITH,
Partner, Corporate Revitalization Partners

"Business is war, and the jargon from Sturgeon's latest work provides a tremendous edge. This required reading for success is highly recommended for those who seek that edge."

FRED P. MESCH, CPA,
Nation's Top Producer, H. D. Vest Financial

"For the seasoned industry veteran or department intern—this book has captured the shamefully funny 'lingo' of the boardrooms and war rooms in organizations across the globe. This book would make a perfect gift for the MBA grad!"

PAM LEWIS,
Associate Director for Development,
The University of Texas Medical School at Houston

"Visitors to another country find a phrase book invaluable when they don't speak the language. If you're venturing into the strange land of business, here's your phrase book. It will tell you what you need to know to sound like you belong there and aren't just a tourist. Green Weenies is the definitive guide to that language, and should be required reading in any MBA program."

BRIAN FARRINGTON,
Attorney (labor law)

"Green Weenies, a truly unique guide of business jargon that no businessperson should be without."

MIKE FARHAT,
CEO, International Business Consultants, LLC

"Ron Sturgeon reveals the secret language of the corporate madhouse with uproarious results in the most trenchant inside-track survey this side of Herman Melville's *Bartleby*. Gahan Wilson's cartoons capture ideally the nervous absurdity of the board-room demimonde."

MICHAEL H. PRICE,
Arts Editor, The Fort Worth Business Press

"Don't let any pencil brain (p. 44) tell you otherwise, but this book is all that and a bag of chips (p. 72). Green Weenies alpha dog (p. 7) Ron Sturgeon has peeled the onion (p. 44) on an area of business you won't learn about in any other book on the market today!"

JOSEPH R. MANNES,
Managing Director, SAMCO Capital Markets

"Knowing these terms would help any of our business customers become our best customers; the book contains intellectual properties that go beyond the mere price on the cover."

DAVID C. KENNY,
Chairman & CEO, RiverBend Bank

"Kudos to Green Weenies. Finally, a valuable tool for women that decodes the language of the 'old boy network.'"

CHERYL GEORG,
Principal, WorldGroup Advisory, Media and Branding Solutions

"As useful as it is entertaining; even the most experienced deal junkie will find new insights."

DON GLENDENNING
Attorney (corporate and securities),
Partner, Locke Liddell & Sapp LLP

"Ron's book is a work of remarkable and useful insight by someone who has toiled in both the trenches and headquarters."

WALT LEONARD,
Attorney (real estate and zoning)

"Green Weenies is not only a humorous, interesting and entertaining read, but also a helpful, serious and valuable overview of current business lingo. A must reference for the board room!"

GEORGE K. ELIADES, CAE,
Executive Vice President, Automotive Recyclers Association

"Thanks to the resourceful and imaginative Ron Sturgeon, we at last have a lexicon of business jargon, hilariously illustrated by the inimitable Gahan Wilson. Some terms will be familiar and some are relatively obscure, but they all serve to give the reader a piercing insight into both the humor and the ruthless nature of conducting business in America today."

STEWART ALCORN,
Market Manager, Frost Bank

"This is a MUST-HAVE reference book for any serious entrepreneur and businessperson—a very fun read."

MICHAEL T. QUINTOS,
Serial Entrepreneur and CEO, First Salvage

"I very much enjoyed both doing the drawings for this book and finding out that businesspeople are just as weird as cartoonists! I am really pleased with the way it came out and proud to be part of it. Well done!"

GAHAN WILSON,
Illustrator

Advance Reviews
5 Star Rating—Amazon's Highest Rating, from top 50 reviewers!

Every term you ever wanted to know but were afraid to ask
Reviewer: Grady Harp

Ron Sturgeon has accomplished far more than he set out to do . . . not only has he unraveled the secret terminology of big business, served up in an astute and often hilarious parody. Using a format that is incisive yet instructional . . . unearths the phrases and terms that make the corporate world sing and defines them then uses them in examples that not only are suitable but also poignant. . . . This is a treasure map . . . imaginative, and thoroughly entertaining. Sturgeon has enlisted the brilliant artist Gahan Wilson to make the whole book visually exciting. Bravo to Sturgeon for an ingenious concept well done! Highly recommended.

A primer on the secret language of business-speak
Reviewer: Daniel Jolly

Those entering the business world no longer have to negotiate the lingo ropes the hard way, as Ron Sturgeon has taken it upon himself to compile a whole book's worth of business jargon that will demystify some of the strange expressions you are likely to hear as you begin your journey up the ladder to success. The Due Diligence section contains short and effective definitions. Sturgeon's not your corporate suit-type; he's a self-made man who knows how to communicate on a level that even laymen can grasp. This book has information anyone can benefit from.

Entertaining introduction to industry jargon
Reviewer: Harold McFarland

Here to rescue the newbie is a compendium of terms and definitions from the world of business. This is fascinating reading. Done in an interesting style that leaves you unable to put the book down as you read entry after entry it is a fun and informative read. Green Weenies and Due Diligence is highly recommended for anyone in the business world who wants to understand the slang used in their industry.

GREEN WEENIES and DUE DILIGENCE

and **DUE DILIGENCE**

Insider Business Jargon —
Raw, Serious and Sometimes Funny

Illustrated by
Gahan Wilson

Business and Deal Terms From an Entrepreneur's Diary
That You Won't Get from School or a Dictionary

RON STURGEON

Mike French Publishing
Lynden, Washington

Published by
Mike French Publishing
1619 Front Street
Lynden, WA 98264
Voice: 360.354.8326 Fax: 360.354.3013
mike@mikefrench.com

For reseller information including quantity discounts
and bulk sales, please contact the publisher.

Library of Congress Control Number: 2005014456
ISBN: 0-9717031-1-6

Library of Congress Cataloging-in-Publication Data

Sturgeon, Ron.
     Green weenies and due diligence : insider business jargon—raw, serious and sometimes funny business and deal terms from an entrepreneur's diary that you won't get from school or a dictionary / Ron Sturgeon ; Illustrated by Gahan Wilson. — 1st ed.
        p.   cm.
     Includes index.
     ISBN 0-9717031-1-6 (hardcover)
     1. Business—Terminology.   2. Business—United States—Terminology.
3. Businesspeople—United States—Language.   4. English language—United States—Jargon.   5. English language—United States—Slang.   6. English language—United States—Terms and phrases.   I. Title: Insider business jargon.   II. Title: Business jargon.   III. Wilson, Gahan.   IV. Title.
HF1002.5.S78   2005   330'.01'4—dc22
                                                                        2005014456

Manufactured in the United States of America
10 9 8 7 6 5 4 3 2 1
First Edition

*Thanks to my three sons and all my friends
who accept and indulge my passion for
business and helping others, but mostly to
my lovely partner of 26 years, Kathi.*

Contents

SECTION ONE

Green Weenies

SECTION TWO

Due Diligence

Table of Illustrations

Credits and Acknowledgments

Thanks to the following for substantial contributions of terms and help:
Brian Nerney, Dixon Thayer, Greg Winfield, Karl Strand

Project Manager
Bette Filley

Senior Editor
Paula Felps

Marketing Manager
Brittany Scott

Research
Cindy Baldhoff

Cover design
George Foster
www.fostercovers.com

Interior design
Desktop Miracles
www.desktopmiracles.com

Publisher
Mike French
www.mikefrench.com

Editing
Erica Meeks, Zak Winfield, Worth Wren, Debra Pope, Kacee Silva
Michelle Woodbury Jones, Patty Quintanilla, Sharron Wagner
Lawanna Haddock, Jennifer Mills, Susan Cook

And to my consumer testing group, dozens of my
friends who voted, edited and advised on everything
from the cover design to the marketing campaign

Foreword

When Ron asked me to write the foreword to his new book, *Green Weenies and Due Diligence*, I was both pleased and honored. I have known Ron for about 20 years, and he is the ideal person to write this book. Ron is the kind of guy who, once you've met, you will remember for the rest of your life.

There are people who get things done, and there are people who have things done to them. Ron is the former; he's a doer. He started with nothing when his dad died while he was still in high school, and has become a success. He has done it by using his brains, imagination, clarity of vision and his boundless energy. Where others look at a situation and see chaos, he sees a pattern and a logical path to take. *Green Weenies* is much more than a book of business terms and their meanings. It is an introduction to a second language—one that can help you accomplish great things. Ron has that kind of vision, and it has led him to achieve amazing things.

The one thing the buyers for big book chains never want to hear is that your book is unique. They've seen so many thousands, probably millions, of books that they don't believe there is such a thing as a unique book. Well, I've got news for them. They'll see one when they see this book. There are many published dictionaries and tomes of quotations, but none on the lingo of the backrooms and boardrooms of America that are this complete. Business has a language of its own, and just as different languages have dialects, different occupations have their own wrinkles and variations of terms and expressions.

What makes this book particularly valuable, whether to a board chairman or young entrepreneur just entering the business world, is that it cuts years off the learning curve of understanding the language and terms of business. How often have we all been in meetings where a term is used that we didn't understand? To raise the question of its meaning would be to announce your status as a newcomer or neophyte and immediately put yourself at a disadvantage. The usual result is that the person not understanding the term decides to clam up rather than speak up and display their ignorance.

Ron is uniquely qualified to write this book, and his "bootstrapping style" gives him an unusual insight and approach to the topic. With only a high school education, he went on to field two successful stock offerings and participate in acquisitions and financings in the tens of millions of dollars. My motto for him is "mission possible," as he isn't afraid of anything or anyone, knows when to hold and when to fold, and has become a skilled negotiator.

In 1985 when I first met Ron, he hired me to do some consulting for his auto salvage yard. With my guidance he computerized the business. I went on to use him as an example of what was possible with determination and focus, as he used his ability and my advice to increase his sales over 100 percent within 120 days. I don't recall anyone accomplishing that before or since. Even back then, he was learning some of the words you see here, and was already quite colorful.

Over the ensuing years, I have enjoyed working with Ron. He displayed one of his many great personal qualities to me on our first visit. That is, that Ron never has been afraid to challenge himself. He has always taken any critical observations, whether from friend or foe, whether presented diplomatically or brutally, as an opportunity to draw a lesson from and to act upon. It is something that very few of us can do—separate the message from the messenger, clinically evaluate it, and take effective actions when the message has meaning. It is a lesson we should all take to heart. Ron's ability to articulate to others what he wanted, sometimes sarcastically, sometimes humorously, always passionately, are the building blocks embodied in these terms.

He is one of the most imaginative people I have ever met and is a genius at advertising and promotion. For example, when Ron decided to open a retail-only used part business, he gave away a free car every day for the first month. Image the excitement it generated! And how much did it cost him? Only about $100 a day, because the cars he gave away were ones he had bought as junk for as little as $50 each. The terms in this book leverage his creativity but they can also make you, the reader, more creative too.

From a distance, I watched Ron expand his salvage empire. One of his many talents is that he is very good at fund-raising and finance. I watched as he skillfully bought a world-class auto salvage yard from a failed public company venture in 1992, with them providing the financing. He really does know these words, what they mean, and how to use them. Used properly, some of the more humorous words can serve to disarm a skilled negotiator, setting up easier negotiations.

As his confidence built along with his vocabulary, Ron executed the best David and Goliath story I have ever heard. In 1997, when he believed that Automatic Data Processing (ADP) had completed a monopolizing acquisition of his computer system provider, he personally mailed letters to more than 4,000 auto recyclers nationwide, asking them to object if they thought the transaction was not in the best interest of competition. Always the self-educator, he studied up on antitrust law. The U.S. Department of Justice received 127 of the complaint coupons he provided his peers and opened an investigation into the transaction. At the Department of Justice trial, when the defendant's attorney asked Ron what he knew about Oracle, he told them he thought it was a planet. I suppose, even then, he could be a bit of a smart alec. To this day he will tell you that he didn't know what Oracle was then. He went on to tell them he was a junkyard dog, a "pothole in the information super highway." In the end, ADP paid a large fine and had to divest the company, loosing tens of millions of dollars. Remember, with the words here, determination and self-education, you too can do *anything*.

Ron went on to rally 320 recyclers to form a limited partnership with a UK company, to develop a new state of the art software program for recyclers, raising millions of dollars. Along the way, with self-study, he learned a great deal about computers and software, and, of course, more of the terms.

Ron sold his auto recycling empire to Ford Motor Company in 1999, and then went on to build a real estate empire. Then, as often happens, he and three other investors bought the subsidiary back from Ford; this included Ron's six original locations, along with 20 more across the U.S. The young "junkyard dog" had indeed grown up to become one of the alpha males in the industry.

And don't forget that his first book, *How to Salvage Millions from Your Small Business* is about to go into its third printing and has now been also published in four other countries.

Ron's legal experiences also exposed him to many of these terms, which he now shares with the world. By the way, he has always been incredibly generous and unselfish with others. It's an attribute that few have; most are proprietary and reclusive with their ideas, limiting themselves. Follow Ron's lead: Use the words here to expand your vocabulary!

Green Weenies and Due Diligence covers a variety of professions and occupations, and I have no doubt it will be welcomed by everyone who was ever too embarrassed to ask what a new term meant.

I especially recommend this book to any business student or person hoping to someday enter the world of business. In this book, Ron tells the story of how he was once admonished not to pass this information on to "outsiders." But again, that person didn't know Ron.

Today he is an incredibly successful businessman, but he has never forgotten the kid who made his first dollar with an old Volkswagen, and he never misses an opportunity to give those on the way up a helping hand.

Prepare to laugh your way through this book, both at the terms and the wonderful Gahan Wilson cartoons. I guarantee it will be the best read you'll have in a long time.

Remember, it's "mission possible," and the words that follow here are tools to help fulfill your dream. Enjoy this entertaining and educational tool. Try to picture Ron as I know him, and imagine him saying these lines in his irrepressible Texas twang when the appropriate business situation presented itself. I am sure you will see why I believe he is the perfect guy to write this book.

Most of us can learn a lot from Ron Sturgeon. Consider this the short course, and we can all consider ourselves fortunate that he's willing to teach it.

HOWARD NUSBAUM
Founder of an Inc. 500 company, and a business consultant/ troubleshooter for most of his life.

Introduction
A Few Words Before We Get to the Words

I suppose it seems odd for an individual such as myself to write a reference guide. I have no college education but lots of scars on my body from practical experience. Those of you who know me also know how passionate I am about business. It pains me to see people who can't seem to get it right and I have a real passion for helping the "little guy." I am proof that success can be obtained without all the college and that you really can be self-taught.

My dad died when I was a senior in high school and I soon had no place to live. He left me $2,000 for college and an old VW bug to share with my twin brother. I soon had a VW repair shop and was drag-racing VWs. I worked seven days a week, lived in a mobile home, and even then was passionate about business. I was like a sponge, soaking up every bit of information I could learn.

In 1977, six years out of high school, I had a chance to buy a mobile home park. My girlfriend told me if I bought it she was leaving me. I did, and she did. Oh well. Later, I branched into collision repair. I accumulated 35 wrecked cars that I was using for parts. When the city told me I had to move them, I rented a parcel of land, bought a portable building and opened a junkyard. (Later they became known as "recycling centers.")

During the early years, I met Brian Nerney and Clint Georg: mentors who helped educate me on financial matters assisting with everything from acquisitions and divestitures to lending, marketing and strategic issues. Clint helped me develop a marketing plan that was featured in *INC Magazine* in 1994. Starting with one employee—my twin brother—I grew the business to 150 employees in six locations across Texas with $15 million in sales. In 1999 I sold out to Ford Motor Company, growing the sales to $25 million in another 18 months. You can learn more about my past at www.autosalvageconsultant.com.

I am 51 now and still learning so much. If you don't feel that you are still learning, you have only yourself to blame. I hope that my first book, *How to Salvage Millions from Your Small Business*, challenged you to continue learning by reading the books that cover topics you need to understand better.

The idea for this book was spawned about six years ago when I first heard the term "green weenie." As I sat in on meetings with other dealmakers, including lenders and venture capital prospects, it became obvious that they had many words and sayings that the rest of the world likely didn't use or even understand. It was embarrassing to ask what they meant; because although some of the words were obvious in context, others were less apparent. I was soon using my Palm in meetings to record another word and partners would stop, laugh, and dutifully give me the definition. I would later ask folks I knew, or was referred to, for new words or words I might have overlooked. Road shows for lenders and equity partners provided many tense but exciting meetings. These folks are not shy, and some of the terms they used were carefully omitted from these pages.

Gathering these words from third parties was harder than I thought. When asked for examples, most people likely cannot think of more than one or two; get them in a high-level meeting, however, and they use them as a second language. They know the jargon and expressions intuitively, but can't just recite them.

I did my first private placement in 1998, just before Ford approached me about buying my business. Since it was done entirely in-house rather than using legal resources, I was mainly learning "serious" words like diligence, disclosure schedules, reps and warrants, as I worked on raising money and dealing with investors. I met Joe Mannes, who was an unbelievable resource for strategic planning and helping me prepare for raising money.

I was soon learning even more new words in the negotiations with Ford. Following that transaction, I continued working for Ford for another 18 months, and then did my second private placement to start a new auto salvage auction pool. Within a few months of opening we were contacted by Copart, the largest public player in that segment, who wanted to acquire us. The CEO of Copart, Willis Johnson, an old business friend, started his career in the auto salvage business as well. Soon we had sold to Copart and I had learned more words.

I look forward to continuing to expand the list. I still have an open Palm file and add words almost weekly. I will continue to update this book with all the new words I am certain to learn. I also look forward to hearing from readers with their updates for new words, or edits to existing definitions. You can email me at rons@greenweenies.com.

In one of my meetings with a venture capital firm, the principal noticed me recording a word. When he asked what I was doing, I explained my mission. He promptly admonished me, saying that the lingo, jargon and language they used had evolved over a number of years amid many millions of dollars of losses and, no doubt, profits. He went on to say that he thought newcomers should have to learn the hard way, the same way he had learned, and that introducing them to words that could give them any edge simply wasn't appropriate. Actually, what he said was "Don't give the bastards the words; make them learn the hard way." Needless to say, I did not heed his advice.

This business of transactions, financing, acquisitions and divestitures is stressful, and there are many colorful people involved. One thing is for sure, as a small businessperson or entrepreneur, you need all the help you can get. Knowing the right words will help you day to day, not to mention make you more colorful yourself. My partners always say they don't know where else they could get as much entertainment value as having me around.

And as I said when I started, I am still learning.

I have divided the book into two sections: the *Green Weenies* section, which has mostly humorous sayings, and the *Due Diligence* section, which has the serious words you are likely to encounter and need to understand. In both sections, I have loosely divided the sayings or words into chapters describing the areas of business where you are most likely to find them used or where they are needed the most.

I hope you enjoy reading and learning from this work as much as I enjoyed gathering the content.

RON STURGEON

Green Weenies

I have, of course, enjoyed writing the Green Weenie chapters the most. These are the terms that initially inspired me to write the book. There are, no doubt, hundreds more terms. In most cases I have added sentences illustrating how the terms are used correctly. I intend to make the book more complete when it's reprinted. Please note that at the end of the book I've furnished information on sending me new entries or clarifications.

1

Jargon and All the Stuff You Really Can't Do Without

Most of the terms in chapter one can be utilized in many parts of a business, so I haven't limited them to any one chapter.

Alpha dog—A natural leader. A person followed by others because of his or her personality, ideas, beliefs, charm, and/or charisma—not necessarily because of rank or position. On a dog sled team the first dog is the *alpha dog* because he is a good leader, even though he may not be the biggest or most powerful.

> USE: "The positive reactions to Mike's commanding presence during the meeting made it obvious that he's the *alpha dog* in our group."

Ambulance chaser—A derogatory term for a professional or service provider who pursues clients that were recently affected by a disaster. It's derived from personal injury lawyers who follow victims to the hospital from the scene of an accident.

> USE: "I can't believe Susan temporarily moved to San Francisco to find clients who want to sue their insurance companies after the big mudslide. She's such an *ambulance chaser*."

Arrow has left the bow—A remorseful or angry way of saying that it is too late to make a change in a deal, project, or operation due to the failure to anticipate the results. (See also: *shoot and then aim* and *toothpaste is out of the tube*.)

> **USE:** "Ted commented that by the time the agency's marketing and distribution plan had been approved and implemented, *the arrow had left the bow*, and perhaps consumer-testing in more markets should have been conducted first."

Arrows in the/your back—Describes the state of bold and daring thinkers, leaders, and risk takers. A lot of arrows go flying in business. Leaders with *arrows in their backs* have a lot of experience; some of it good, some bad, some expensive, but all of it is valuable. (See also: *scars on my body* and *dirty fingernail person*.)

> **USE:** "Having all those *arrows in our backs* is an expensive way to learn that we can't always buy real estate and turn a profit. There are too many market variables that can change."

I tell you about **rules of engagement**, but not the rules of marriage or divorce. Sound confusing? No not really, and you can discuss with your wife or girlfriend, it's not an issue at all, see page 210.

Assholes and elbows—Refers to people having their head down working VERY hard. As in a sinking boat, all one can see are their butts and elbows as they bail water out.

> **USE:** "The situation got so tough as we got closer to the deadline that it became *assholes and elbows*."

Bake your noodle—Provide a service needed, usually as an extra or favor.

> **USE:** "Brian asked David, 'If I *bake your noodle* and prepackage the part, then will you buy it?'"

Balloon—Synonymous with an idea or concept; often represents out-of-the-box thinking. A *balloon* is floated in the same way that a *straw man* is presented, so it can be shot down if the idea is weak or doesn't make sense. (See also: *out of the box* and *straw man*.)

> **USE:** "Sylvester, our doggedly persistent *balloon* guy, floated several ideas at our staff meeting, but most of his *balloons* on boosting efficiency were rejected as unworkable."

Banana problem—A project so simple that a big, dumb gorilla could handle it. Commonly used in the industry in increments of "one banana" for very easy and "two banana" for easy.

> **USE:** "What's taking him so long to get your office set up? It's a two *banana problem* at most."

Baptism of fire—A difficult situation faced by a company or individual that will result in either significant success or failure. Examples include Initial Public Offerings (IPOs), a new CEO hired to manage a struggling company and hostile takeover attempts. A person surviving a *baptism of fire* is indeed a leader and survivor.

> **USE:** "Pete, having saved at least five plants from closure, had surely proved that he could survive a *baptism of fire*."

Be careful what you ask for, you just might get it—Almost literally what it says. Be cautious about what you seek or demand because you might get it and it might not turn out the way you expect. I served on the board of an Internet game company that desperately wanted a shot-in-the-arm influx of new subscribers. Unbeknownst to the company, Microsoft named the firm's latest creation the "Game of the Day" and posted the honor prominently on the Microsoft website. In one day, more than 100,000 people tried to download the game, causing the firm's server to shut down, thus disconnecting the firm from the web, which is not a good thing when trying to earn a livelihood online. (See also: *dog chasing and catching the car.*)

> **USE:** "In my early negotiations with Ford Motor Co. I told my friend and negotiator Brian to tell Ford 'to shove it.' He quickly asked me if that was what I really wanted. Brian warned, '*Be careful what you ask for, you might just get it,*' and pointed out that I was risking a lot with my words, as Ford might walk away forever."

Bee with a bone—An individual that is obsessed with something which is none of his concern, and which is likely way out of his league. Imagine what it must be like for a bee planning on carrying a bone, now that's an impressive goal.

> USE: "Jerry is a real *bee with a bone*. He's only an intern, but he complains about our recent executive restructuring."

Belt and suspenders—The extra resources needed to support an ambitious or difficult business plan. Extra research, for example, would be the *belt and suspenders* to provide macro analysis of all the items in a budget. Once such analysis is complete, you can rest assured that the numbers or other findings are correct and won't let anyone down. It also refers to the need for a *Plan B* (a backup plan or safety net in case of failure). It can also describe a really helpful person or team, as they can indeed be the *belt and suspenders*; without their implementation skills, the plan may fail. (See also: *Plan B*.)

> USE: "Although the manufacturing division had all the required capability for our new product lines, the distribution channels would surely need a *belt and suspenders*, including more trucks and drivers, as this division was low on several resources."

No a **Tranche** isn't where they put
Uncle Joe after he passed, see page 262.

Between the devil and the deep blue sea—A decision-making situation when all alternatives are unpleasant or undesirable. This is similar to being between a rock and a hard place and is also called a "Hobson's choice." Indeed, would you rather have a meeting with the devil or the deep blue sea? (See also: *devil you know is better than the one you don't, probable death is better than certain death,* and *pile of shit that stinks the least.*)

> USE: "We were faced with continuing the old product line that was still breaking even, or dumping it and starting over with a more expensive but more promising lineup of new products. We were caught *between the devil and the deep blue sea*."

Bigger than a breadbox or smaller than a car—Often used to describe costs, a market, or other operating factor when it's unknown or uncertain. The term can also be used to discuss an opportunity or threat when little is known about it. It is typically said when giving instructions, such as an attempt to help with researching or understanding the situation, so that the next steps can be decided. I often use this term when someone tells me something should be low cost, as "low cost" can be subjective. In an early-stage discussion, understanding whether the item is *bigger than a breadbox or smaller than a car* can sometimes end a discussion and prevent wasted energy.

> USE: "Greg thought the idea of selling the add-on product was a good one, but no one really knew whether the market was *bigger than a breadbox or smaller than a car,* so more studies were needed to decide if it was feasible."

Binaca blast—Derived from the popular breath freshener of the 1970s. In business, it describes a "bomb" event or announcement or other occurrence that comes as a "breath of fresh air." It is almost the opposite of a *turd in the punchbowl.* (See also: *turd in the punchbowl.*)

> USE: "The introduction of sexier and sportier hybrid electricity-gasoline powered vehicles is a *Binaca blast* which has re-ignited America's love affair with cars."

Bio break—A restroom break during a meeting. Need I say more?

> USE: "Wouldn't you know it, all day at work I passed by the restroom several times and didn't have to go, but the one hour that I have a meeting, I couldn't hold it—I had to take a *bio break.*"

Blind man and the elephant—A metaphor for not seeing the whole picture, assuming that the part you are in touch with is representative of the whole. It is derived from the story of the same name by Rudyard Kipling. (See also: *close to the trees, can't see the forest for the trees, weatherman syndrome, open the window and see the weather, sitting on the nickel,* and *chasing nickels around dollar bills.*)

> USE: "His situation was just another case of the *blind man and the elephant,* claimed Ken Lay of Enron fame. He said he was guilty of not seeing the whole corporate picture and was under-informed or misled by others who committed the fraud."

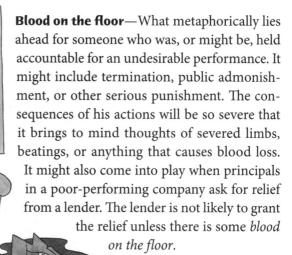

Blood on the floor—What metaphorically lies ahead for someone who was, or might be, held accountable for an undesirable performance. It might include termination, public admonishment, or other serious punishment. The consequences of his actions will be so severe that it brings to mind thoughts of severed limbs, beatings, or anything that causes blood loss. It might also come into play when principals in a poor-performing company ask for relief from a lender. The lender is not likely to grant the relief unless there is some *blood on the floor.*

USE: "When Mr. Dell hears that 15 percent of his brand-named PCs are crashing in the first year of service, the *blood on the floor* will be that of the quality control staff."

Boil out—Take some action in order to determine something. (See also: *bake-off, beauty contest,* and *last man standing.*)

USE: "We need to *boil out* our best candidate for the CEO position."

Booth bunny—A disparaging name for an attractive woman that is hired to work in trade shows.

USE: "GM had more *booth bunnies* than all the other exhibitors combined. You would think their female marketing executive would notice what other companies are doing to attract buyers—building better cars!"

Break your pick—Fail to complete a tough or perhaps impossible business goal. It is usually a task that many have tried but failed at doing, so their picks are likely still stuck in the rock. Lessons learned from previous failures can be very valuable. Where many have broken their picks, extra care and planning is needed, and the probability of success is low.

USE: "Many marketers have tried to understand what the ultimate customer niche is, but all have *broken their picks* on this classic business puzzle."

Buttoned up—Refers to a plan, a company's financial health, or even a person's background or operating philosophy that has been thoroughly vetted, researched, or documented. Such a reference is generally good, as *buttoned-up* items or persons are carefully prepared and don't spring many surprises. Some of my colleagues accuse me of being anal, but I think I am just *buttoned up*. (See also: *vetted* and *sand below our feet*.)

USE: "We've done our due-diligence homework to ensure that we're *buttoned up* on this acquisition."

Can't be the arms and legs—A caution usually issued by an executive or manager indicating that although he can make a plan, he cannot do the work to implement it. "Arms and legs" refer to those workers and resources that will do the real work of implementation. Often there is a need for more *arms and legs*.

USE: "Brent said he could train the top sales administrators in new selling skills, but *could not be the arms and legs* to make sure the required follow up and sales successes were achieved."

Chair plug—Someone who attends meetings, but contributes nothing.

USE: "Geoff never gives us his opinion. He's not much more than a *chair plug*."

Changing the tires while the car is going down the road—Refers to making adjustments in the fast-paced business world. Often the rapid pace does not allow for measuring results before plotting the next step, so the next moves must be decided while the venture plows ahead. In a perfect world, cars and business would stop for changes and decision-making. (See also: *drinking from a fire hose.*)

> **USE:** "Our sales turnaround was so intense that we were often *changing the tires while the car was going down the road,* making alterations before we even knew the effects of our last changes."

Chew on my leg—A commentary or action focused on the foolishness or erroneous thinking of an associate on the wrong side of the argument. When your cause is lost and you nonetheless continue to defend the "wrong side," you had better be ready to have your boss *chew on your leg.* It can also refer to management constantly demanding better performance, more data or reporting, or other changes or improvements by one or more associates. The process is typically, but not always, associated with an insufficiently performing company, department, position, or employee.

> **USE:** "Don't *chew on my leg* as you have for the last 10 months regarding our production cost per unit, which has already beaten your goal."

Chipmunking—This describes someone in a meeting holding a hand-held device, feverishly typing with their thumbs, perhaps sending a text message or entering data. (See also: *thumb expert.*)

> USE: "David wasn't paying attention to the projection charts, he was too busy *chipmunking* on his Treo or Palm."

Close enough for government work—A snide remark applied to something that likely isn't of the highest quality; but since *government work* is even worse, it's adequate.

> USE: "Sarah commented that the trim and paint work, which was definitely substandard, was *close enough for government work.*"

Were you a boy scout at one time? Are you still a **boy scout** in your heart? Are you sure that's a good thing? Check it out on page 132.

Close only counts in farts, grenades, atomic bombs, horseshoes and pregnancy—I suppose this one is self-explanatory, but the bottom line in executive circles is that "close" doesn't really mean very much in most endeavors and is generally unacceptable. In short, you either achieve the success you planned for or you don't. In any of the above events, close does count, but not in any other instances. I leave it to your imagination to coin a sentence, but it is really a good way to tell others that "close" will not be accepted.

Close to the trees or Too close to the trees—A reference to being too close to an issue, problem, operation or project to have an overall view of the picture solution, impact, benefits or drawbacks. It's a condensed version of "can't see the forest for the trees." When you're six inches from a tree, what do you see? The bark, of course. But you do not have a clue about how many more trees there are or what you're getting into. (See also: *blind man and the elephant, weatherman syndrome, sitting on the nickel, open the window and see the weather, can't see the forest for the* trees and *chasing nickels around dollar bills.*)

> USE: "You're so *close to the trees* that the daily operating woes prevent you from seeing one of your employees failing to do his management job."

Coasting will only get you to the bottom of the hill—Applied to slackening efforts and work habits or overly cautious and passive business plans. Those that coast on their "laurels" or past successes will get somewhere, but only *to the bottom of the hill*, not to the top of the next hill. (See also: *coast.*)

> **USE**: "We've had great success with our aggressive sales promotions, but your new strategy amounts to *coasting, and that will only get us to the bottom of the hill.*"

Color commentary—As in sports announcing, a utility term used like a vocal footnote. It's added description, musing or clarification during a discussion or conversation. Adding some color to a black-and-white drawing adds character and makes the drawing more interesting or informative.

> **USE**: "Following the sales talk, Joe's *color commentary* included an insightful observation regarding how many fast-talking salespeople hit their sales goals but fail to maintain margins."

Company cholesterol—The buildup of information, staff, or other bottlenecks that impede a company's ability to perform.

> **USE**: "The Chief Restructuring Officer said he had never seen so many excess employees and it was no wonder *company cholesterol* had dramatically slowed down the decision-making in every department."

Cone of silence—From the old TV series, "Get Smart." You remember, right? Secret agent Maxwell Smart would meet with his colleagues under a large glass dome so that only the party he was talking to could hear what he was saying.

> **USE**: "The VP of HR Donna called her friend Lori, an HR director at another company, to verify a job reference. Lori gave her the straight story, but told her to keep it under the *cone of silence*, as the company wasn't supposed to release that information."

Cool hunting—Searching out younger prospects while conducting market research in order to see "what's cool."

> **USE**: "Apple spent lots of time and money *cool hunting* before they finalized the design of the iPod."

Corvette to buy milk—Used to describe a system that is very robust and probably expensive, but underutilized. If a new printing press costing $750,000 only runs two hours a day, it's a good example of this situation.

> USE: "The new computer system was very powerful and was capable of doing much more than we could utilize. I know management said they bought an impressive one, but it seems to me like it's like having a *Corvette just to buy milk*."

Did you find a mistake in one of the terms?
Or just want to add additional "color" to the definition?
Submit it to keep all of us better informed
at **www.greenweenies.com**

Crash the car—It is roughly what it sounds like and obviously not a good thing. *Crashing the car* can be causing the company to fail or taking an initiative that has failed. Usually a car has a single driver who's responsible for the crash, and that applies in the business context as well: someone is accountable for the wreckage.

> USE: "When the director from corporate came to visit, we knew the purpose was to find out who *crashed the car* and made all of our profits drop."

Crusader—Similar to an evangelist, it is a person who crusades for a cause. (See also: *evangelist.*)

Curing cancer—Typically used to describe an initiative that is impossible or just too difficult to achieve; tantamount to finding a *cancer cure* or negotiating world peace.

> USE: "Considering how few employees we have, our boss is asking us to *cure cancer* with his unrealistic demands."

Cutting the dog's tail off one inch at a time—Typically used as a warning, as in *never cut the dog's tail off one inch at a time*. It would be torture to a real dog, and eventually the critter is likely to retaliate. The term is often used to warn against administering adverse or traumatic change a little bit at a time. Such prolonged "treatment" or agony can have negative consequences. Obviously this method should be contrasted with doling out too much change at once. (See also: *shovel instead of a spoon*.)

USE: "When someone needs to be terminated, don't *cut the dog's tail off one inch at a time* by demoting him continuously until he quits; just make the cut quickly and humanely."

Dance with the one who brought (brung) you—Stick with the lender, vendor, business partner, executive or investor who has a proven track record of contributing to the success of your ongoing venture. Sometimes we have no choice but to change our close associates, but in general we should remain loyal to, and if necessary, patch things up with, "them that brung us" as the old codger might say. (See also: *don't change horses in midstream.*)

USE: "If you *dance with the one who brought you*, you're likely to have a business and personal friend for life, as well as a valuable asset in your company."

Death from a thousand cuts—Termination of a proposed deal for many small reasons as opposed to one major cause. Following the drafting of a letter of intent, deal proposals don't usually fail because of only one issue or barrier. More often, it is a multitude of issues or problems that lead to the failure to reach agreement. It can just as easily refer to any plan or person that fails, not because of one misstep or problem, but because of a confluence of many factors or events. (See also: *last straw.*)

> USE: "Following months of negotiations, the merger proposal suffered a *death from a thousand cuts,* although there was no single deal-breaking component."

Burping the elephant, now that sounds messy, right? Wrong, see page 158 for the gruesome details.

Devil you know is better than the devil you don't—Your existing associates may not be ideal, but a new arrangement could be even worse. It is sometimes better to deal with familiar problems than to replace them with a new, possibly more troublesome, batch. (See also: *don't change horses in midstream, pile of shit that stinks the least.*)

> USE: "He didn't like either employee's performance, but he had to make a choice, so he decided that *the devil he knew was better than the one he didn't,* and kept the one that he knew was at least capable of producing the goods."

Dirt in the oyster—A gem that is just waiting to grow and be discovered.

> USE: "Our widget is *dirt in the oyster.* It just needs some tweaking."

DNA—What made the company successful in the first place; the business roots or origin of what made you flourish.

> USE: "Dave knew if we could stop adding product lines unrelated to our core business and get back to focusing on our *DNA,* we would achieve record profits."

Dog chasing and catching the car—Ever wonder what a dog would do with a car if he caught it? Imagine the dog hanging onto the tailpipe, then taming and controlling the car! A similar scenario often arises in business. It is easy to be excited about a pending transaction, but after the deal closes, realizing that you must actually execute on the plan can be overwhelming, like *drinking from a fire hose*. (See also: *be careful what you ask for, you might get it.*)

> **USE**: "We closed the deal for the delivery of additional parts, and then, like a *dog chasing and catching the car*, we suddenly found ourselves actually working through the logistics of cramming 15 trailer loads per day into our tiny warehouse."

Dog's breakfast—An outcome that is far from the desired results. More broadly, it can refer to any outcome, process or practice that causes problems or is not up to standards.

> **USE**: "When we discovered our advertising campaign was offending a large sector of our market, we knew we'd be eating a *dog's breakfast* once the quarterly report came."

Dog years—A derogatory reference to the amount of time someone spends on completing a task. Dog's age at a ratio of about six years per one human year, so that employee is being accused of taking six times as long as necessary to complete a task.

> **USE**: "Ted said he had applied for the permit at the city over six months ago and it should have been done in one month at most. But, he opined, 'They do everything down there in *dog years*.'"

Don't change horses in midstream—(See also: *dance with the one that brought you.*)

> **USE**: "Even if you are frustrated by the slow pace of progress, *don't change horses in midstream*; stick what is working for you instead."

Don't change the dog food without talking to the dog—In other words, do not go to the market with your new product or service (or change the existing one) before you fully understand what the customer wants. (Note: Do not ever let the customer know you're referring to him or her as a dog.) It can also describe making personnel policy changes that might adversely affect employees without thinking through the changes first.

> **USE**: "We knew we had *changed the dog food without talking to the dog* after sales plunged on our revamped formula, which we had not consumer tested well enough."

Don't have a dog in the fight—No direct involvement or stake in a business conflict or a pending action. When the fight is on or soon to start, sometimes it is better to just steer clear, especially if you don't have anything to win or lose. Whether it is a feud between department heads, bosses and subordinates, or competing companies, it might be better for you to just ignore it. It can also refer to a situation that you simply don't care about, as you have no stake in the outcome.

> **USE**: "I could see the board fighting over firing our marketing chief, but since I didn't know him or *have a dog in the fight*, I didn't really care."

Don't leave for Chicago until all the lights have turned green—A pejorative term for one who can never get started. Wait until all the lights are green before leaving for Chicago. All the lights are never green at the same time, so you would never leave. This describes someone who is afraid to start on a venture and is hyper-cautious to the point of dysfunction.

> **USE**: "Jim will never pull the trigger and close on this deal. He won't leave for Chicago until all the lights have turned green".

Give copies of ***Green Weenies and Due Diligence***
to your customers, employees, even vendors!
We can personalize the cover with your company's information.
Any sophisticated business associate will love this gift!

Don't (or can't) know what you don't know—It is easy to make big plans and think you've covered all the business bases, but you can't know everything, and what you don't know can hurt you. You won't notice that a piece of knowledge you never knew about is missing. In order to plan thoroughly and ask pertinent questions, you must have a basic grasp of the subject, and always be aware that more information might be needed. Never assume that you've already covered every angle. The real solution is to be more collaborative; bring in more people to *pick their brains,* and as I always say, do more "consumer testing" by asking others what they think.

> **USE**: "The launch of disposable diapers worldwide was well planned, but since Bill *didn't know what he didn't know,* sales in Korea only trickled. That's because the product's brand name means 'trash' in Korean."

Drinking from a fire hose—A situation where there is more work to do than any human can accomplish. I learned this term firsthand in several of my ventures. Imagine trying to cope with your mouth clamped to a running fire hose. It's a vivid description of business at its most intense level and particularly applicable to turnarounds. (See also: *coming up or going down, changing the tires while the car is going down the road.*)

> USE: "The CEO was *drinking from a fire hose*; all of his company's departments were failing, and since the CFO had abandoned ship, he now had to fill those shoes, too."

Dry hole—A speculative venture that turns out to be a huge loss. This originally referred to an oil well that cost a huge amount of money to drill, but didn't yield a single drop of oil. Now used to describe any fruitless business initiative.

> **USE:** "Everyone knew it was a *dry hole* when they saw the quality of the employees; they couldn't execute on anyone's plan."

Eat the elephant one bite at a time—Either solely undertake the mammoth project in its entirety or head toward the monstrous goal one step at a time while delegating some of the responsibilities to others. Big projects and goals can be intimidating, but you have to start somewhere. For instance, to resolve a quality issue caused by problems in multiple departments, one must: choose a starting point, progress logically through one problem before trying to tackle the next one and follow the same pattern across each department, one at a time.

> **USE:** "Keith knew that it wasn't going to be easy penetrating the national wholesale market, but he vowed to *eat the elephant one bite at a time* by systematically calling on every potential customer."

Eating your own dog food—A company testing a product on itself.

> **USE**: "We've got to *dog food* that product before selling it to the general public."

Elvis year—This is the year that a product, service or employee thrives. As years go, it's the king!

> **USE**: "Profits are up, spending is down, this is our *Elvis year*!"

Emotionally invested—Committed by heart and pocketbook. Being financially invested is one thing, but the ultimate commitment to success requires *emotional investment* as well. *Emotional investment* is empowering, and when there is a failure, the heart suffers a loss as well as the pocketbook. Investors in public companies hold financial stakes but have no opportunity to be *emotionally invested*. (See also: *skin in the game* and *head in the game*.)

> **USE**: "Monty had bought some shares in the ESOP (employee stock option plan). However, he wasn't *emotionally invested* because he didn't care how the company produced results so long as his stock didn't lose value."

Surgical hiring—sounds painful, and expensive.
Is it really? See page 212 to find out.

Emperor's new suit or Emperor's new clothes—From the Hans Christian Andersen fairy tale of the same name. In the original story, con artists convince the emperor that the beautiful clothes they are tailoring for him are invisible to people who are foolish or unworthy; of course there are no clothes at all, but no one in the town is willing to admit that they can't see them. The term now refers to anyone who goes along with something which is obviously incorrect in order to avoid appearing stupid or out of step. Once they are forced to face the sham, people generally act even more convinced of their decision.

> **USE**: "Even though the rest of them wanted to go along with the pretense, I could see through the *emperor's new clothes* right away."

Empty shirt or suit—A person who has nothing important or meaningful to say, or isn't as smart as they act and thereby has little or no credibility. An *empty shirt* or *suit* doesn't communicate valuable information. He is a real "nowhere man" who gives the impression of being important, but has no substance; there may as well be no person in the suit at all. (With a nod to the Beatles.) (*See also: all hat and no cattle.*)

> **USE**: "The guys from corporate seemed like *empty suits*, because they weren't listening to us; what they talked about accomplishing simply wasn't achievable, and everyone knew it."

End zone—Just as in football, this is the place where you score. Refers to the point one wants to get to, or the end point that one actually did get to.

> **USE**: "After months of striving for his sales goals, he finally reached the *end zone*."

Evangelist—Someone who is always spreading the news about the company, much like a preacher. Anyone with a zealous belief in the company and the product. (*See also: crusader.*)

> **USE**: "Sammy was so proud of the company and the new line of dishwashers, he was the best *evangelist* we ever could hope for. He sold more by word of mouth than the advertising did."

Eye candy—Any type of graphics used in packaging, marketing material or on a website to make it look better. I know, I know, you thought I was going to use it in a sexist form, but that's old news.

> **USE**: "The website had the best *eye candy* I had ever seen. The pages flowed, and the ordering process was crisp and friendly. There was not one sexy girl on the site, and it worked great."

Feed the ducks when they are quacking, don't look for ducks to feed—Used in regards to looking for investors or partners. You would always rather have them come to you hungry than chase them around with the bread. Be ready for investors when they come to you showing interest, don't go after them trying to sell.

> **USE**: "Brian advised, rather than trying to go to every potential lender, that we should *whisper down the lane*, as it was a small community of prospects and we should let them come to us. Then we could *feed the ducks when they are quacking*, rather than just looking for ducks to feed."

Filling in the potholes—Tactics or strategies implemented in a defensive mode to redress strategic weaknesses. The term also refers to correcting unexpected problems in a plan or operation. Potholes often appear with little or no warning, and if not repaired (or filled), they grow to be big problems.

> **USE:** "The mechanics spent many extra hours *filling in the potholes* caused by the lack of a preventive maintenance program."

Financial gigolo—A prominent person who is recruited to serve on a board of directors solely to bring credibility; he only does what he is asked and poses no real threat to management. It was coined by future U.S. Supreme Court justice William O. Douglas in 1934.

> **USE:** "Everyone knew when Clinton's ex commerce secretary was appointed to the board of our diaper subsidiary that he was just a *financial gigolo* and would do whatever the president of our division wanted. He darn sure knew nothing about diapers."

Flying circus—A tour of operations or a *dog-and-pony show* by executives on an airplane. It often pokes fun at their attempt to justify the cost of the corporate jet. (See also: *dog-and-pony show*.)

> **USE:** "We knew the *flying circus* would leave the corporate headquarters when we heard that they were going to be making a follow-on stock offering."

Foam the runway—A last-minute loan or capital infusion arranged by a company about to run out of money. Without "foaming the runway," their plane will certainly crash and burn.

> **USE:** "If that big loan last week hadn't *foamed the runway* for us, we definitely would have gone out of business."

Fortune cookie—A witty way to refer to something you heard that is very insightful.

> **USE:** "When I heard that idea on how to build sales, I said 'What a *fortune cookie.*'"

From your lips to God's ears—A way of telling someone "may whatever you just predicted come true." It's a little like wishful thinking.

> **USE**: "We knew that $20 a share was none too probable, but we breathed, 'Please God, make it so.' When we made our first initial public offering of stock during the 9/11-driven bear market, it went *from our lips to God's ears* and never was heard again."

F**ed up beyond all repair/recognition (FUBAR)—Military slang from WWII, meaning just what it says: a truly messed up situation. Can apply to anything that is botched or chaotic. (See also: *abortion*.)

> **USE**: "Corporate HR records were *FUBAR*, and none of the confused staff could find the files telling us what share we'll have to pay for our medical insurance premiums even though that was decided months ago."

FUBAR—(See: *F**ed up beyond all repair/recognition*.)

Fully baked—Thoroughly developed or realized, usually referring to a plan or program. Much like a pie or casserole cooked and ready to eat, a *fully baked* plan is ready for implementation. You've surely heard of half-baked schemes? (See also: *soup to nuts* and *making the soup*.)

> **USE**: "When James and Jane plan a corporate meeting, you know it's going to be thorough, efficient, productive and fun—*fully baked*."

Fuzzify—To make something less clear, usually with the purpose of trying to hide the true message or bury a potentially embarrassing or damaging effect or fact.

> **USE:** *"Fuzzifying the tax deductions won't stop the IRS from wanting to audit your income tax return and get straight answers."*

Get (the hell) out of Dodge—Refers to westerns, and perhaps the Old West itself, wherein escaping Dodge City, Kansas with your life and your liberty required luck and good timing. In business, it is a near miss, like hitting the sales goal at deadline, barely meeting a target or narrowly escaping a calamity.

> **USE:** *"Instead of continuing to operate the OSHA-violating factory, we decided it would be better to get out of Dodge by shutting it down just days before the inspectors arrived."*

Getting blood out of a rock or stone or turnip—Trying to get a result out of something or someone who cannot possibly deliver.

> USE: "Convincing the failing insurance company to fork over a big settlement on our flood losses would be like *trying to get blood out of a turnip.*"

Gift from God—A wonderful or exciting surprise; unexpected and unearned but very much appreciated.

> USE: "When our largest competitor abruptly announced that they were filing for bankruptcy, it was a *gift from God*, making increased sales a certainty."

No, **macaroni defense** has nothing to do with a food fight. See page 173 to get the whole story.

Glazing—Corporate terminology for sleeping with your eyes open. This usually occurs at early morning meetings and conferences.

> USE: "The speaker barely looked up from his notes, so he never noticed that half the room was *glazing.*"

Gravy on the steak—This is a positive result which was unintended but not totally unexpected; the little added extra that really makes things great. That chicken fried steak might taste pretty good, but the gravy on top makes it even better. (See also: *Lucky Strike extra.*)

> USE: "Ronnie's quality control upgrades won accolades from investors and customers alike, but the real *gravy on the steak* was reduced production downtime. Hey, our workers and our executives are happy!"

Head down—(See: *assholes and elbows.*)

Herding cats—This one is my second favorite term, after *green weenie*. *Herding cats* is a tough chore. In business, it translates as managing a group of people that are hard to control or direct. Imagine trying to keep dozens of cats all headed in the same direction focused on the same results. I first heard it applied during a discussion of a consolidation of a bunch of mom-and-pop salvage yards. The owners stayed on. They all had their own ideas of how to run the consolidated business.

Though not technically wrong, as most of them had been successful managers, they held sharply different ideas on running the business. Following the consolidation, each previous owner continued running his operation as a freestanding unit and resisted standard practices and directives issued from headquarters. Now that would be a CEO's herding nightmare!

The term can also mean trying to direct employees who don't work well together. My favorite use of the term, however, came in a memo about private stock placements. A decision was needed on whether to offer $1 million either in $250,000 shares to four investors or in $10,000 shares to 100 investors. Investors always have their own ideas about how things should be done, what went wrong and how you could have done better. Each will want to have his or her hand held and get regular progress reports. The business decided that if you're going to *herd cats*, four is much easier, so he turned down all the small investors. Herding 100 shareholders is impractical, if not impossible, and will definitely drive one crazy.

USE: "Trying to coordinate all those investors has been as hard as *herding cats*—and about as effective."

Holding your breath under water—Describes the suspense of dealing with a problem that has gone on far too long. Can be the frustration that occurs when a supposed solution is not working or is working too slowly, or the impatience caused by repeated failures. If you try to hold your breath too long, eventually you die. It's applied to executives who, for instance, are working in a turn-around, and the results aren't as expected or required, so they are close to death.

> **USE:** *"We're holding our breath under water* to see if Franklin can turn around 10 years of drooping sales."

Honeymoon—Similar to *champagne phase*, the time period right after the project has begun. In this phase, people have fun, and like all newlyweds still blissfully believe it will be like this forever. (See also: *champagne phase*.)

> **USE:** "When the new CEO's *honeymoon* is over, he'll have to produce big new profits."

Honeymoon before the wedding—Getting to experience the benefits before the product even hits the market.

> USE: "We needed some prospects who wanted a *honeymoon before the wedding* and didn't mind the risk of ruining clothes by testing the new detergent before wider release."

House of termites—A negative term used to describe a business that isn't doing well and is starting to crumble, much like a home that is being eaten by termites will eventually fall down.

How many teeth a (the) horse has—An old Arabian proverb stemming from three wise men sitting around a tent arguing over how many teeth a horse has while the horse stands outside. It would be much easier to just go count the teeth. It means do not sit around arguing, debating or philosophizing about something that you can go find out. Often, the answer is somewhere in your database, so don't waste time theorizing; go get the correct answer. (See also: *open the window and see the weather.*)

> USE: "It was a classic example of arguing over *how many teeth the horse has*: We debated which monthly sales ploy worked best when all we had to do was check our monthly sales figures against each strategy."

I can run faster than my wife, but that doesn't mean I am fast—This one cracks me up. It's literally true, but in business it means that just because one division or department is doing better than a similar division or department doesn't mean it's *really* doing well if *both* of them are way under their goal.

> USE: "Pete was so proud, he had increased production more than 10 percent, which was more than either of the other plants, but Brian explained that it didn't matter, that *just because he could run faster than his wife* (the other plants) *didn't mean he could run fast.* Unfortunately, Pete was still missing the target and budget by more than 20 percent, so the company was still way under water."

Ice cracking—Be careful if someone tells you they hear the *ice cracking*; you might be about to fall through. Usually it describes the tension around someone who is trying to justify bad performance or simply make excuses for a bad result. Although there can be legitimate reasons for the problem, often someone is just on the wrong side of the argument and is better off being quiet instead. (See also: *wrong side of the argument.*)

> USE: "After losing his second major account, Marshall warned him that where he had been standing was now thin *ice cracking.*"

If you can't (or don't want to) play with the big dogs, get (stay) on the porch—If you don't think you can compete, don't bother trying. (See also: *if you can't stand the heat, get out of the kitchen.*)

> USE: "Netscape constantly whined about Microsoft's cutthroat competition pushing Internet Explorer on PC buyers. Well, as they say, *if you can't play with the big dogs, stay on the porch.*"

If you can't stand the heat, get out of the kitchen—Similar to the previous saying; can also refer to a company or individual under intense scrutiny or criticism. Sometimes such heat just comes with the job; if you do not want it, quit. (See also: *if you can't (or don' t want to) play with the big dogs, get (stay) on the porch.*)

> USE: "He was nearing retirement when his company was acquired by new owners who cracked down hard on all the employees. He complained to his co-worker, who told him, 'If you can't stand the heat, get out of the kitchen,' so he decided to retire."

Incoming or incoming round—Response to a criticism or complaint, often a sarcastic barb or verbal jab. In the military, it is shouted to warn of impending enemy bullets or artillery shells. In business, "*incoming*" is typically uttered in meetings when someone feels under "attack."

> USE: "The meeting focused on blowing John's ideas out of the water. He remarked to me as the vocal barrage started: '*Incoming!* Will my plan survive? We'll see when I return their fire.'"

Invite me to the meeting—Make me an equal or substantial partner/leader/shareholder of an initiative. It can be the same as being *invited to the table.*

> USE: "*Invite me to the meeting* and I'll resolve all your communications problems. I want an equal share, and I'll contribute a greater effort to the cause."

Jury out—A comment about the uncertain status of results or an idea. The final judgment won't be known until the jury comes back in from deliberations. It's a good way to say we don't really know yet. (See also: *jump ball.*)

> USE: "We won't know if the new idea will be used as long as the *jury's out.*"

Kiss your sister—Usually kissing your sister is a pleasant courtesy but there is nothing particularly exciting about it; it's a non-event. *Kissing your sister* in business describes some action which has no excitement or result; generally seen as a waste of time.

> USE: "After returning from yet another attempt to land our biggest potential client, which resulted in the status quo of them still not choosing a vendor, my boss asked 'Did you *kiss your sister* again?'"

Last man standing—This is the winner, survivor, or best performer. (See also: *bake-off, boil out,* and *beauty contest.*)

> USE: "Steven will be the *last man standing* when the blueprint drafting contest is decided. Nobody can beat him on precision or quality."

Lemon squeeze—A meeting wherein all agree they are there to talk about the bad stuff, but also agree that when it is over, it is over! Comes from the idea of drinking something bitter.

> **USE**: "During that *lemon squeeze*, we came up with some brilliant ideas to solve all our problems. We need, but don't want, more of those tough sessions."

Lemons into lemonade—It simply means turning something that is bad (sour) into something good. After being laid off, you can *turn lemons into lemonade* by taking the opportunity to find the job you really wanted. If sales are weak, but better than the last period, you can *turn lemons into lemonade* by announcing that sales have increased over the prior period. (See also: *optics*.)

> **USE**: "Mike knew that after his shop burned to the ground one day after the insurance policy expired, he could make *lemons into lemonade* by selling the land for a tidy profit."

Lipstick on a pig—Sometimes, no matter how hard you try, you can't make something ugly look any better than it is. Usually the term refers to dressing up an old plan or product. Even if you put *lipstick on a pig*, it is still a pig and everyone knows it. This one has to rank in my top 10 favorite sayings.

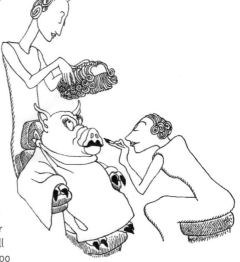

> **USE**: "Radio stations are constantly putting *lipstick on the pig* by running temporary promotions to give away money to listeners, but otherwise their format doesn't change. They still play the same music and run too many commercials."

Lower than whale crap—Depressed or low in value or spirit. Can describe either a psychologically depressed person or a business statistic that's way too low. When a whale drops feces, it falls all the way to the bottom of the ocean.

> USE: "Enron's stock price dropped *lower than whale crap* after the Justice Department announced a full-scale investigation of Enron's accounting practices."

Lucky Strike Extra—Something good which was unexpected. (See also: *gravy on the steak*)

> USE: "We knew that interest was going to go down and lower our costs, but we didn't expect the real *Lucky Strike Extra*, that the portfolio would increase in value over 10 percent."

Mickey Mouse—A term used to describe something that is undeveloped or poorly thought through. A *Mickey Mouse* system is unsophisticated and ineffective on many levels. (See also: *quick and dirty* and *shake and bake*.)

> USE: "Their management system has a lot of flaws, it's really very *Mickey Mouse*."

Mix some water with that and it will really stink—A "nice" way to call someone's idea bullshit. The nonsense in this reference may be a little old, stale or dry, and by reviewing—mixing in the water—you reveal how much it really stinks all over again. It seems likely to me that the saying originated in Texas.

> USE: "Some idealists say that always trusting trained employees to do the right thing will boost production—*mix some water with that and it will really stink*."

Moose head on the table—The big, obvious thing that no one is talking about. Some issue, problem or challenge we all know exists right in front of us, but we try to ignore. Similar to "the elephant in the room."

> **USE**: "The federal deficit running amok was the obvious reason for our surging inflation, but no one wanted to discuss the *moose head on the table*."

Mouse milking—A project or venture that requires maximum effort for minimum returns. It's nearly impossible to *milk mice* and you won't get much out of it.

> **USE:** "Selling computers door-to-door to senior citizens may not be as hard as *milking mice*, but I bet it's close."

Mystery house—Slang for a new business that appears to be highly profitable but has not announced any products yet, or doesn't appear to have viable revenues. It also refers to an office layout where cubicles are hard to navigate around.

> **USE:** "Enron was hawking its sales of broadband and touting the potential for huge sales and profits with more than 20 traders. But to all of the salespeople, it was just a *mystery house*, since there wasn't a single sale made."

New kid on the block—An upstart, newcomer or novice to anything in business. Usually a new competitor.

> USE: "The *new kid on the block* in our consumerniche was giving us a run for our money."

NHL—Acronym for No Heavy Lifting. It applies to almost any position in a company where an executive isn't required to do much of anything and can delegate all necessary tasks. I suppose that makes the job a cakewalk or gravy job, and calls into suspicion both the executive's true skills and the need for the position.

> USE: "Adam was well-liked as an executive, but his was obviously an *NHL* position, and all that work could probably be accomplished without him doling it out."

Nibbled to death by ducks—Your project or job getting killed or taken away little bites at a time. Problems can nibble, time can nibble, coworkers can nibble, and suddenly the project is no longer viable. (See also *death by a thousand cuts*.)

No such thing as an accident, only premeditated carelessness—So true that it needs no explanation.

> USE: "When he neglected to tell Cheryl about their meeting, he apologized for forgetting, but she knew there was *no such thing as an accident, only premeditated carelessness*."

Not in my back yard (NIMBY)—Used to describe people who believe something has a right to exist, but not where they have to deal with it; also a vow to overcome a new competitive threat on a company's home or established marketing turf.

> USE: "An Australian lamb purveyor wants to come into Texas, our nation's number one lamb-producing state, and swipe our lamb market share. I say '*Not in my backyard*'."

One-eyed king in the land of the blind— I love this one almost as much as *green weenie*. Imagine a world full of blind people. Now imagine that their new king has one eye. He's the only one who can see anything. He's revered and worshipped, if you will. It's used to refer to an employee— either newly hired or an existing one with talents just discovered or rediscovered—whom everyone is looking to for great, unbelievable, unachievable or even magical results. The term can also be used sarcastically, referring to someone who is stuck on him or herself. He or she is likely overrated but might enjoy his or her brief day in the sun. Can also have a negative connotation; someone with minimal competence (one eye) will still seem like the best when surrounded by those with no competence (blind).

> USE: "When the other football players saw Ted perform on the field, exceeding all expectations, it was obvious that the coach thought he was the *one-eyed king in the land of the blind.*"

One-trick pony— A company with one product.

> USE: "Aunt Fanny's Fire-Licked Barbeque Sauce is the No. 1 favorite in the South, but the company is a *one-trick pony*. They need more products."

One-way ticket—This is a job or assignment with an end in sight. It usually describes an assignment, perhaps in a turnaround, where the job has an ending date before it ever starts.

> USE: "Greg was hired to shut our widget division down. It's a *one-way ticket*, because when it's finally closed, he's out of a job."

Open the window and see the weather—A point in time when analysis will not get the answer, but observation will. It can also refer to a situation where we cannot see the solution because we cannot or will not look for it. (See also: *can't see the forest for the trees, chasing nickels around dollar bills, how many teeth the horse has, too close to the trees, sitting on the nickel, weatherman syndrome* and *blind man and the elephant.*)

> USE: "We repeatedly hired expensive analysts to tell us how to boost employee morale and productivity. Finally, we *opened the window and saw the weather.* All we had to do was practice the Golden Rule: Treat others as we want to be treated; love thy neighbor as thyself. Over time it has worked, and productivity is up 50 percent."

Optics—The way something appears or is seen vs. what it may actually be; looks or perception vs. reality. This word is more useful than it might appear at first glance. It can refer to the way an executive compensation presentation is perceived, and perception can still be everything. Corporate America thinks of optics at every juncture. Changing the optics can make something that was bad look good (or at least less bad). I once saw it used in a board meeting where a company had missed their goal of 200 percent growth by a large margin. To make the *optics* better, the presenter didn't address the missed goal, only that growth was up 150 percent. (See also: *lemons into lemonade.*)

> USE: "The *optics* of Ted's loan request could have been improved if he hadn't gone to the bank in his new Ferrari and announced that he had just returned from Vegas."

Optionaire—A millionaire on paper, as a result of options that could, should or might vest. The reality is that the options won't vest, so the probability of becoming a real millionaire is not very good.

> USE: "None of us thought it was wise for Kim to start building a new house, because at this point she was nothing but an *optionaire.*"

Ozone thinking—Wrong thinking, weak reasoning, poor judgment; if your head is in the *ozone*, you can't think clearly. You might say or do things that don't make sense or haven't been well thought out. (See also: *breathing our own exhaust, don't forget what stage of the process you're in* and *altitude sickness*.)

> **USE**: "It must have been *ozone thinking* when Coca-Cola decided to mess with its drink formula and come out with New Coke."

Peanut gallery—A derogatory reference to someone whose opinion we just don't care about. It refers to the cheapest seats in the theatre and therefore the patrons whose judgments are valued the least. (See also: *armchair quarterback*.)

> **USE**: "Donna told Ron to just be quiet; his opinion from the *peanut gallery* didn't count."

Peas and carrots—Two business options that are usually different but still equal in importance or potential.

> **USE**: "Quality control and cost control are crucial to any manufacturer's success. Like your *peas and carrots*, you shouldn't favor one and ignore the other."

Peel the onion—Dig deeper into an issue, deal, problem, etc. As you *peel the onion*, you see more flaws (if they exist), or may even discover bugs! (See also: *drill down, fishbone analysis, granularity* and *layer(s) of the onion*.)

> **USE**: "Let's *peel the onion* to get to the root of the problem."

Pencil brain—Derogatory reference to a critic of a business or financial plan. *Pencil brain* implies that the critic is distorting the financial footings with bad assumptions or inaccurate calculations. This is attributed to Franklin Raines, the embattled (and then ousted) CEO of Fannie Mae.

> **USE**: "Don't listen to that *pencil brain*! Our numbers are fine."

Pencil whip—To criticize someone in a written report instead of ver-
bally.

> **USE:** "That supervisor is notorious: He'll act like nothing is wrong, but then
> he'll *pencil whip* you in his review."

Picking your brain—Allowing someone to learn from you, lending
them the knowledge you have upstairs. Sometimes it can be flattering
have someone *pick your brain*, but it can also mean a competitor is
trying to find out something he shouldn't have access to.

> **USE:** "Tim doesn't know what direction he'd like his company to go, so he
> wanted me to ask you if he could pick your brain for ideas."

Pirate—A nice way to say someone is greedy; a businessperson interested in large profits and showing few altruistic motives. Although
pirates are certainly greedy, many will usually have some code of
honor and won't profit solely at the expense of others. In the venture-
capital Wall Street world, *pirate* is often too nice a word. (See also:
greenmail.)

> **USE:** "Wall Street *pirates* often use *greenmail* to grab big returns without
> having to buy a company or deal with any corporate management
> chores."

Stay informed! Get your free weekly Green Weenie with
Gahan Wilson's art via email. Register at **www.greenweenies.com**

Piss and vinegar—Brash attributes that can include high energy, articulate and usually salty language, a sarcastic attitude and bold decision-
making. Although generally a positive description, the term can also
refer to someone who is fussy, cranky or egocentric.

> **USE:** "Full of *piss and vinegar*, the new vice president didn't care what others
> thought of her. She was headed to the top with her aggressive manage-
> ment style."

Plane money—Refers to the size of executive signing bonuses, which are rumored to be enough to buy a plane.

> USE: "The employees, who were given no raises last year, were clearly aggravated when a new CEO was hired and given *plane money* rumored to be over $3 million for a signing bonus."

Playing football without a helmet—Playing without a helmet can damage a person's head and cause them to make poor decisions, like a boxer becoming "punch drunk." It can also describe someone who is taking too much risk. Maybe they don't have a *Plan B*, or just aren't properly prepared for execution of their plan. (See also: *Plan B*.)

> USE: "Everyone brought their research reports with them to support their ideas, except the new salesman, who thought he could wing it. The rest of us knew better than to *play football without a helmet*."

Pollyanna syndrome—The title character from the novel by Eleanor Hodgman Porter, *Pollyanna* was a relentlessly optimistic and enthusiastic girl who always believed the best of people. While such spirit may be motivational, this is generally a condescending term in a business context; like a *boy scout*, a *Pollyanna* may be seen as simple or naïve. (See also: *boy scout*.)

> USE: "The boss showed his *Pollyanna syndrome* by having complete certainty that everyone was trying their hardest. That meant that employees could get away with anything."

POS (piece of shit)—In business and social circles, the acronym can be used more politely than the term to refer to some nonsense, stupidity, bad decision making, poor performance or other unwanted result. Of course, it can also refer to a person of low morality or few ethical standards, someone behaving badly or someone you just dislike for any number of reasons.

> USE: "Tell the *POS* that if he wants to stay here, he's got to stop harassing the female executives."

Prettiest girl at the dance—A reference to the most attractive or aggressive salesperson, negotiator, proposal-maker or other participant in business talks; it is also the most tempting offer, proposal or product in said talks. It comes from that sage old advice: Don't skip the dance because you're afraid a certain boy won't ask you to dance; instead, go determined to be the 'prettiest girl' there and see who does ask you—then decide whether to accept. In business, don't be the one to truncate your own opportunities. Always "go for it." Sell hard and then decide if you want to accept any offer made. Work on making yourself, your company, offer or product, etc. the *"prettiest girl at the dance."* If you succeed, you can negotiate from a position of strength. (See also: *the dance.*)

> **USE**: "Ted Turner's CNN empire was, hands-down, the *prettiest girl at the dance* when buyout options were being considered by Time Warner and other suitors."

I defined **starter marriage**, but not finish marriage, why is that? See page 150 for the details.

Printed on soft paper—(See: *soft paper report.*)

Promised land—A wonderful place; the ultimate goal, reward or destination. Most of the time it is hard to believe that we can get there.

> **USE**: "Ted, the eternal optimist, was the only person in production who thought he could actually hit the goal, because he believed in the *promised land.*"

Psychic income—This is non-monetary, non-cash compensation, such as the pride that comes from a job well done.

> **USE**: "You can't pay some people enough; they want *psychic income* to motivate them in their job."

Push the button, turn the crank—From my good friends Dixon and Greg, a term that originated at Scott Paper Co. and then evolved. Scott's clientele didn't want their customers to use too many paper towels or too much toilet paper. The more the dispenser made you work, the less paper you used and the longer supplies lasted. Now the term is used to describe the process of making it harder for customers or potential users to get a product so they will not overuse it. The term is also used to describe a barrier to entry or sharing, whether intended or not.

> USE: "Software can be easy to share or swap, but XYZ Cyberspace Tools opted for a security barrier that curbs sharing and forces would-be users to buy, register and retain programs for their own use. This is innovative *push the button, turn the crank* software. "

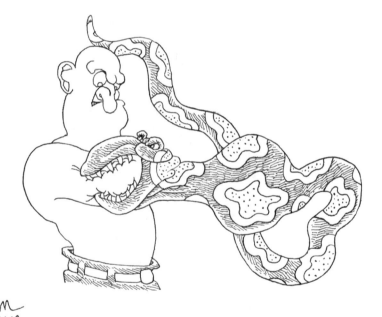

Pushing a bowling ball through a snake—Some things are just hard to do and painfully slow. Watching them happen can be like watching paint dry; it is very boring and seems to go on forever. It is often used in turnarounds when it takes time for the solution to demonstrate itself, or for the final results to be favorably impacted.

> USE: "Solving a sausage-extruding production line jam can be like *pushing a bowling ball through a snake:* You can see it coming, but at a snail's pace. Everyone must be patient."

Pushing a string/rope—Have you ever tried *pushing a string*? It's too flexible and never goes where you want it to go. *Pushing a string* is often used to describe a plan that will never succeed or any action that's unlikely to get results.

> USE: "We all knew that breaking into that market was virtually impossible; we'd be more successful if we were *pushing a string*."

Raggedy Ann/Andy Syndrome—These are classic stuffed dolls; they can't stand up because they have no backbone. In business, it is used to describe someone who won't make hard decisions or stand up for themselves or others.

> USE: "I used to have a cohort that all of our subordinates would complain about because he had *Raggedy Andy Syndrome*, which caused him to make empty promises because he didn't want to tell anyone no."

Radioactive—This is something or someone that no one wants to touch: Such an item or person evokes bad feelings or is simply shunned due to a reputation for problems, however inaccurate that reputation might be. I learned this word when I worked for one of the largest companies in the world. Typically, entrepreneurs are not liked by bosses with lots of college and multiple letters after their title. The culture at large companies makes those entrepreneurs *radioactive*.

> USE: "Ron is *radioactive*, because his entrepreneurial approach runs afoul of the stodgy corporate bureaucracy and his ideas just haven't been accepted."

Red herring—A misleading distraction, a false clue or lead; something that distracts attention from the real issue. Mystery writers long ago adopted the idea as a literary device in order to throw the reader off the scent leading to "whodunit." Ironically, *red herring* were once used to train hunting dogs to follow a scent. In business it's a preliminary prospectus, signified by red type on the cover, noting that the stock shares or bonds cannot be sold yet, pending Securities and Exchange Commission approval. (See also: *red herring* in the *Due Diligence* section, chapter eight.)

> **USE**: "Our *red herring* was designed to be a classic false clue. The business plan effectively focuses potential investors' attention on our accelerating growth and away from our decelerating profits."

Red Cross money—A financial bail-out of a high flying company, where the "donors" know they likely won't get their money back.

> **USE**: "Everyone was aghast that the CEO would put more money in the fledgling division. We all opined that he knew it was *Red Cross money*, but he had enough that he didn't mind making the 'donation.'"

Rifle shot—A precise and decisive action; a directive, decision or enterprise that's precisely and dramatically on target; opposed to the "shotgun" approach in which you hit or affect a wider target area but without much force.

> **USE**: "When we learned the plant was polluting its site, we fired a *rifle shot*, shut that factory down quickly, and began our own massive cleanup."

Ring the bell—This happens when you win, or the project is a success. As with the old carnival game, where you tried to hit the platform hard enough to make the bell ring at the top, it is often hard to ring the bell. Sometimes you see a bell in a business that the employees ring when some goal is met.

> **USE**: "Ann pointed out that the goal was quite ambitious, and it was going to take a lot of effort from all the team members to ring the bell on this one."

Rot at the head—A manager or management doing a poor job, causing the rest of the organization and overall company performance to suffer. It is derived from a dead fish, wherein rot starts at the head and spreads over the body.

> USE: "As we discussed the previous department manager's poor performance and how that negatively affected the results for the past year, Stu said 'Yeah, it always *rots from the head*.'"

Running on the hub—Out of money. The tire is ruined, the wheel is destroyed, and now we are *on the hub*. It can be a slow process or a quick one.

> USE: "When they were late paying their rent three months in a row, then gave us a bad check, we knew they were *running on the hub*."

Sand in the gears—Something gumming up the works. Whatever it is, something isn't working quite right; it is usually a small problem that can lead to big problems. Although sand is small, if enough of it gets in the gears, a much bigger problem occurs.

> USE: "The order fulfillment department kept throwing *sand into the gears* by missing deadlines, making it harder and harder to sell."

Scalping—One may think it describes what the Indians would do to the "white man." Actually, white settlers did the first scalping! The Indians learned it from French trappers who skinned their enemies and sent the scalp home to show their prowess. They would sometimes leave the scalp behind as a trophy to scare others and demonstrate their bravery or to show that they had prevailed. In business, executives may get *scalped* as part of a restructuring or realignment of a business or because of a manager who failed to deliver. Often, a lender or other stakeholder requires a *scalping* of an executive to show others that a change was necessary. As painful as it can be, change is often good. (See also: *blood on the floor* and *public hanging*.)

> USE: "One of the disadvantages to working for large corporations is the sometimes-necessary practice of *scalping* during downsizing."

Scars on my body—Considerable business experience. We get scars on our body and mind from the incidents we suffer through. Typically, the term is applied to an entrepreneur who has actually built a business, or to a faithful employee who has lots of experience. (See also: *arrows in our back* and *dirty fingernail person.*)

> **USE:** "I built this business from scratch, no small feat for a computer software firm. I've got the *scars on my body* to prove it."

Scorched earth—Refers to an action that wipes everything out. In business, it might be laying-off everyone, closing a plant, or even demolishing it. It's a *scorched earth* initiative, but it can increase profits.

> **USE:** "We could see no better alternative than to execute our *scorched earth* plan to get rid of everything unprofitable."

See some wood—Get some backlogged or previously scheduled tasks or projects done. It derives from the idea that the wood of the workstation surface cannot be seen due to the clutter of unfinished chores. The term can be good or bad.

> **USE:** "Mr. Jennings insisted that he *see some wood* in Theresa's work space by having her complete and clear out all the projects she had started."

Send a Christmas card—This means after we're done doing business, don't call us, we'll call you; if you must contact us, just send us a Christmas card—literally. This one makes my top 10 list of favorites. Often the seller doesn't want to hear from the buyer after the transaction closes. This term translates as a belief that "no news is good news." Of course, the seller wants his or her money and the buyer's other obligations fulfilled, but doesn't want to hear about any problems. The term can also be applied to anyone you don't really want to hear from again.

> **USE:** "After the long negotiations ended with a deal, Ted made it clear to the buyers that all he ever expects going forward is for them to *send a Christmas card.*"

Sevareid's Law—This is from former broadcast journalist Eric Sevareid's observation that "the chief cause of problems is solutions." In other words, solutions often cause more problems than they solve. In fact, the so-called solution may be worse than the original problem.

> USE: "We just thought we had it bad some time ago when our old machines needed repairs every month or so. Now *Sevareid's Law* applies to the new replacement machines which can't duplicate the quality we got from those old standbys."

Shake and bake—Describes a product that is developed and produced too quickly or poorly.

> USE: "That product design, manufacturing and sales cycle was so fast that it troubled everyone, and their fears were validated when the returns started coming back. It was clear that it was worse than *shake and bake*. The moral to the story was that easy and fast isn't always the best." (See also: *quick and dirty* and *Mickey Mouse*.)

Don't you wish you'd have had this book when you first started work?

Sharing teeth—This one cracks me up. Imagine three old geezers, trying to eat dinner, but they only have one set of teeth to share. Dinner will be slow, and it's not a pretty imagine, passing the teeth around. When you don't have enough resources to go around and you have to share, that's *sharing teeth*.

> USE: "The dismantlers were very inefficient as they spent a lot of time standing around waiting for a forklift, since there was only one for the six of them, and it was a lot like sharing teeth."

Shit doesn't stink—Used to refer to an egocentric. They think there's nothing negative about themselves, but they find plenty negative about others. Everyone has something imperfect about them, but these people don't think they do.

> USE: "Jill never fails to let you know that she's better than the rest of us, especially when it comes to job performance and her love life. Why, she even thinks her *shit doesn't stink!*"

Shitdisturber—As you can see from some of the more basic jargon here and elsewhere in this dictionary, business often gets down and dirty. A *shitdisturber* is a constantly complaining or otherwise less than desirable employee/associate, often someone who's too confrontational or combative. (See also: *stirring the pot* and *union delegate*.)

> USE: "Ken has always been a *shitdisturber* in our shop. He just can't get along, or stop arguing long enough to be very productive."

Shout from the tower—Sometimes the louder you talk, the less you're heard. By the time you're shouting to make a point, you won't be heard at all. By then, another communication method will be needed.

> USE: "Blaring our work safety tips over the intercom every morning didn't lower our accident rate. Since *shouting from the tower* didn't work, we tried small-group safety meetings with donuts and coffee, and our accident rate plunged."

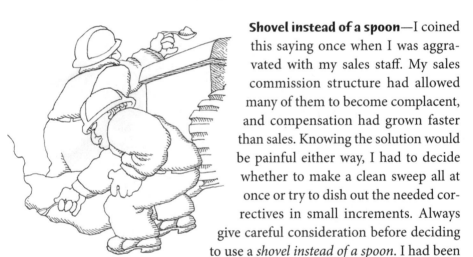

Shovel instead of a spoon—I coined this saying once when I was aggravated with my sales staff. My sales commission structure had allowed many of them to become complacent, and compensation had grown faster than sales. Knowing the solution would be painful either way, I had to decide whether to make a clean sweep all at once or try to dish out the needed correctives in small increments. Always give careful consideration before deciding to use a *shovel instead of a spoon*. I had been tweaking the plan, but there was constant tension and it finally seemed like it was time to use the shovel. I discarded the old plan and installed the new one in one swift move. The high tension lingered for a while, but a few weeks later, everyone had settled in, sales exploded and soon the changes were producing favorable results. The months I had spent using that spoon were wasted. (See also: *cut the dog's tail off one inch at a time*.)

> USE: "I wished I had used a *shovel instead of a spoon* much sooner, but at least I did finally decide to attack the problem in one swift move."

Silent war—From the book of the same name by economist Ira Magaziner. The book addresses the reality that many manufacturers and their distributors talk publicly about the importance of teamwork yet fail to heed their own advice behind the scenes. Whatever business "war" is occurring—such as both sides trying to wrestle more of the total margin stream into their pockets—is silent because it takes place behind closed doors.

> USE: "In the collision repair world, insurance companies say they want to work in partnership with repair shops, but then squeeze them on payments for services performed. It's a *silent war* as opposed to a 'declared war.'"

Sister Mary's home for boys/girls—A reference used in warning newcomers that the business world is a tough one, not a place to be coddled or pampered. At Sister Mary's, the peanut butter must be spread equally on each boy's (or girl's) bread. Not necessarily so in business, where parity may or may not be required between parties in a deal.

> USE: "The last time I checked, this was not *Sister Mary's Home for Boys*, and our new partners need to quit whining. Terms will never be equal between vested and non-vested partners."

Skin in the game—A stake or share in the venture, enterprise, etc. "Skin" doesn't have to be money. It can be a career, reputation, or other personal stake in the results or performance. To fail can easily spell a CLM or CEM. (See also: *emotionally invested, CLM* and *CEM.*)

> USE: "When a person's own *skin is in the game,* they have something important to lose and will usually perform at a higher level to protect it."

Slip the noose—Escape the consequences or impact, like the outlaw dodging the hangman.

> USE: "J.J. insulted the client and lost the account, but somehow *slipped the noose* by not getting fired; we're still trying figure out how she got away with it."

Smoke test—A reference to almost anything that has been tested (a theory, process, product or employee) and passed. Comes from the idea of supplying electricity to a product to see if it works without belching out a puff of smoke.

> USE: "It was a good thing we crash-tested the car; without that *smoke test* we wouldn't have known that the rear window popped out every time."

Snake bit—Prone to bad luck.

> USE: "He's *snake bit* if he had two auto accidents in one day; that's the worst luck I've ever seen."

Soak time—A period to mull it over, ruminate, chew your cud, etc. (See also: *percolate*.)

> USE: "After the offer, some *soak time* was taken before making the decision."

Soft paper report—A negative reference to a report, indicating disbelief or a lack of confidence in the report's facts, or just general disrespect for the report or its author. It's called the *soft paper report* because it needs to be written on soft paper, so that it will have another use, ahem, like in the toilet.

> USE: "Craig's presentation had no substance; it was a *soft paper report*."

Spin him up—Get someone or something up to speed; update someone on the current stage or status of a project, proposal or idea.

> USE: "We knew the new CFO would be lost when we first brought him into our 2-year-old project and that we would need to *spin him up* as quickly as possible."

Stick to your knitting—Keep doing what you do best and stay focused on core competencies.

> USE: "Sorry, Robert, I thought you knew how to do this! Why don't you just *stick to your knitting*, and I'll hand this assignment over to Nick."

Stirring the pot—Deliberately causing problems when things could otherwise be peaceful. (See also: *shitdisturber* and *union delegate*.)

> USE: "When the office action slowed or dulled, Billy Bob always felt he had to *stir the pot* to make things more exciting, but he also caused unnecessary problems."

Superstitious knowledge—Intuitive knowledge or insight gained from experience rather than research; also, questionable information that we suspect may be true, but which hasn't been corroborated. The term is often applied to things that experienced people know or think they know. This type of "knowledge" may be found to be incorrect when studied objectively.

> USE: "Men are always convinced they can handle management emergencies better than women, but there's no scientific basis for this *superstitious knowledge*. Indeed, many studies show the opposite."

Surgery with a butter knife—A botched job or performance; also refers to a job or task that doesn't require finesse or high skills. Medical surgery, of course, requires ultra-sharp scalpels and precision. Using a butter knife—large, dull, and indiscriminate—in surgery would leave ugly scars, if not kill the patient. However, when precision isn't required, a butter knife or another object might be the quick and easy tool for the simpler task. It can be used in a turnaround. If 10 percent of staff must be eliminated, select a group indiscriminately rather than taking the time to determine which 10 percent most deserves to go. (See also: *cutting bone and muscle*, and *laser gun vs. bow and arrow*.)

> USE: "You wouldn't perform *surgery with a butter knife* to cut outlays on quality control when making emergency medical equipment. But when time is critical, you might announce a 10 percent across-the-board budget cut with your old *butter knife*."

Sycophant—Someone who employs flattery in order to gain favoritism; a suck-up or brown-nose. You hear it a lot in upper level meetings, especially if there's an attendee unlikely to know what it means.

> USE: "That *sycophant* in the meeting today kissed so much ass. I can't believe the CEO didn't see right through her act."

Take away—What the participants *take away* from their meeting and down the *path forward*. It can be an assignment or a tidbit that's expected to be useful later. Often, the presenter plans a *take away*. Otherwise the meeting is just a waste of time. (See also: *path forward*.)

> USE: "Charlie's *take away* from the meeting was simple, he had to increase sales in the blue territory or lose his job."

Ten dollar solution—A reference to any old solution, process or technology that works better than the expensive one that replaced it.

> USE: "I am normally receptive to change, but it was obvious that the new software didn't work as well as our old *ten dollar solution*, which was simple and cheap."

Testosterone poisoning—An initiative ruined by a lack of females on the team.

> USE: "The marketing campaign seemed to be geared exclusively toward young men, which was odd for a product like orange juice. Looked like a case of *testosterone poisoning*."

The dance—What potential suitors do prior to making the deal. (See also: *prettiest girl at the dance* and *tired of dancing, ready to f**k*.)

> USE: "During *the dance*, they discussed some of the details of the proposition."

The farmer died—A term to describe a major change or shake-up in something which has been the same for as long as anyone can remember.

> USE: "When the manual line was automated and computerized, we knew the *farmer had died*, and we didn't even have a funeral!"

The lick log—Something that brings together adversaries, if only temporarily. Animals, even some natural born enemies, gather around a *lick log* and enjoy this salt lick or mineral block without killing each other. They all need it, so they let their guards down long enough to stand side by side at the *lick log* until they get their fill.

> USE: "The prospect of reducing federal banking regulations has drawn lenders of every sort, even some cutthroat competitors, to feed at the *lick log* and lobby side-by-side in Washington."

Theatre—Acting like something is bigger than it is; making a big deal out of something inconsequential or of low priority. (See also: *academy award performance.*)

> USE: "Johnny wanted to reap maximum effects from his cost-cutting suggestion for paper clips, so he created a 36-slide PowerPoint production with music and recruited a pretty office intern to start the show. It was great *theatre* for paper clip fans."

Thrown under the bus—What happens to a scapegoat when hit by a barrage of criticism or blame. It's one of those nasty things that some people do to others to save their own rear. In my world, one of the first business lessons learned in successful transactions and fair dealings is that one rarely benefits from *throwing someone under the bus.*

> USE: "CFO Jane found herself taking the full brunt of analysts' criticism of the firm's accounting practices. She felt like she had been *thrown under the bus* by the CEO, who kept tight reins on all the company's bookkeeping practices."

Ton of money—Did you know that $908,000 in $1 bills weighs exactly a ton? It's loosely used to refer to a million dollars.

> USE: "No one knew exactly how much the executive's retirement package was worth, but rumors were it was about a *ton of money.*"

Tone deaf—Often applied to a high-level controller or financial officer whose only job is to gather and present the numbers strictly by the book, with no bias or opinion. It's also used with highly technical people, like computer programmers or inventory personnel. These employees can be very valuable in their own departments and roles, but typically aren't good at interaction as they don't see the bigger picture; they are *tone deaf* to everything other than their own specialty.

> USE: "The *tone deaf* CFO said we must lay off 10 percent of the sales staff to achieve our sales per employee goal, but he hadn't considered that some of the salespeople sold more than others, or what a drop in morale might do to sales."

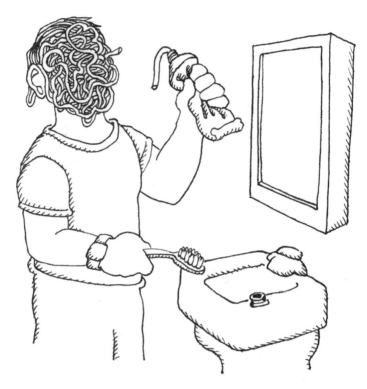

Toothpaste is out of the tube—Something said or done prematurely or without adequate planning, which is now difficult to undo. Like trying to get toothpaste back into a tube, it's pretty much an impossible task.

USE: "Only after we announced the acquisition did we realize the financing wasn't approved; the *toothpaste was out of the tube*, and we were in big trouble."

Toxic boss—A boss who's so bad that no one wants to be around him or her. He can be mean, profane, unfair, lazy or any of hundreds of other nasty things; in the end, those toxins just make his subordinates miserable.

USE: "Kelly dreaded going to work each day because Terri was such a toxic boss that she typically had everyone upset by the end of the morning meeting."

Train wreck envelope—The envelope you are handed that contains bad news, perhaps the worst news you will ever get. It also refers to a sealed envelope that someone would open if a disaster occurred. When I sold my company to Ford Motor Company, I handed two *train wreck envelopes* to the manager, Bill Stevens, as I was leaving. The two sealed envelopes were marked "open first when something bad happens" and "open second when something bad happens." The contents of the first envelope had a single sheet of paper that said "Blame it on Ron, he's gone." The second envelope had a single sheet of paper that said "Prepare two envelopes."

> USE: "The messenger always gets the short end of the stick when they have to deliver the *train wreck envelope*."

Tree falls in the forest—. . . but do we care? From the classic philosophical question: If a *tree falls in the forest* and there's no one there to hear it, does it make a noise? In business, this may be used to imply that managers or executives are too far removed from the daily action to know exactly what's going on. The forest is a big place and in many cases no one would hear one tree fall. Unfortunately, that fallen tree may have been important.

> USE: "We often wonder about that *tree falling in the forest* when we think about our senior executive. He spends a lot of time so far away from the shop floor and daily operations that he rarely understands what's going on back at the ranch."

Tripping on midgets—Being undone by small details. (See also: *can't see the forest for the trees, too close to the trees, devil is in the details, weather man syndrome, open the window and see the weather* and *blind man and the elephant.*)

> USE: "We suspect the CEO was *tripped by midgets,* because she didn't understand the details of our cost-accounting system and screwed up all of our cost analyses."

Trying to catch a falling knife—An effort that's extremely risky and almost certain to hurt anyone trying to handle it. Close your eyes, imagine a sharp knife falling, and now try to catch it. Who would want to even try? It means risking failure or other setbacks while trying to manage, rescue or resolve a really bad initiative or venture. Few want to have anything to do with it. The *falling knife* is similar in theory to an extremely "hot potato." You definitely want someone else to handle this item.

> USE: "Coming before our boss to defend a male employee who harasses female co-workers is like *trying to catch a falling knife*."

Tszuj—(pronounced "zhoozh") An expression made popular by TV stylist Carson Kressley, meaning to add a special flare to an outfit or hairstyle. In general, it means to tweak or finesse something.

> USE: "*Tszujing* the cost-benefit tables can get you in a lot of hot water if you're not a math whiz who loves to tweak via trial and error."

Tuition—The price you pay for the mistakes you make. Everyone makes mistakes in business, but when you actually learn from them, you can think of the cost as being *tuition*.

> USE: "Ron paid a lot of *tuition* in the early years by making bad buys, but now his experience lets him get prices below anyone else."

Turd in the punchbowl—Is another of my personal favorites, slightly akin to *green weenie* but even more repulsive. It's an ugly problem that pops up suddenly and must be taken care of as swiftly as possible. Although unexpected, it usually isn't hidden like a *green weenie*. Also, it can refer to something done intentionally in order to foul you up. (See also: *Binaca blast* for the opposite.)

> USE: "At the July sales recap meeting Shawn bragged about his division's results, but CFO Garry threw a *turd into* Shawn's *punch bowl* by noting that the bulk of those results were due to an accrual for the next quarter."

Turn the lights out—. . . the party's over; the last step in shutting down a business, plant, division, etc. It's a little nicer (but not much) than saying "Close them down."

> USE: *"Turning the lights out on our 100-year-old boot-making firm required a lot of chores, from ensuring that every employee got another job to linking all our clientele with other reliable boot-makers."*

Use a gun on our private parts—This is where we shoot ourselves in the foot, or, ahem, somewhere else a bit more sensitive. Many times in business, when something goes wrong, we want to say that something or someone did that to us. The reality is that we often do things to ourselves. We don't plan or execute well enough, don't get people in the right positions, etc.

> USE: *"When Rick started blaming this month's shortfall on Bob, not knowing Bob was the owner's son-in-law, Rick basically was using a gun on his private parts."*

Value stream—This is a term that encompasses every step in the production and delivery of a product or service (whether it adds value or not).

> USE: *"Our accountants used some great graphics to outline our company's complex value stream: From the farm, through processing, packaging, marketing, delivery, then finally to dinner tables."*

Vapor ware—Any idea that doesn't work as promised, or may not work at all. It really can apply to any proposed plan, process or initiative. (See also: *holloware.*)

> USE: *"It's just like Microsoft products to be vapor ware."*

Velvet coffin—The corporate practice of maintaining lifetime employment, usually in family-owned businesses. It's the first thing to be buried following a takeover.

> USE: *"Clint had been with us for more than 55 years but hadn't produced any work in the last decade. I guess it paid to be the son of the founder, as he got a velvet coffin."*

Verbal powder—Language which is explosive, yet does not trigger any action.

> USE: "Instead of being that quiet little mouse we always thought Samson was, he recently unleashed his *verbal powder.* Now he's got to convince everyone that it's not just *powder,* but rather a step toward changing obsolete policies."

Victory lap—A time for praise, cheers, flowers and maybe even a champagne toast for a job well done.

> USE: "Sales of Pete's new product creation were much better than forecasted; he knew the boss would give him a *victory lap.*"

Wallet biopsy—Likely coined by hospitals, but used in any business where a potential customer is sized up for their financial capability before trying to sell to them.

> USE: "Sam had the whole credit department, plus two investigators, doing a *wallet biopsy* on the three prospects. He wanted to make sure they could afford the planes, and wasn't going to let all three drive us down on price if they weren't bona fide buyers."

Watching the sausage being made—Another description of an unpleasant task. This is a metaphor for anything you don't want to be present for, or witness. You want others to do this. I don't know anything about making sausage, but I have images of what goes in, all the leftovers, etc, and everyone always told me that if I could see what was involved, I would never eat sausage again.

> **USE:** "Ted told his team he did not want to participate in the early negotiations, it was too much like *watching the sausage being made*, and he would wait for the second round of negotiations when he could add value."

Watershed event—An event that saves, redeems or just plain blesses the recipients; a turning point.

> **USE:** "The aerospace division experienced a *watershed event* when it received an order for new technologies worth over $10 million."

Weatherman syndrome—Someone isolated from the real world while making forecasts. My friend Dixon Thayer gave this illustration: "People standing in the rain watching a TV in a shop window while the TV weatherman is saying 'Doppler Radar shows us a beautiful sunny day.'" Thayer added, "Sitting in a windowless broadcast booth and looking at data is not enough! Open the window and look outside (at the real world) when making forecasts." (See also: *close to the trees, can't see the forest for the trees, sitting on the nickel, open the window and see the weather, chasing nickels around dollar bills* and *blind man and the elephant.*)

USE: "No one has ever accused Federal Reserve Chairman Alan Greenspan of having the *weatherman syndrome*. His inflation and other forecasts are wise to the ways of Wall Street, Main Street and the world."

What you don't know is worse than what you know—Sometimes in business one doesn't want to know certain things because the new knowledge is burdensome. In environmental matters, does one really want to know if there's a hazardous chemical below his factory site? Perhaps not. CEOs and other high-ranking company officials sometimes make a conscious effort to stay ignorant of some things, although other employees may very well know about them. If an executive knows about something, he must then either act on the matter or be prepared to lie and face the possible legal or financial consequences.

> USE: "The President halted discussions about prisoner abuse and left the room. Some observers wondered if perhaps *what he didn't know might be worse than what he did know,* and so he wasn't interested in finding out more. His staff knew to shield him from too much of the truth, so he would never have to decide whether to lie."

When pigs fly—Extreme skepticism; a declaration that something will never happen.

> USE: "We will all be happy at work, yeah, sure, *when pigs fly!*"

Where the rubber meets the road—Where or how the outcome will be decided; where the execution of some job, plan or project actually succeeds or not, where we find out whether our plans, equipment or methods actually work. There is friction between the road and the tire, and road conditions are a surefire way to test a tire.

> USE: "When we get down to negotiating interest rates, that's *where the rubber will meet the road.* We'll find out if the deal is doable and affordable."

Whisper down the lane—A surreptitious way of letting someone know something without coming right out and saying it in front of everyone else; also, gossiping. It's tantamount to our government "leaking" information they want reported but don't want to be attached to as the source. It's also used to describe giving someone early information, perhaps to see how they will react. In business, the term also refers to rumors and their tendency to get out of hand while making the rounds.

> USE: "Even corporate executives are known to *whisper down the lane*—to air ideas without actually proposing them, and then see what reactions develop as the low-key message becomes gossip."

White elephant—Something which is rare but not so valuable, often costing more to keep or maintain than it is worth; a formerly prized possession no longer desired or any investment that nobody wants because it is unprofitable.

> USE: "The company's 1899-vintage headquarters building is classic Main Street architecture, but it's a headache to maintain; this beautiful *white elephant* is even harder to heat and cool for our workers' comfort."

Why keep a dog and bark yourself?—Refers to the premise that there is no reason to surround yourself with talented people if you aren't going to listen to them, but instead just bark orders to them, stifling their ability to perform using their talent. Such a person, of course, is an autocrat.

> USE: "The R&D Department came up with a lot of exciting concepts, but the VP of R&D invariably overruled them with his own inferior ideas. '*Why keep a dog and bark yourself?*' they wondered."

Wiggle our hips—Do a little jig, so to speak, by embellishing what otherwise might be a weak presentation, plan, etc. It has sexist overtones.

> USE: "We all knew that even if he *wiggled his hips*, the board just wasn't going to be impressed with his detail-deficient expansion plans."

Win or win—Often heard as a sarcastic comment, "we're behind you, win or win." It pokes fun at an initiative or other plan that likely has some risk, which everyone supports in a guarded manner. If it fails, support will likely vanish, as this isn't the same as win or lose.

> USE: "We told Sam that his idea sounded good, and we were behind him, *win or win*. Sam knew he better go think through this one well, as he really might not have our unqualified support if he didn't succeed."

Won't hear the bullet leave the chamber—Referring to someone who's likely not smart or sensitive enough to realize that his idea is about to be shot down or "killed." He or she moves ahead as if everything is normal, totally unaware. It can also refer specifically to someone who has been identified for termination but doesn't have any idea it's coming.

> USE: "Everyone but Ted knew as he opened the presentation that *the bullet had already left the chamber*; there wasn't any chance his lackluster, ill-conceived initiative would receive funding."

Green Weenies and Due Diligence makes a perfect gift for that business student you know!

Wood is still rotten—A problem still exists despite extensive work to fix it. It's a bit like termites in a piece of wood; the more you look, the more damage you seem to find. It usually refers to employees that just can't flex to new market demands or employer expectations, or to some portion of a business that was previously thought to have been fixed, but still has problems.

> USE: "Everyone agreed that the *wood is still rotten* in the U.S. steel industry. After four decades of effort, neither the steelworkers nor the steel makers have found a way to compete effectively with cut-rate foreign steel."

Wrapped our fish in that one—This describes a plan that is questionable or suspect (and yes, smelly); not good for much except wrapping a fish in. (See also: *doesn't amount to a hill of beans.*)

> USE: "Clint suggested we hire an all-male sales force, but it was ridiculous, and we could have *wrapped our fish in that one*."

Wrong side of the argument—A lost cause that is best dropped and replaced with a better one. Sometimes no matter how persuasive one is, his ideas and solutions are just doomed because his position is flawed. For instance, arguing that a product launch already delayed for a year should be delayed again—when everyone knows that further delays could bankrupt the company—is on the *wrong side of the argument.*

Delaying under other circumstances might have been wise, but not in this instance. If the consequence is bankruptcy, the argument is doomed. In this case the correct side would be to present a plan for moving ahead with the product launch but proposing contingencies for flaws that could pop up. When a cause is lost and one nonetheless continues to defend it, he had better be ready to have his boss *chew on his leg.*

USE: "The new manager had already been granted two extensions on the project which led to a loss of a major client. For him to argue that delaying further made sense would put him on the *wrong side of the argument.*"

You don't know what is right, but you know what is wrong (or vice versa)—Meaning it can be easier to know what's wrong than what's right in a plan or project. For instance, when the trucking department wanted 10 new trucks, they asked the manager to review Chevys, which cost $45,000, and Ford, which cost $75,000, but no further study was needed. He didn't know if $45,000 was right, but he knew $75,000 was wrong. (See also: *directionally correct,* and *lens hasn't been installed.*)

USE: "The consultant said he didn't know for sure exactly how many salespersons were required to do $200,000 per month in sales, but he knew based on industry metrics that the 10 currently employed was wrong, and likely was about double the needed amount. With just a small amount of work, he knew what was wrong, and with more work would know what was right."

2

Management and Strategic Issues

2x4—(See: *nails in the 2x4.*)

30,000 feet above—A high-level strategic or analytical perspective, typically held by a business executive, owner or manager. Smaller numbers, such as 10,000 feet above, can also be used to refer to a certain long-range or broad view of a business operation, plan, goal, idea or suggestion. Good executives are trained to think from *30,000 feet above* in most cases because it is the optimal strategic perspective. At times, however, they also need to consider short-range tactics and understand more details in order to make the correct decisions. (See also: *helicopter skills, lens hasn't been installed,* or *granularity, layer(s) of the onion,* and *drill down* for the opposite meaning.)

USE: "The ideal production line manager is one who can see the forest from *30,000 feet above* and can focus on the individual trees close-up from ground level."

Academy Award performance—(See: *theatre.*)

Acid test—A conclusive test. Before you release a new product to the public, you need to give it the *acid test*. (See also: *acid-test ratio* in chapter nine.)

> USE: "It looks good on paper, but we should give it the *acid test.*"

Air cover—A situation in which a senior manager agrees to take the flak for an unpopular decision, while someone lower on the chain of command does the dirty work. The term evolved from World War I and World War II wherein Doughboys, GIs, or Marines were given bomber or fighter aircraft support before and during attacks on enemy forces. You sure wanted your "boys" above keeping enemy aircraft from coming down on you.

> USE: "The CFO will provide *air cover* while you reduce staff by half."

All that and a bag of chips—A reference to an unexpected twist or benefit that usually comes with a bit of sarcasm and perhaps a tad bit of envy, but can also be a sincere compliment. The "*bag of chips*" can be either an unexpected bonus or an unexpected drag on the company.

> USE: "Although many service policy options had been proposed, some are good and some are downright lousy, Pam's unique plan seemed to be *all that and a bag of chips.*"

"A"–who has it?—"A" stands for accountability when determining who is going to make sure the required follow-up on a project occurs. Too often in meetings, items are discussed and everyone opines or muses about them, but without an "A" the items never get done. This is often taught in business school. Similarly, an "R" stands for resource. If one person is accountable, another (or others) will be the resource. Another person will have the "C" to communicate, and another the "I" to inform. (See also: *RACI.)*

> USE: "Dale made it clear following the discussion of cost reductions in pallet usage that Ronnie would *have the 'A'* to present potential solutions at the next meeting."

Bagged—What you do to a bad idea; just like throwing out trash.

> **USE:** "Tim's idea for salesperson compensation was *bagged* when the CEO heard about it. He felt it would be too disruptive to sales."

Bagging the tiger—Catching, finding or creating something that is hard to hold. It might be a new technology that no one else has. The bag is some sort of restraint that could be manufacturing or distribution bottlenecks, lack of capital or sales constraints.

> **USE:** "Ted said we were *bagging the tiger* by not solving the legal issues surrounding the promotional material for the new baby seats, and we should let it go ASAP to get the sales during the season."

Big and easy analysis—This is a process of assessing different strategies or projects in order to determine priorities.

> USE: "Here's how we do our *big and easy analysis*. First we draw a square, and then we divide it into four equal portions. We mark it like a graph: One side being 'big and small' to indicate size of expected results and the other side being 'hard and easy' for how difficult the task will be. We bullet each strategy or project within the quadrants. Soon, it's easy too see which items will be the easiest to do while yielding the biggest results. Then we set our priorities accordingly."

Blamestorming—A discussion wherein the goal is to avoid responsibility for a failed initiative, and pin it on someone else if possible.

> USE: "The meeting was mostly just a *blamestorming* session, with everyone trying to figure out who could be held accountable for the project's disastrous results."

I want a really big **tombstone**, how about you? I actually would like to get, say, one per year for the next 10 years. Sound gruesome? Maybe not, see page 124 to know for sure.

Blocking and tackling—The most basic tasks of any good business team. In the business world, *blocking and tackling*—such as meeting production, quality and logistical goals—are often overlooked. Someone has to do the *blocking and tackling*, also referred to as heavy lifting.

> USE: "Cheryl said, 'The marketing plan looks great, but without *blocking and tackling* in the factory and distribution trenches the new product launch would be a failure.'"

Camel's nose under the tent—This speaks to someone or something that is getting into the details of your business. Although it could be welcome, it's more likely something that is creeping in slowly, being nosey.

> USE: "Tim said he felt like our competitor's *nose was under our tent*, as they just knew too much about the marketing program."

Can't see the forest for the trees—(See also: *too close to the trees, weatherman syndrome, open the window and see the weather, blind man and the elephant, sitting on the nickel, chasing nickels around dollar bills,* among others.)

Closing the loop—Bringing everyone who's needed into the management or operating circle of associates on a given project. *Closing the loop* means getting the last requisite person involved.

> **USE:** "After we decided on the sales goal, Sam pointed out that because of the need to hire more salespersons, we needed to get HR involved in order to *close the loop.*"

Come-to-Jesus meeting—A disciplinary or other meeting where bad news is announced or discussed. The jargon implies that some participants may cry, wring their hands and have soul-searching moments during the meeting. Of course, it also applies to a meeting with just one employee where performance is discussed. (See also: *prayer meeting.*)

> **USE:** "Pete knew when he missed the sales goal by a wide margin that a *come-to-Jesus meeting* was surely in order."

Cool beans—A favorable and humorous reference to something good, often a surprise business development just discovered or identified. *Cool beans* carries the same meaning as saying "That's good news" or "That's good."

> **USE:** "When I told him that we had actually hired one more salesperson than expected without any additional increase in payroll, David said 'That's *cool beans.*'"

Cowboys—Used to describe employees that are somewhat out of control, or hard to control. Rebels, if you will.

> **USE:** "We always said our auction buyers were cowboys, as they were always reluctant to use new methods, and just wanted to do things their way."

Dawn patrol—A stroll or tour through the workplace shortly after arrival (for the day or for the first time) to greet co-workers, check on progress and see who's in and available for consultations or big meetings later. Sometimes recommended as a time management tool. It can get socializing out of the way before settling down to work. It also can be intimidating, especially for those that don't get to work on time or are caught not working.

> USE: "The store owner finds his long-standing *dawn patrol* through the store effective in minimizing employee tardiness."

Dead wood—Employee, department or division of a company that no longer plays a role in company output. In the ocean *dead wood* floats, but in business it sinks.

> USE: "Profits are down. It's time to let go of the *dead wood*."

Decision rule—A term used to describe the rule(s) that will be used to make a decision. For instance, what is considered success of a new product can be in the eye of the beholder. In order to get everyone on the same page and eliminate subjectivity, *decision rules* are laid out at the outset. All those parties that will be called on later to make a decision on whether to eliminate a product line agree in advance that if the sales are above X amount of dollars, the product line passed the first *decision rule*. Typically, multiple rules are applied as agreed. (See also: *decision tree*.)

> USE: "When we still weren't making a profit after the second quarter, we knew the product line would be closed for not even making it to the first *decision rule*."

Decision tree—Just like it sounds, it's a tree with limbs and branches. At each branch, a decision is made to go right, left, up, etc., on to the next junction. At each of the junctions, a decision is made indicating the next branch to take, often using a *decision rule*. (See also: *decision rule*.)

> USE: "The branches of the *decision tree* show the appropriate directions we've taken and the growth the company has made as a result."

Denial—As in all areas of life, this is an inability or refusal to accept the truth about something (especially oneself). But it is not a river in Egypt.

> USE: "Greg called Mike on the carpet about his cost-cutting results, which Mike defended despite the obviously bad performance. Greg reminded him that *denial* was not just a river in Egypt."

Dollar waiting on a dime—When high-priced executives are delayed due to the actions of hourly-wage workers.

> USE: "Our corporate attorney had to delay the meeting for 15 minutes because Ron's secretary hadn't copied all of the attachments yet—just another case of a *dollar waiting on a dime*."

Drag an oar—Dragging an oar will slow the boat down. In business, those that *drag an oar* may be lazy or unwilling, and they slow down rest of the team. (See also: *pull an oar*.)

> USE: "Everyone hates those who *drag an oar*, bringing everyone down with them while the rest of the team is working hard."

Driving without a dashboard—Managing a business without the requisite gauges and guidance systems. Imagine driving a car without a dashboard! Yet many companies do basically the same thing—operate without the tools to steer and monitor performance. I am a huge advocate of using operating metrics, which are the gauges for guiding the company, and devoted an entire chapter to their use in my book *How to Salvage Millions from Your Small Business*. Operating metrics tell you how many items you made, shipped, and sold yesterday. Without these basics on inputs and outputs, you can't possibly understand how the company is performing, where you're headed or when you might arrive. (See also: *gauge, Key performance indicator (KPI)* and *operating metrics*.)

> USE: "It was obvious to Bill that the previous owners had been *driving without a dashboard*, as there were no reporting systems in place for understanding the company's performance."

Ear candy—Usually issued from a CEO or other high-level executive. Providing *ear candy* is embellishing things beyond belief; exaggerating in order to satisfy the target listeners, such as stock analysts or employees.

> USE: "Everyone knew that all the talk about someone buying the company and saving our jobs was just *ear candy*, but it sure did 'hear good' to us."

Empty vessels make the most noise—An insult implying that people of low intelligence talk the most and the loudest but have little credibility. Often they are just plain annoying. An empty vessel is just that; it has nothing to offer.

> USE: "Dennis wasn't even a high school graduate, but he spoke as if he was a brain with a Ph.D. He was really an empty vessel making the most noise in the monthly meetings. Everybody cringed when he stood up to speak."

Epidemic vs. Isolated—Widespread or common vs. rare, limited or unusual. Problems can be described as either of these two extremes. *Epidemic* problems are pervasive and obviously hard to solve. *Isolated* problems are focused in one area and are much easier to solve.

> USE: "Morale at the Atlanta plant was at an all-time low, but fortunately it was *isolated* to that site rather than *epidemic* to all the southern factories."

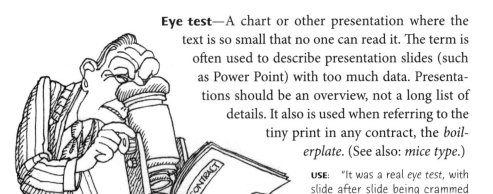

Eye test—A chart or other presentation where the text is so small that no one can read it. The term is often used to describe presentation slides (such as Power Point) with too much data. Presentations should be an overview, not a long list of details. It also is used when referring to the tiny print in any contract, the *boilerplate*. (See also: *mice type*.)

> USE: "It was a real *eye test*, with slide after slide being crammed with text."

G2—This is a military term for reconnaissance. It refers to seeking and collecting information, often secrets. In business, it means to search for some deal-related data that would be helpful in making a key decision or in clinching the deal. It can also refer to any number of other types of reconnaissance, such as a secret search for a new CEO.

> **USE:** "Our campaign to hire salespersons away from competitors was code named G2."

Greenwash—Pokes fun at the way a company plays up environmental benefits of a product or service in order to deflect attention from less savory aspects.

> **USE:** "We all knew they were going to *greenwash* their announcement; they had to appear environmentally friendly, as they killed all of the native vegetation."

> How about a gift that is treasured, passed around
> and reminds your customers of you?

Hands on the wheel—The state of being in control, usually referring to an executive or manager. The best leaders always keep their *hands on the wheel* or delegate this duty to a trusted and skilled subordinate or peer. Having your *hands on the wheel* simply means keeping an eye on what's happening by using the gauges and making necessary adjustments to keep the *car out of the ditch*. (See also: *car in the ditch.*)

> **USE:** "Following 23 quarters of successive growth in sales and profits, no one doubted that Chairman Warren Buffet had his *hands on the wheel*."

Hawthorne Effect—The phenomenon whereby productivity improves in any organization being studied due to the added attention (whether positive or negative). It was first identified and observed in the Hawthorne Plant of the Western Electric Co. in the 1920s and 1930s. When the added spotlight dims or goes away, the improvement ceases.

> **USE:** "When the corporate team of efficiency experts began studying our factory operation, our output jumped 10 percent overnight. They told us it was the *Hawthorne Effect*, and that they wanted us to do even better."

Head in the game—In order to do a good job, an employee always has to have his head in the game. (See also: *hands on the wheel, emotionally invested* and *skin in the game.*)

> USE: "After having led a successful business for 50 years, the CEO still had his *head in the game.*"

High-class problem—This is an issue or challenge that has arisen under favorable circumstances; a problem to be thankful for.

> USE: "We're short on product to ship for now, because demand is way up, but we'll gear up and catch up. If only all our challenges were such *high-class problems!*"

Hit-and-run management—In some ways, may be a good thing. You can be sure the boss doesn't hang around very long. It can certainly be a bad thing as well, when the boss just runs through, giving you some information but not enough, or admonishing you but not being clear about why. It's not unlike a car accident, where it happens quickly and the person leaves the scene. (See also: *seagull management.*)

> USE: "We only see the boss every six months; he is a classic example of *hit-and-run management.*"

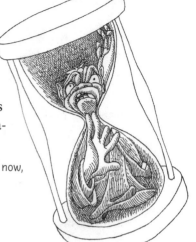

Hourglass mode—A derogatory reference to an executive or other boss who takes forever to make a decision. It comes from the hourglass icon in Microsoft software, which is always aggravatingly slow.

> **USE**: "I've been waiting on Stan's input for days now, he must be stuck in *hourglass mode*."

Idea hamster—A derogatory reference to a manager or peer who is constantly generating new ideas, but leaving the feasibility analysis to others, and likely taking credit for any favorable results.

> **USE**: "Tom is our *idea hamster*. I've never seen him follow through on any project, but he's always ready for a pat on the back if one of his ideas pans out."

Jekyll and Hyde—A reference to literature's most famously dual-personality character, the meek Dr. Jekyll and his sinister alter-ego, Mr. Hyde. It can be used to describe a senior manager's extreme good and bad qualities or the polarized views between two key officers within a corporation.

> **USE**: "The night and day bosses where I work are so different; they're like *Jekyll and Hyde*."

Jump ball—Borrowed from basketball. If something is a *jump ball*, it is still undecided. (See also: *jury out*.)

> **USE**: "We're not sure how well the toy will sell, it's still a *jump ball*."

Key performance indicator (KPI)—Used synonymously with operating metrics, meaning a major gauge of performance or results. For instance, the number of units produced in a given period is a *KPI*. They are invaluable for comparing companies' performances but equally valuable for benchmarking departmental, individual and other performances within a company and comparing past with current or projected performances. (See also: *gauge, driving without a dashboard* and *operating metrics*.)

> USE: "The shipping department's *KPIs* differ from quality control's gauges: Shipping must move products quickly, efficiently and safely; quality control must detect defects, which slows product movement down."

Kill the messenger—Refers to the tendency to want to punish the bearer of bad news, even though that individual isn't responsible for it. *Killing the messenger* won't change the message.

> USE: "The CEO sounded like he wanted to *kill the messenger*, my friend Amy, even though she did him a favor by telling him that the board intends to fire him."

I don't think **helicopter skills** are going to get you flying, but if you aren't sure, see the definition on page 140.

Kremlin syndrome—A term used to indicate "Them vs. Us," with at least two meanings: (1) an obsessive disrespect for authority. It may stem from anger or frustration that the people at headquarters are disconnected from actual operations. (2) A mania for or fixation on exerting authority. Typically, it refers to a company's headquarters thinking it can control everything from a single point, while others view the bosses as having their heads in the sand.

> USE: "Billy Joe was exhibiting a bad case of *Kremlin syndrome* when he said, 'Those highfalutin' corporate suits up there in New York think they know how to run a business in Texas. Hell, they don't bother to show their faces down here 'cept when they think somethin' is goin' wrong!'"

Lay cards on the table—To be perfectly honest and up front. Ironically derived from the language of poker, a game of deception. If someone calls your bluff, it might be time to *lay your cards on the table*. (See also: *peek under the tent*.)

> USE: "Negotiations had been dragging on, with neither Cheryl nor Kyle trusting what the other was saying. Finally, seeing that they weren't making any progress, they both agreed to lay their cards on the table so they could move ahead."

Leg your way into it—Kind of like getting into a Ferrari: You put your leg in first and then work your body in. It's a way of describing going in slowly or working your way through obstacles as you tread carefully to minimize risk.

> USE: "We should test our product in the smaller market first as we *leg our way* into the major metropolitan area."

Lifeboat discussion—A negative description of what managers do when layoffs are planned. In this unfortunate situation, hard decisions must be made regarding who will stay on the boat and, ahem, who will be thrown overboard to die in the cold, shark-infested waters.

> USE: "We knew that a *lifeboat discussion* was going on in that conference room, and sat nervously wondering which of us would have to go."

Lion's share—The biggest slice of the pie, it's usually reserved for the *alpha dog* or the *800-pound gorilla*. If you want the *lion's share*, well, you better start acting like the lion.

> USE: "Greg is the king of our office jungle, so he always gets the *lion's share* of the profits."

Managing the blood supply—A term used to describe managing the highest producing, but also high maintenance employees, or those who are especially innovative, such that their departure or burnout will not adversely affect the company.

> USE: "When the company lost Nate, the managers knew that they'd have to *manage the blood supply* to make up for the absence of such a creative contributor."

MBA jerk-off—A derogatory name for a Master of Business Administration graduate who thinks he or she knows it all, typically a younger person who hasn't learned to listen and be a team player or manage by consensus. This egotist wants to argue about everything and believes he or she has all the right answers despite having no actual experience.

> USE: "You can always recognize an *MBA jerk-off*. This loud-mouth is never wrong, can fix any business problem, and doesn't mind telling you he's from Haahhhvaahd or Yale."

MBWA—An acronym for *Management by Walking Around*. It's often used to criticize a manager that spends too much time on the floor with workers or can refer to a *dirty fingernail person* who has no college education. There are plenty of subscribers to a theory that *MBWA*, with some non-collegiate training, can be more effective than having an *MBA*. This management style is sometimes encouraged because it gives the manager exposure to his subordinates so they don't think he's just hiding behind a desk. It gives subordinates a chance to talk to their manager and see that he is approachable. (See also: *dirty fingernail person*.)

> USE: "Jim didn't seem to be able to meet his project deadlines. He claimed it was because he had too much to do, but his underlings blamed it on the fact that he his *MBWA* style prevented him from getting his real work done."

Mice type—The fine print, very small writing. (See also: *eye test.*)

> USE: "I didn't know what kind of contract I was signing until after I read the *mice type.*"

Minion—A loyal subordinate, typically one who will follow instructions to the letter, sometimes slavishly and usually without question.

> USE: "Wouldn't it be a wonderful business world if most employees were good conforming *minions?*"

On-the-job training (OJT)—Speaks for itself and is still the best teacher in many sectors.

> USE: "Many blue-collar jobs of manual labor offer *on-the-job training* to new employees."

One hand in the air—It's reminiscent of raising your hand to be recognized or to vote in the classroom. Now it means that someone is almost convinced. When that person is convinced, she or he will have two hands in the air.

> USE: "I had *one hand in the air*, but stopped thinking it over when Halliburton came to town offering tenfold U.S. wage rates to work in military support jobs in Iraq."

Order and priority (O&P)—Qualities emphasized by management, because too many employees can't seem to get a handle on either directive.

> USE: "Workers too often do the tasks at hand in the wrong *order*, without considering company *priorities*. An *O&P* education campaign is in order to train these slow learners."

Overdressed, overfed, overhead—Corporate excess.

> USE: "XYZ Inc. has big fancy headquarters, where the execs are *overdressed* and *overfed*, all leading to too much *overhead.*"

Ox in ditch—(See: *car in the ditch.*)

Prayer meeting—(See: *come-to-Jesus meeting.*)

Problems older than whores—Most problems have been around for ages. Being compared to the so-called "oldest profession" means everyone knows the problems, they've been around forever. Solutions are much more valuable and harder to come by.

> USE: "One of our problems that is *older than whores* is that we can't find enough qualified salespeople."

Pull an oar—In a boat, *pulling an oar* will propel the boat along. In management, those that are willing to *pull an oar* are praised, as it helps move a project along. (See also: *drag an oar* for the opposite.)

> USE: "The best workers are the ones who are willing to *pull an oar* to ensure that the company reaches the corporate goals."

Pull him through a keyhole—An activity that is obviously stressful and potentially painful. It's used to describe an action that must be undertaken to get results, often in a short amount of time or with limited resources. It can also apply to a situation where someone has failed to perform and now must have extra pressure applied in order to reach a goal.

> USE: "It was obvious that we would have to *pull Ted through a keyhole*, as there were only two days left to finish the code, and there was not a *Plan B*."

Pushing a ball uphill—Used to describe a difficult task that you just can't seem to accomplish.

> USE: "It seemed like no matter how we tried to avoid problems, the new sales plan had us constantly *pushing a ball uphill*. We never could quite hit the goal, and it was such a continuous struggle."

Put the scotch to—When you *put the scotch* to something, you make it stop. You probably want to *put the scotch to* projects that are costing you money and not creating profit. Comes from Shakespeare; the relevant line from *Macbeth* is, "We have scotch'd the snake, not killed it." The verb also means "to block (a wheel) with a scotch."

> **USE:** "Our dry cleaning service is hemorrhaging money, it's time to *put the scotch to it.*"

RACI—A structured approach to formally assigning responsibilities, particularly during meetings. The "R" stands for responsible, the "A" for accountable, "C" for consulted and "I" for informed. (See also: *"A"—who has it?)*

> **USE:** "When *RACI* assignments are designated and maintained, things are more likely to get done between meetings."

Did you think you had a **square headed girlfriend** in high school?
Maybe not, see page 211, depending on your age,
there may have been no such thing back then.

Rome burning—Refers to ancient *Rome burning* to the ground. In business, it refers to a business that isn't doing well, or one that has a "fire" (big problem) in one area or system wide.

> **USE:** "After the 9/11 disaster, it wasn't just one or two airlines that were detrimentally affected; it was more like *Rome burning.*"

Save from bacon—To remove yourself or your company from a potentially damaging or dangerous situation. Is a pig happy to be headed for the bacon factory? That's probably something he wants to avoid, and so do you.

> **USE:** "We were near broke, so that loan really *saved us from bacon.*"

Seagull management—Ken Blanchard's characterization of a style in which managers behave like seagulls: They swoop down, pick up a scrap of data, an error or something different, squawk loudly, crap all over the people in the vicinity and then fly off. (See also: *hit-and-run management.*)

> USE: "We didn't see the CEO often; when he showed up, we knew he'd find something to carp about, unload on a few of us for being so careless, and then, as suddenly as he appeared, he'd be gone. This was his classic *seagull management.*"

Septic tank level—Ughh! Don't read this one if you have a weak stomach. The *septic tank level* refers to common laborers, because, ahem, the bosses (or big chunks) always fall to the bottom. In this instance, the laborers are actually above the bosses, if that can be good. I tried my best, but just couldn't come up with a sentence.

> USE: "In the Army, the officers run the show, but it's the enlisted men who get the job done, proving they are not *septic tank level.*"

Shoot and then aim—The way an unworkable plan is formulated. If you *shoot a gun and then aim* it, you probably won't hit the target. It can also describe the execution of a plan without proper training, planning or resources.

> USE: "If you do all your homework first, you can prepare an effective airline operating plan. With ours, however, someone *shot, then aimed* and left us with no contingencies for rising fuel costs."

Shotgun approach—When you have no clue what the solution to a problem might be, you try anything you can think of in the hopes that something might work.

> USE: "Ron first tried marketing with a *shotgun approach*; sending out mailers, running Yellow Page ads, having outside salesmen, advertising in newspapers and doing anything else he could think of to get the phones to ring."

Skyscraper curse—A curse on an initiative that is just too ambitious. It stems from the issues involved in trying to build the tallest building in town; it can cost more than expected, and end up with lackluster returns or even bankruptcy.

> USE: "If successful, this campaign would be a huge boon for the company, but many are worried about the *skyscraper curse.*"

Smoke and mirrors—These are deceptive tricks used to obscure the reality of the situation. Someone using *smoke and mirrors* is trying to pull the wool over your eyes.

> USE: "Larry could see instantly that the presentation had no real financial numbers to back it up, but that it was relying on *smoke and mirrors.*

Solomon—Leaders use this as a way to describe what they must do when they don't have enough information to go on and those around them don't agree. In the Bible, *Solomon* had to decide which of two women was telling the truth about being the mother of a baby. He told both women he would just cut the baby in half. The true mother (who was eventually awarded the baby for her demonstration of true love) immediately begged him to give the baby to the other women rather than have the baby cut in half. In business, being *Solomon* is difficult, and frequently no one gets what he wants. When the leader has done well, he achieves the appropriate result by creating an event that exposes the correct path to take. Good leaders have to be Solomon at times. The alternative is to not make a decision—a very bad thing.

USE: "Bosses sometimes need to play the role of *Solomon*, even though it is unpleasant, in order to discover how to achieve what is necessary."

Stalking horse—Similar to a Judas goat, it's something to draw others out of the bushes. In business, this is used as a metaphor for something or someone that serves as a benchmark, a goal or something to follow. Its roots are in hunting: Birds would fly away from humans, but not horses or cattle; therefore, the hunters would hide behind a horse in order to stalk the birds.

USE: "The *stalking horse* was always there to remind us of how much we needed to achieve."

Take a roll call—Used to discuss who is paying attention or who was present at a meeting.

USE: "Perhaps *taking a roll call* would have helped, as it was obvious no one heard anything that was said at the weekly sales meeting."

Too close to the trees—. . . to see the forest. It means perspective is lost by getting too close to an issue. In this case, a manger loses all ability to be objective. (See also: *can't see the forest for the trees, weatherman syndrome, open the window and see the weather* and *blind man and the elephant.*)

USE: "J.R. was *too close to the trees* to see that her team was the main reason the company wasn't hitting its sales goals.

Top of the tower shouting—(See: *shout from the tower.*)

Training Wheels—Used affectionately to describe someone new at a task. Giving them some temporary extra help can benefit them in the beginning, when it's most difficult. Just like training wheels that come off, you can't prop them up forever.

> **USE:** "Tim assigned the retiring sales manager to work with Susan, his replacement, as *training wheels.* She'll be around for the first month or so, to help her get past the learning curve."

Violent agreement—Their words may differ and their arguments can get heated, but the parties are in basic agreement. They simply haven't slowed down and considered each other's perspective, so they don't realize it. Or they know they're in agreement but don't want to admit it for political, prideful or other reasons.

> **USE:** "Bush and Kerry sure had some *violent agreements* during their three debates, mostly with regards to Afghanistan policy."

Wallpaper the meeting—To stack a meeting with people who are in favor of your position. Most likely, they are *yes men.* (See also: *yes man.*)

> **USE:** "Of course they loved his idea, he'd *wallpapered the meeting.*"

Wide eyed—Used to describe someone who has so much enthusiasm for something that it may affect his ability to be objective. A young child is *wide eyed* when he sees a candy jar in the store, and many people are *wide eyed* when they go looking at new cars. Employees can be *wide eyed* about a rumor of better insurance; if a buyer at an auction gets *wide eyed* easily he may pay too much for the item he is bidding on. It's a typical problem with entrepreneurs; when they prepare a business plan, they often get wide eyes, overestimating sales or underestimating expenses. (See also: *eager beaver.*)

> **USE:** "The director of HR was *wide eyed* after hearing the initial presentation from the insurance provider, which offered better coverage and lower rates."

3

Sales and Marketing

80/20 rule—Marketing principle stating that about 20 percent of a company's customers will account for about 80 percent of its sales. It can also include other issues, such as when 20 percent of the employees cause 80 percent of the problems. It is also referred to as the *Pareto Principle*, which states that there are a vital few (20 percent) and the rest (80 percent) are trivial to the bottom line. The value of this guideline serves only as a reminder that one should focus on the few important aspects that will have the most effect. (See also: *Pareto Principle*.)

Acres of diamonds—Describes a business situation, endeavor or market condition with many opportunities just waiting to be "mined" or taken advantage of.

> **USE**: "Once upon a time Bill Gates foresaw *acres and acres and acres of diamonds* ready to be plucked along the so-called 'information highway.' His market-leading software proved that his premonition was correct."

Alpha pup—Market research lingo for the "coolest kid in the neighborhood," a trendsetter, peer leader, early adopter who isn't afraid to spend money on the latest "cool" product or innovative technology. Possibly a future *alpha dog*. (See also: *alpha dog*.)

> USE: "If the *alpha pups* go for it, we'll sell millions of them."

B2b e-commerce—Business to business buying and selling conducted over the Internet.

Baby seal—Refers to subordinates, often salespersons. I got this from my good friend Larry Reeg, who is a salesperson. It's also used to describe meetings (baby seal meetings) for these employees where they are clubbed. I suppose it can apply to any employees who don't meet their goals. (Sorry, don't shoot the messenger, all I do is gather the terms and document them, however repulsive they may be.)

> USE: "The sales crew exited the meeting feeling like baby seals. All who attended had been browbeaten harshly for not hitting the sales goals."

Bird nest on the ground—An easy target and/or an easy target for competitors. It's an uncommon occurrence in business, particularly where markets are concerned. (See also: *low-hanging fruit.*)

> USE: "Fred opined that the Tampa market would be a *bird nest on the ground* and easy to enter, as he saw no serious competitors there."

Breathing our own exhaust—Listening to or feeding off one's own ideas to the point of excluding other information crucial to making better decisions. Many times, as part of strategic planning, participants hear so much about their own ideas that they forget to consider weaknesses and threats that they are certain to encounter. They get so enamored with their concepts that they recycle or breathe in their own ideas or "exhaust" over and over, ignoring outside forces and other folks' input. This problem can be alleviated by a *devil's advocate*. (See also: *altitude sickness, ozone thinking,* and *play devil's advocate.*)

> USE: "Donna was *breathing her own exhaust* as she continued ignoring others' concerns about the market size being unable to support the new project."

Bullet proof—Typically used to describe a plan that can't fail; something that is invincible.

> USE: "The consumer testing of the product, in conjunction with the excellent marketing, made the sales plan *bullet proof.*"

Green Weenies and Due Diligence—
the textbook for business communication

Cheesecake—A term for PR releases, memos or other communications that are old-fashioned, too cute or too simplistic for the audience. As a common perishable food item, it also describes the short "shelf life" of management ideas that aren't seriously thought out or sustained.

> USE: "Our *cheesecake* mail-outs to clientele seemed as if we were communicating to first graders about our CEO's *cheesecake* plans for long-term profits based on old technologies."

Cockroach theory—A business theory stating that bad news tends to be released in bunches.

> USE: "They sure proved the *cockroach theory* when they made announcements of accounting problems four days in a row, then their CFO was indicted."

Co-evolution—Theory that a company can create new business, markets and industries by working with direct competitors as well as customers and suppliers.

> USE: "Though routinely competing for customers, grain marketing cooperatives have adopted *co-evolution* strategies such as forming joint ventures to build flour mills, promote exports and develop products."

Company rag—An internal newsletter or newspaper put out by the company for its employees. (Side note: Paper stock for newsletters and other publications often has some rag cloth content.)

> USE: "Her true age was exposed in the *company rag* along with the other birthday announcements."

Dead Fish, Idaho—A fictional town in America used by marketers when describing the worst place to sell anything.

> USE: "The product was so bad that when we demonstrated it in *Dead Fish, Idaho*, the citizens jeered at us."

De-horse—Rumored to have come from the car business, where the goal is to get the customers out of their old car and into a new one. Many times, if they can just get the person in the new car to drive home for the evening, they have been *de-horsed* and will almost certainly buy the new car. It's used in business to refer to just about any situation where we want to get the customer to stop using their current product or service so they will start using and eventually buy the one we are offering.

> USE: "As a jewelry salesperson, I knew that if I could just get her to remove her old dull ring and put on the new shiny ring, she'd be *de-horsed*."

Demo-monkey—A derogatory name for a person who gives a good product demo.

> USE: "The salesperson was the most talented *demo-monkey* I have ever seen, and his prospects always bought after the product demonstration."

Dial it back—Tone down the rhetoric or advertising.

> USE: "Your sales pitch is too aggressive. *Dial it back!*"

Dialing and smiling—Refers to the practice of cold calling, as in sales.

> USE: "The boys in the sales department were *dialing and smiling* as they worked their targets, and they knew that when they stopped smiling, sales would fall."

Dialing for dollars—From the early telethon fund-raising days. It's used in business to mean raising investment funds, seeking bank loans or pursuing other financial support.

> USE: "An initial public offering of stock is one method of *dialing for dollars* in the corporate world."

Don't order yet—A comment used when selling, meaning that the seller is about to throw in something extra that the buyer wasn't expecting to get. (See also: *throw in some Ginsu knives.*)

> USE: "'Don't order yet,' Ginny told her husband, knowing that when Sam stalled in making his order, the company threw in a free service warranty."

Drag the prize to the front door for someone else to kill, drag the skins to the front door for someone else to clean, drag the kills to the front door for someone else to skin—Regardless of which version, it's a "*rainmaker*" term. Each translates to this: "I'll go get the prospects, but then you have to close the deal, not me." Thus, it could refer to an executive team landing a prospective buyer for the company, offering a tentative deal or letter of intent, and then bringing the prospect and plan to the "*rainmaker,*" the deal closer who arranges the financing. As used in sales, one party is responsible for landing the prospect, but another has to close the sale. (See also: *rainmaker.*)

> USE: "Ted knew he could *drag the prize to the front door for someone else to kill,* but it wasn't clear to him that any of the incompetent sales staff could handle such a large order."

Feet on the street—A marketing term for employees visiting customers in their places of business.

> USE: "We put more *feet on the street* than any other insurance company, and our clientele appreciate the personal contact."

Fish in the boat—A reference to an old fishing thought which says it's hard to get the *fish in the boat*, and until you do, it's not caught. A salesperson, for instance, may be trying to reel in a customer, but until he closes the sale he doesn't have the *fish in the boat*.

> USE: "Don't get too excited about their touring of the factory, because it isn't until he signs the contract that the *fish is in the boat*."

Future-proof—An adjective usually referring to a product, idea or improvement to an existing product that won't be made obsolete by the next wave of technology or other advancements. It can also be used as a verb, meaning to make a product that won't become obsolete with the next new innovations.

> USE: "We have to *future-proof* our global-positioning software so that GM won't turn to the next competing innovator to outfit those Cadillacs in the coming years."

Hit and run—A term with at least three business meanings: (1) to make a quick, hard sell but then not follow up with the prospect; (2) to use short, intense advertising campaigns; and (3) in management, to criticize subordinates quickly and insightfully, then quickly leave them to stew about it. (See also: *hit-and-run management.*)

> USE: "As one of our marketing tools, we *hit and run* with snappy 20-second prime-time TV commercials aired only four nights each month. We dovetail those with dozens of personal *hit-and-run* calls on prospective clients."

Kickback marketing—Any form of marketing agreement where companies refer customers back and forth to each other. My kids and other friends in their business consortium give out $10 coins good on any purchase at any of their businesses.

> USE: "Spitzer was concerned that, in addition to contingent commissions, there was significant effort to steer customers to favored competitors, which didn't always help the customer get the right coverage at competitive prices. It looked like a *kickback marketing* scheme to him."

Lipstick indicator—A barometer based on the theory that when consumers feel less than confident about the future, they turn to less expensive indulgences such as lipsticks. Therefore, lipstick sales tend to increase during times of economic uncertainty or a recession. The term was coined by the chairman of Estee Lauder, and it has proven to be quite accurate.

> **USE**: "The *lipstick indicator* supported our information that reflected high sales due to the high unemployment rate."

Market cannibalization—Occurs when a company's new product competes with and negatively affects sales of existing, related products. In short, a company eats some of its own market share. Sometimes this can be a good thing, because it may be the only way to bring the newest products to market. In fact, the approach can be a send-off for a new or replacement product line.

> **USE**: "When Bayer made a debut of its 'maximum strength' aspirin, the new product ate into sales of classic old standby Bayer Aspirin. Bayer officials said *market cannibalization* was the only way to retain and build market share against new Extra-Strength Tylenol."

Pareto Principle—(See: *80/20 rule.*)

Popcorn and peanuts—This term is used to refer to almost anything that sells easily and has quick returns. It can be used to describe the company's best-selling product or something that sells in high volume. Everyone wants popcorn and peanuts because they taste great and are inexpensive!

> **USE**: "In my company, it's almost entirely our *popcorn and peanuts* that keep us alive."

Press on the flesh (from press the flesh)—An old term with a relatively new marketing tweak meaning to literally or figuratively touch or affect the customer. The old term meant to shake hands.

> **USE**: "We had so many salespeople on the street that it was obvious we were going to *press on the flesh*."

Reaching critical mass—This means getting enough sales, customers or market share to become profitable. It might also refer to reaching the breakeven point.

> USE: "To *reach critical mass*, Dell Computers had to go with big sales promotions in addition to cutting-edge products."

Rent-a-crowd—These are the folks that a company will hire to pose as customers for a new business opening, such as a restaurant or other retail business.

> USE: "Sammy assured the owner his first night would be busy, but didn't tell him that some of the people were actually *rent-a-crowd* customers."

> **Sucks like a Hoover**, sounds like a vacuum cleaner sales pitch, right? Wrong again, see page 183.

Repurposing—Taking content from one medium, such as books or magazines, and repackaging or revising it to be used in another medium: brochures, in-house newsletters, etc. It can also apply to a factory or other building that is converted from one purpose to another.

> USE: "Our newspaper ad campaign became a series of public service announcements. It was a stroke of genius; *repurposing* led to cost saving."

Reverbiagizing—This is rewording a proposal, advertisement or other language with the hope of getting people to respond to it.

> USE: "It's the same ad concept; we have just *reverbiagized* it to make it sound better. Now it's selling our products."

Sell it or smell it—Used to describe any perishable goods a company might sell. If they aren't sold quickly, they will surely rot and smell, causing big problems.

Sound bite—From TV and radio broadcasting, brief but articulate and snappy news or other comment, often prepared in advance and often spoken by politicians for an interview. In business, this tidbit is spoken like the source really knows a lot about the chosen subject, when in fact the source's expertise may be limited. It's difficult to get an accurate impression when only an excerpt of their verbal communication is heard. It's also known as a buzzword.

> USE: "Our PR director sure knows how to give a *sound bite* every time Channel 8 shows up for interviews. He can talk about anything and sound like he's an expert, but it takes preparation, he says."

Stop selling—As odd as it might seem, there is a time to sell and a time to *stop selling*. Some salespersons continue to "sell" when the customer is ready to order. Most of the time, the salesperson has good intentions; he is simply trying to offer more information. This sometimes aggravates customers and could cause the customer to not buy at all. The term is usually used, however, to describe a person who is trying to convince someone else that his idea is good. Once he has convinced the person of that, he needs to stop; over-selling is a waste of time. The best people, whether just salespersons or employees, can sense when it's time to close or that the customer doesn't need closing, they are ready to buy.

> USE: "The customer seemed likely to order until Bill refused to stop selling and kept offering more and more information. When he finally mentioned that the part was blue, the customer changed his mind, saying he didn't want a blue one."

Sweet spot—When an occurrence is at its most advantageous point. The *sweet spot* in product pricing is the point at which the price allows good margins but also generates maximum sales. At a higher price, sales may decrease. At a lower price, sales could be great, but the profit may not be. Two examples would be when an optimum number of customers can be served without adding extra labor, or getting the most miles before replacing a truck fleet.

> USE: "We knew we had hit the *sweet spot* in the market, as our price was right in the middle of our competitors, and sales exploded."

Throw in some Ginsu knives—From the old infomercials, to include something of added value at no extra charge when making a sale. It can be linked to products or even business plans or selling the business itself. You recall the old line: "But if you order now, we will throw in this wonderful set of Ginsu knives!" It's not uncommon for an experienced negotiator to hold back and make sure he has something extra to throw in to close the deal. (See also: *don't order yet.*)

> USE: "If you'll clinch the deal today for our company, we'll *throw in some Ginsu knives* and, literally, the kitchen to go with them. By that, I mean the company-owned lodge on the lake at no extra charge."

Value migration—The movement of growth and profit opportunities from one company to another, one industry to another, or one country's industry to a similar industry in another country. It's often used to discuss industries from which value has migrated, leaving a scarcity of growth opportunities.

> USE: "*Value migration* has been an ongoing pattern for the U.S. apparel manufacturing industries because the cheap labor is the ace in Chinese mainland's super-sized deck of growth opportunities."

We eat our own dog food—The company selling the product actually uses that product because it is so good.

> USE: "It wasn't just another product endorsement when the pro basketball player touted Airy Shoes on TV. He owns the shoemaking company, so both he and his employees *eat their own dog food*: They wear their own shoes."

Whale—From the casino gambling world, a large volume customer or buyer. Winning this person's business is a coup.

> USE: "Ted announced that the new fishing lure had been picked up by the largest *whale* we could have imagined, Wal-Mart."

Woody—A strong and quick upward movement in the market, a security or sales.

> USE: "After receiving an ultimatum due to poor sales, I'm relieved we finally picked up a *woody* in our division, or I would have been replaced as manager."

4

Accounting, Investments, Contracts and Technology

Aggregated eyeballs—A term describing the total amount of hits on a website; the total number of prospects that looked. Obviously conversion to sale is the next metric to measure.

> USE: "Based on the site's *aggregated eyeballs*, we have a very hot product on our hands."

Air pocket—This is a condition in which the price of a stock or the value of a company plunges unexpectedly, similar to an airplane when it hits an air pocket. The term can also describe a deal that goes sour quickly and without warning.

> USE: "Jim knew that the announcement of his company's major customer filing bankruptcy was a huge *air pocket* that would also kill the sales contract and send his own company's stock reeling."

Alligator property—Real estate that develops excessive taxes, soaring maintenance costs, and/or prohibitively high interest rates and becomes predatory in the sense of eating up the owner's profits. It can also be used to describe a facility that is closed and standing empty, while taxes and other costs go on.

> USE: "The inheritance tax on that family-owned newspaper made it an *alligator property*, so the prospective heirs were forced to sell it to a wealthy media conglomerate."

Back of the envelope—A swiftly or hastily prepared agreement. (See also: *on a napkin*.)

> USE: "It was one of those *back of the envelope* deals, since we were in such a hurry to complete the transaction."

Backing the truck up—A reference to the figurative or literal vehicle that will be delivering proceeds (money) from a transaction. When the money truck hits us or arrives at our door, it means the transaction has closed and the money has arrived. Often the money *truck is backing up* but is not ready to unload, which can be frustrating. In most deals, the money truck backs up several times before it finally arrives (hitting us). Many businesspeople are superstitious about discussing it until the money is actually in hand. (See also: *money truck.*)

> **USE**: "Bob felt that the truck would back up next Tuesday, and the closing would occur at 2 p.m. on that day; 'In this business, you never know for sure,' he said."

Bare pilgrim—A naïve investor who loses all of his money in a private investment or by trading equities in the stock market.

> **USE**: "He thought he was going to be wealthy, but because of his ignorance he lost it all, and now is a *bare pilgrim.*"

Bleeding edge—Beyond the so-called cutting edge, latest technologies or developments in a business sector. So new and hazardous that the company risks injury.

> **USE**: "*Bleeding-edge* manufacturing technologies must be proven on the factory floor and are often too risky for companies with small R&D budgets."

Bo Derek—A slang term used to describe a perfect stock or investment. Named for the actress known as the "Perfect 10."

> **USE**: "I was always leery of investing in the stock market, but my broker told me not to worry because he had a *Bo Derek* for me."

Bottom fisher (or feeder)—A person, group or company always look-ing for the cheapest or best below-market value in transactions such as acquisitions and stock deals. Rather than pursuing a blue chip deal or opportunities in which many other bidders will also be participating, they look for value in obscure opportunities that others might over-look. With few or no other bidders, the largely ignored seller is likely to accept a lower price or more demanding terms.

> USE: "Known as a *bottom feeder*, Luther never looked at the biggest deals because he felt that it was easier to make a larger profit on the smaller overlooked deals." (See also: *gunslinger*.)

Boys in the backroom—A group of prominent or powerful people making decisions behind the scenes, behind closed doors. They may be the company's principal stockholders.

> USE: "If the *boys in the backroom* don't agree, our publicly held company's CEO and chairman won't make any deals."

Breakup fee—A fee associated with a breakup or decision not to stay with a given lender or partner. *Breakup fees* are set early in negotia-tions, as are the mechanisms defining how a breakup will proceed. Such fees can be very costly, reaching into millions of dollars, and are generally seen as a deterrent to *breaking up*. The fee is paid by the party wanting out of the transaction. Oftentimes the fee is escrowed by either or both parties at the beginning of the transaction, with certain rules for its disbursement.

> USE: "The *breakup fees* in our Bank of America contract are so exorbitant that we'll never look for a new banker."

Breeze-in-your-face marketing—An expression for all marketing and promotional spending that creates no sustainable competitive advan-tage and lasts about as long as a *breeze in the face*. It comes from the title of a *Harvard Business Review* article.

> USE: "The promoters' *breeze-in-your-face marketing* campaign didn't reach enough fans, so the opening box office results were disappointing."

Burn rate—The rate at which cash is used up by the business. For instance, if the business has $2 million in available cash, but is losing $500,000 per month, and its cash flow is not covering costs, the company will likely fail in a matter of months. It's important to understand the *burn rate* and not confuse it with operating losses. It is cash used, not necessarily a bottom-line measurement. Bottom line measurements, including operating earnings, include many non-cash items, and many items not in bottom line measurements like capital expenditures affect cash. (See also: *runway* and *how big is the hole and how are we going to fill it.*)

> USE: "Ted reported that our *burn rate* of $400,000 per month meant we probably had two months left to keep the doors open."

Call the loan, but it won't come—Addressing the reality that in many cases you can call a loan, but it won't do any good. *Calling a loan* means to declare it due. Generally speaking, a loan is called due to maturity or a default; in default situations, it's rarely paid off. You can't call a loan and expect it to come like your trained pet.

> USE: "Gary said he wants to *call the loan, but he knows it wouldn't come* so he's holding off for now."

Carry the abacus—A reference to the person counting the money, measuring results, keeping the books, etc. The abacus was an ancient way to count money, and is now used to describe more modern systems.

> USE: "Tom has agreed to *carry the abacus* for us since his department would be responsible for delivering the sales and receiving the funds."

Chasing nickels around dollar bills—When cutting expenses, going after the smaller, easier savings and overlooking larger, more difficult reductions. It's easy to do when cutting expenses is the only focus and the person in charge is myopic about the task. The term can also be used when the company focuses on one customer niche for sales, while ignoring other segments that are much larger. (See also: *can't see the forest for the trees, too close to the trees, weather man syndrome, sitting on the nickel, open the window and see the weather* and *blind man and the elephant.*)

> USE: "Our controller was *chasing nickels around dollar bills* when he directed everyone to trim orders for paper clips and pens but neglected to recommend the needed layoffs."

Chips and salsa—Computer lingo: *Chips* = hardware. *Salsa* = software.

> USE: "Most new computer users prefer to pay a price that includes *chips and salsa.*"

Clicks and chicks—A tactic wherein websites use sexy females to attract business.

> USE: "The HR department is all upset that we decided to go for *clicks* with *chicks* by hiring Pamela Anderson to pose for our website, but I thought it was pretty fine."

Clinton bond—A bond that is said to have no principle, no interest and no maturity.

> USE: "Wouldn't you know my luck. I saved up my money to make an investment and it turned out to be a *Clinton bond.*"

Clipping coupons—Describes the way the best products and services seem to sell or run themselves, generating a steady stream of profits. Like *clipping coupons*, these returns eventually come with very little effort or attention.

> USE: "The Marta acne treatment product line was selling like hotcakes, allowing us to just *clip coupons*, generating large cash flows with minimum outlays or attention."

Code 18—Refers to mistakes made by a computer user (who was 18 inches from the screen).

> USE: "The whole IT department had a *Code 18* yesterday; the data was all lost due to the one mistake they made in coding."

Comb the hair—In data analysis, meaning sort through (*comb*) the data (*hair*) several times and in several directions to ensure exposing all aspects and interpretations of the information. In planning, the process finds loose ends as well as logic problems, and generally improves the accuracy of the plan. *Combing the hair*, however, can also kill the plan if too many problems are found.

> USE: "We had to *comb the hair* six times, analyzing our plan's data from buyers' and sellers' perspectives to reassure our partners, bankers and stockholders that we knew what we were doing."

Cookie jar accounting—Remember Grandma's cookie jar? She filled it, and you helped yourself as you wanted. In corporate America, this saying refers to accountants putting earnings aside to use later, sometimes disingenuously. It's rarely practiced by entrepreneurs, except occasionally to pay taxes. Public companies use their "cookie jars" in many ways to manage earnings from quarter to quarter, including covering charges and write-downs. The funds may serve as reserves or be used to boost earnings to meet expectations or to offset losses. (See also: *cooking the books, creative accounting, voodoo math, gaming the numbers,* and *window dressing.*)

> **USE:** "Freddie Mac uses *cookie jar accounting* to manage earnings from quarter to quarter and to help smooth out wide bottom-line swings stemming from complex interest swaps and derivatives, making the company's earnings look like they have had steady growth."

Cooking the books—Refers to bookkeeping entries or methods intended to mislead auditors, investors, or analysts. Methods include overstating income, capitalizing expenses to overstate profit and hiding adverse financial issues. Cooking food always changes the product and *cooking the books* changes them as well. (See also: *creative accounting, voodoo math, cookie jar accounting, gaming the numbers,* and *window dressing.*)

> **USE:** "*Cooking the books* to hide earnings shortfalls from outside investments will eventually bring the IRS—and perhaps the Justice Department—knocking on your door."

Corn/hog ratio—The difference between the price that could be obtained by selling a component of a product and the price that could be obtained by selling the finished product. The saying is derived from the farming practice of deciding whether to feed the corn to the hogs and then sell the hogs, or to just sell the corn separately.

> **USE:** "Our study and application of the *corn/hog ratio* said that selling the scrap computers whole for the gold in the circuit boards brought in more net sales than hiring extensive labor to disassemble the units."

Cradle to grave—Describes a process or person that handles something from start to finish. In auto recycling, we used the term to describe how we remade a process that called for many employees to dismantle cars, clean and stock parts into a system where one employee did it all. This increased accountability, lowered cost, and allowed variable costs in the dismantling department without complex job descriptions and overlapping work. (See also: *soup to nuts, making the soup,* and *end-to-end.*)

> USE: "Once we installed *cradle to grave* along with *pay for performance,* our costs dropped by 30 percent and productivity increased 20 percent."

Green Weenies and Due Diligence makes a perfect gift for that business consultant or financial planner you know!

Creative accounting—Some people think of it as accountants "making something out of nothing." (See also: *cooking the books, window dressing, gaming the numbers,* and *cookie jar accounting.*)

> USE: "Some Enron executives were accused of highly *creative accounting* when it became apparent that the items they sold were really just rented."

Cycle back—This means to make a second pass at understanding a component of a business plan; to reconsider the fundamentals and assumptions in the plan. This process can be applied to most any business decision.

> USE: "Mike was not satisfied with the plan and wanted to *cycle back* and reconsider its cost projections."

Dead cat bounce—A temporary recovery in a stock's price after a large drop in value. Since the "cat" is dead, the rise is really just a bounce, and it will soon drop again and stay down.

> USE: "Those dot-com stocks were plunging sharply, but suddenly XYZ.com stock's value took a *dead cat bounce*, regaining 80 percent of its lost value, only to lose it within hours when everyone realized the news about the company's prospects for survival wasn't real."

Dead tree version—A written or published version of anything that is also available electronically. Refers to the fact that paper is made from trees.

> USE: "Our CEO wanted more electronic versions, as it cost nothing to store and deliver them, rather than copying and filing the printed *dead tree versions*."

Deal toy—A plaque, paperweight or other trophy specially designed to commemorate the closing of a transaction. Typically these are made of Lucite, but can be metal or glass and are often shaped liked a tombstone or monument. They're generally presented to all parties who were responsible for consummating the deal and can be a source of great pride. (See also: *tombstone.*)

> USE: "Many merger negotiators are superstitious and don't want to discuss or design a *deal toy* until after the transaction has closed."

Deals that fund [close] quickly, fund [close], those that don't, don't—This is really true for most transactions, including buying, selling, borrowing, and funding. Most of the time, the deal either gets done fairly quickly or it doesn't get done at all. Deals that don't close quickly don't always die, but as negotiations drag on, the chances of not closing increase dramatically. (See also: *deal fatigue.*)

> USE: "He thought he could take his time closing, but his boss told him to wrap it up before he lost the deal, explaining that *deals that fund quickly fund, those that don't, don't*."

Devil is in the details—Formulating a business strategy can be easy, but developing and executing the details can be much tougher—possibly even killing the initiative. Many good plans have failed due to management's inability to deploy or maintain the employees that are necessary to handle the details and do the job. All of us have been tripped up by a detail. I learned this early on from my mentor Brian Nerney. (See also: *tripping on midgets* and *the big print giveth and the small print taketh away.*)

> USE: "Even though the plan looks achievable, Ted knows the *devil is in the details,* and that strict quality controls will be required for the plan to work."

Dog-and-pony show—A major investment presentation or loan request to lenders or investors. The management team parades the business plan, trying to impress the prospective lenders or investors. The reference to dogs and ponies evokes thoughts of a circus with all the glamour and glitz captivating people's attention. (See also: *flying circus.*)

> USE: "When the Burlington Northern and Santa Fe railroads proposed merging, they trotted out the financial *dog-and-pony show* to tout the deal to investment bankers, stockholders, big bank lenders and federal anti-trust regulators."

Drill down—An effort to understand more details of a business plan. (See also: *fishbone analysis, granularity* and *layer of the onion.*)

> USE: "Dale insisted that we *drill down* further in the plan, because he suspected that when we examined all the details, we'd discover that the production numbers couldn't be substantiated."

Dry powder—A broadly used term usually referring to cash, but can mean virtually any resource needed for success. When gunpowder is dry, it's explosive and powerful, but after the powder gets wet or is used it's no longer ready for action or potent enough to have serious impact. After employee morale is gone, there's no *dry powder* to launch a turn-around. Similarly, if all the cash is gone, the company can't possibly recover, even with a new initiative.

> USE: "We knew we had to give up our expansion plans when we understood that we simply did not have enough *dry powder* to survive and also open the new distribution center."

Dueling data—Data that should be the same but aren't, data that should point the same direction but don't; generally data that can be misleading. Sometimes two different sources report different data that represent the same information in the company, yet both purport to be accurate. For instance, the manufacturing division reports that X units are produced and the distribution division reports that it shipped Y units over the same time period. The correct number has to be known and usually the answer will reveal problems within the company. It can also be used to describe consistent data being discussed by two parties who differ as to the meaning of the data.

> USE: "We produce only what we've sold. When marketing claimed that it sold 444 widgets and manufacturing claimed that it produced 494 widgets, we had to explain the *dueling data* for May. As it turned out, the difference was the defective parts."

End-to-end—Used largely by technology vendors to imply that whatever they build for one part of your organization will work in harmony with whatever they build for another. In short, their computer and mechanical systems will network from one end of your business or process to the other. It can describe any process or person where something works from one end to the other end. (See also: *cradle to grave.*)

> USE: "Our *end-to-end* computers talk seamlessly with each other, linking production, accounting, engineering and design, inventory management, payroll, sales and distribution."

Fishbone analysis—A thorough analysis diving into the foundational issues, also called an "Ishikawa diagram" after its Japanese originator. To solve a problem, one must understand all the root causes. Such an exercise reveals the "skeleton" of the subject by going all the way to the bone to uncover root causes and issues. (See also: *drill down, layers of the onion* and *granularity*)

> USE: "We paid for the complete works, a *fishbone analysis* that will tell us the origins of the ongoing labor dispute and all the factors leading to the strike by our truckers."

Flaming e-mail—E-mail that includes expletives or otherwise offensive, sarcastic or nonproductive language.

> USE: "Our attorney, 'boiling mad' over unproductive negotiations to settle claims against our company, sent a *flaming e-mail* to the plaintiffs' attorney. When the judge heard about it, he also used some coarse language to chastise our attorney."

Foot and tie—Used in a financial or operating plan to mean the numbers appear reliable, the math seems accurate, the numbers compute logically from one analysis to another, or the data match in comparisons. All the numbers should *foot and tie* together.

> USE: "It was obvious as we studied the plan that the financial numbers didn't *foot and tie* to the operating metrics, which were exorbitant."

Friends and family—A group of close-knit associates, friends or relatives of the seller in a deal for stock or other assets. The term is commonly used when talking about a private placement stock offering wherein one sells it to *friends and family*. I have closed two of these deals, one for my salvage yard chain just before I sold it to Ford, and one when I started the salvage auto auction. These offerings are limited in size. My first one was raining $1 million, my second at $2 million. The SEC restricts how such an offering can be distributed with strict guidelines on how one can market it and how many investors are allowed. The deals may also be regulated by states. Regulation varies from state to state, so seek good advice because there are many legal traps. Additionally, in most cases the investors are required to be accredited. The *friends and family* connotation comes from the reality that if the stock isn't going to be publicly traded, it will be closely held, and will likely only be sold to folks that are known personally.

> USE: "Don't think that because you are placing shares of your company stock with *friends and family* that you are immune from due diligence, buttoning up the documents, proper disclosures and handling all the legalities. Sometimes relatives will yell even louder than strangers if things go south and they lose money."

Gaming the numbers—Playing with assumptions, statistics, or other information to project what one wants the forecasts, data or plans to show; likely in contrast to what one thinks is actually the most likely outcome. Managers can play this dangerous game to get bonuses they might not deserve. It's also used to describe accounting misstatements. (See also: *cookie jar accounting, cooking the books,* and *window dressing.*)

> USE: "We wanted to buy our major competitor so badly that our CPAs were *gaming the numbers* to prove to our directors the wisdom of consummating the acquisition."

Gap analysis—A detailed examination of gaps between what's in operational or financial reports and what's in the budgets and goals. It's a close look at what we said we would do and what we're actually doing. It looks at the numbers line by line to understand where the problems are and/or uncover weaknesses in the forecasting process. It can also be used to analyze operational data including production and distribution.

> USE: "When the June results were announced, it was obvious that a *gap analysis* would be required to understand where we missed our targets and why."

Gauge—One of the measures of a company's performance; one of the reporting mechanisms for operating metrics; a measure of any of the company's vital components. As in a car or machinery, the gauge is the visual tool used to understand what is going on. (See also: *driving without a dashboard, KPI* and *operating metrics.*)

> USE: "The CEO wants an up-to-date *gauge* on what's happening in every major division of the company, as well as equally current measures of every vital financial statistic—weekly."

Gazelle—A company growing at an annual rate of 20 percent or more.

> USE: "That company opened its doors five years ago and it's been running like a *gazelle* ever since."

Go back to the well—Go back to a lender, partner, the boss, board of directors, shareholders or other investors for more money, other resources, or approvals for new initiatives. Generally a bad thing. If you *go back to the well* too often, it runs out of water. Good business planning in conjunction with superior execution will prevent you from needing to *go back to the well*. Regardless, you will not go back many times, as this trip is a *CLM* or *CEM*.

> USE: "If you *go back to the well* just once too often, it totally dries up for new venture capital, operating loans or even nods to hire more employees."

Granularity—The need for more detail, or a situation short on necessary details. When studying a situation, budget, deal, or metric, you may need more details to understand the matter. (See also: *drill down, fishbone analysis, layer of the onion* and *color vs. play by play.*)

> USE: "It was a *granularity* case. We knew the rate of production for our widgets, but we needed to know more—like how many minutes were required to apply a decal to each widget and how much glue is used to do it."

Gravity filing system—Stacking or piling files around the office, instead of putting them in alphabetical order in file cabinets or using another more organized storage system. I once had a controller who filed things horizontally instead of vertically. It was a nightmare to find anything.

> USE: "Some CEOs are notorious for their *gravity filing systems*, either stacking files on the floor or in corners of their offices, instead of returning them to the file clerk for storage."

Greenmail—A legal but perhaps unethical stock market profit-taking strategy. A buyer takes a significant stock position that enables him to state plans for taking over a publicly held company. The buyer doesn't really want or plan to complete the takeover, however, and hopes that the target company will buy back the stock at a premium to avoid the takeover. The maneuver isn't blackmail; it's *greenmail*. (See also: *anti-greenmail* and *pirate.*)

> USE: "Some corporate raiders like to use *greenmail*. They buy up shares until they have 20-30 percent of a targeted publicly held company. Then they announce plans for a takeover, but they choose only targets they know will avoid a takeover at almost any cost. Hence, the target company's directors agree to a stock buy-back at a premium. The raiders go away richer."

Hacker—A *hacker* is a computer expert with a knack for breaking through or getting around computer defensive systems. A *hacker* is not to be trusted—unless, of course, he's on your payroll—in which case they make mighty fine security experts. Some companies hire *hackers* to make sure they are hack-proof, and of course all the virus companies have hackers as employees.

> USE: "A *hacker* broke into our computer systems last night. The servers will be shut down all day."

Haircut—A reduction in price or compensation, usually forced on the seller or payee by another party. In stock offerings, companies routinely enter the process with a stock value number in mind, but by the time the final price is dictated by the underwriters, the seller usually gets a *haircut*. Even in normal bargaining on business products and services, it isn't unusual for a *haircut* to appear at the last second of negotiations to seal the deal. Many times a *haircut* is unexpected and almost always bad for the seller.

> USE: "As they discussed the final deal, Scott said if the vendor would take a *haircut* of 5 percent off the quoted price of their work uniforms, he would sign up."

Hockey stick—In financial and operating plans, a change in the numbers that appears unrealistic, like a hockey puck being slapped from a standstill to a jillion MPH in a split second. If last year's sales were $1 million, this year's are unlikely to be $10 million. Bankers, lenders and even partners or investors like to see reasonable profitable growth and are likely to discard anything that looks like it was inspired by a *hockey stick*. Although there are many valid exceptions, growth of much more than 10 to 20 percent annually is rare. If a company is expecting a *hockey stick* increase in sales to make a turnaround, investors will look at it dubiously. The term is also used because a hockey stick trails the ice flat for a second, then takes off up. If your graph of sales looks like that, you may be in trouble. (See also: *nosebleed numbers.*)

> USE: "The manager presented a budget with a forecast for growth like the company had never seen before, and it was dismissed as a *hockey stick* projection."

Holloware—Software that is supposed to be the best, but in fact doesn't perform as advertised. (See also: *vapor ware.*)

> USE: "Cory realized that even though his new accounting software promised the world, it was nothing but *holloware* and couldn't make good on that promise."

How big is the hole, and how are we going to fill it?—In other words, how big is the financial deficit and what plan can we devise to erase it? The size of "the hole" is similar to the *burn rate*, but not exactly the same thing. The *burn rate* can be either a current or projected cash depletion rate. The size of "the hole" is an estimate of how much sales, income or cash is needed to solve a problem or potential crisis. Such a hole was likely created by cash depletion or other unexpected event. It can also apply quite nicely to production, shipping and other areas. If you miss production numbers, how big is the hole and how will you fill it? You may have to shift production to another plant. (See also: *burn rate* and *runway.*)

> USE: "Although the company is quite profitable, the pending asbestos litigation forced everyone to ask 'How big is the hole, and how are we going to fill it?'"

In the penalty box—Time period when a company's stock price is in the doldrums and has yet to rebound because of weak sales, poor earnings, government regulation, or some other reason. It's not unlike hockey, where a player gets penalized for doing something bad!

> USE: "If we don't show a profit by the end of this quarter, we'll be *in the penalty box.*"

Jennifer Lopez–J-Lo—A technical analysis term referring to a rounding bottom in a stock's price pattern. For those who are unaware, the bottom on Ms. Lopez is infamously round.

Layer(s) of the onion—Level(s) of detail, depth of the research or study. To get to the core of an onion, you peel back the layers. (See also: *fishbone analysis, granularity* and *drill down.*)

> USE: "Getting to the heart of marketing research is like peeling the *layers of the onion;* you go one step at a time to dig deep for the best information."

Levers of profit—Tools, actions, or items to be used (i.e., pushed or pulled like levers on a machine) to control sales and profits. For instance, lowering prices almost always increases sales but typically lowers the margin per item. If you pull the price lever down too far, the margins fall below cost and losses occur. If you push the lever up too far, the margins rise but sales may drop again possibly causing losses. Price and margin are but a few of the levers available to managers. Advertising, other promotions, finding lower-cost suppliers and renegotiating vendor prices are just a few of the others. Learning to use many levers simultaneously is an accomplishment mastered by only a few.

> USE: "Greg knew that price and product mix were the *profit levers* he wanted to use to achieve the sales and margins needed to deliver record operating income."

Losing your virginity—Refers to the first time you give up equity to outside investors. When I did my first private placement and no longer owned 100 percent of the company, I had to take my Ferrari and other perks off the company books. (See also: *lose virginity* in chapter five.)

> USE: "I *lost my virginity* when I completed my first private placement, selling 15 percent of my company to others. It was a bad feeling, especially when I realized that the company would no longer make the yacht payments or pay for the insurance."

Massage—In accounting, manipulating the numbers to get a desired result; in planning, making an initiative feasible, or killing it if that's the agenda. Not unlike a massage, it kind of moves things around.

> USE: "Bill said that given some time he could gather more data and *massage* and refine the numbers, which would determine whether the project was borderline or just plain unfeasible."

Meatloaf—Unsolicited personal email from friends and relatives, not Spam. Both, of course, are types of meat, but the meatloaf tastes better than the Spam.

> USE: "My friend sent more *meatloaf* than I could handle; I almost wished I could get Spam instead, since it comes in a smaller can."

Money truck—Its arrival is always hoped for. (See also: *backing the truck up.*)

> USE: "Ever since the first draft of the contract, they had waited anxiously for the *money truck* to arrive."

More water in the bucket to offset holes in the bucket—Adding more resources to offset a drain on cash, administrators, workers or other resources; possibly not the best strategy, since it does nothing to repair the problem (fix the holes). For instance, if the company is losing too much money, it will need additional sales, or perhaps divestitures of assets, to replenish the cash lost by negative income.

> USE: "Our movie theater chain was bleeding cash from our rapid expansion, fierce competition and rising costs to screen new releases. We had to pour *more water in the bucket to offset holes in the bucket*. That's not easy when our ticket and concession prices were already on the high end."

Nosebleed numbers—Sales, productivity, or financial numbers that are so high or unbelievable they make your nose bleed, as if at a high altitude. It is a reference to the nosebleed section of an arena, very high up in the stands. In business, they are part of a business plan or projection that just doesn't make sense or is wildly optimistic. *(See also: hockey stick.)*

> USE: "Patty predicted that she could rent all the spaces in less than three months, which were obviously *nosebleed numbers*, since it took over two years on her last project to accomplish the same goal."

Pain points—A favorite saying of consultants used to describe company units, enterprises, operations, or site vulnerabilities due to poor operating structure, technology, or inefficiencies.

> USE: "Delta Air Lines has been hit hard by rising fuel prices, a shrinking leisure flying market and regional low-cost carriers. Those are the airline's biggest *pain points*."

Pays like a judge—Can be counted on to pay the bills on time without taking inappropriate discounts or asking for special favors. Judges are generally predictable, fair and (we hope) honest.

> USE: "Mennonite businessmen are known for *paying like a judge*. They're never late on a bill and they even hand-deliver the check or cash to the creditor."

Placeholder—What it sounds like: something or someone who's just filling space; the opposite of dynamic. In the same vein, it can also be a budget number that is unproven, with no one having confidence in its accuracy. A *placeholder* is usually temporarily holding the place until the qualified replacement can be found. It also applies to a space left blank in a financial plan or an operating plan.

> USE: "Paul was asked to be a *placeholder* in the CEO position until a replacement for the deceased officer could be found."

Plan B—A plan of action if and when plan A fails or falters; an alternative. Good executives always have a *Plan B,* and they are often needed. Murphy's Law states: "Things that can go wrong, will, so always have a backup strategy." You can probably figure out what a plan C is as well. (See also: *playing football without a helmet* for the opposite.)

> USE: "We have a *plan B* so that if the building doesn't sell by the deadline, we can draw some cash from our credit line."

Pothole in the information super highway—A derogatory term used to describe someone who is not computer literate. The term was used by Senator Gore when he wrote some legislation, and also was used in his political rhetoric.

> USE: "Did you see Mary trying to do research online? She could barely even open the browser—talk about a *pothole in the information super highway!*"

Ragged edge—Being out of control or going too fast; always trying the newest things even though there's greatly increased risk. It can be a good thing or a bad thing.

> USE: "Pauline's nearly *ragged edge* R&D has management worried that she won't check our new pharmaceuticals for all potential hazards."

Rainmaker—The person, department or firm who makes everything happen or come together. Usually the term is used in a financial sense to describe the person that can make the money appear, but it can also be applied to a star salesperson who brings in a big sale at the end of the period, helping to reach a goal. (See also: *drag the prize to the front door for someone else to kill.*)

> USE: "Everyone agreed that if he stayed focused, J.C. could be the *rainmaker* we were seeking to spur the sales increase in Seguin."

Revenue leakage—Disappearing sales revenues or profits resulting from known or unknown problems. It can also be used to describe theft or just lost opportunities for sales due to weak salespersons.

> USE: "Bill told us our single biggest source of *revenue leakage* is excessive price discounting by the staff."

Runaway email—Any email that inadvertently went to the wrong recipient, often with dire circumstances.

> **USE**: "Ted knew the second he hit send that the objectionable attachment was going to get him in trouble with the HR director, and he wished he hadn't sent the *runaway email*."

Runway—A business or an individual can have a short or long *runway*, and for both, the big questions are: How far will the cash carry us? Will we have enough to do what needs to be done? You always want the *runway* to be longer than you could possibly need in order to allow for errors. If the *runway* is too short, of course, the airplane crashes. (See also: *burn rate* and *how big is the hole and how are we going to fill it?*)

> **USE**: "If you only have $20 in cash to last you six days until payday, and it's going to cost you $5 per day for gas, your *runway* is too short!"

Scalded cat—An investor, lender or partner who heads for the exits at the slightest hint of trouble.

> **USE**: "After just one quarter of bad numbers, Sarah sold all her stock like a *scalded cat*."

Sitting on the nickel—Too thrifty, cheap, Scrooge-like, etc. Goes beyond conservative and wise budget controls. (See also: *chasing nickels around dollar bills, can't see the forest for the trees, too close to the trees, weatherman syndrome, open the window and see the weather*, and *blind man and the elephant*.)

> **USE**: "Fred was always *sitting on the nickel*. He felt secure with the cash in the bank even though he knew that by not spending it, he was costing himself sales and business growth."

Skunk costs—Expenditures or investments that cannot be recouped by a decision to abort a project. (See also: *sunk costs*.)

> **USE**: "We had already spent over $100,000 when we realized that we were never going to perfect the product, so we chalked it up to *skunk costs*."

Slop guy—The person who is willing to take whatever amount is remaining in an equity raise after the other participants decide on their participation level. It's often a disadvantageous position. Additionally, the *slop guy* has the disadvantage of not knowing in advance the amount of money he may have to bring to the closing table.

> **USE**: "Brian made it clear he won't be the *slop guy*. He wanted everyone to sign up for the amount of equity they wanted, including him. He wasn't going to just stand by and take what was left."

Sunk Costs—(See: *skunk costs.*)

The big print giveth and the small print taketh away—The *big print* refers to the titles and other main text in a contract, the *small print* refers to the *boilerplate*. The *small print* is always where the deal breakers and covenants are. (See also: *boilerplate* and *devil is in the details.*)

> **USE**: "After getting burned on selling his first invention, the young entrepreneur knew that *the big print giveth and the small print taketh away.*"

Tired of dancing, ready to f**k—This needs little explanation. It means you are tired of the talk, negotiations or delays and are ready to consummate the deal or move to the next step. It's time to *stop selling*. (See also: *the dance.*)

> **USE**: "Venture capital principals can have short attention spans. Once they've decided they've heard enough, they take decisive action because they're *tired of dancing, ready to f**k.*"

Tombstone—An ad memorializing a transaction or a *deal toy* (which is similar to a trophy). A *tombstone* is usually printed in an official financial magazine like the *Wall Street Journal*. (See also: *deal toy.*)

> **USE**: "Years later, he still had the *tombstone* announcement that had been published in the *Financial Times.*"

Totem pole—A ranking based on any number of factors, metrics or results as applied to employees, processes, financial results and many other business concepts or operations. Atop this pole is the best. Think of American Indian *totem poles*: they tell family or tribe histories. Company totem poles are often distributed or posted, so everyone knows who is doing the best and who is at the bottom doing the worst.

> USE: "As for our company's list of top salary makers, our CEO is always on top of the *totem pole.*"

Voodoo math—Math that's suspicious, spurious or just so complicated that everyone questions its accuracy. Though not illegal and sometimes the simplest method, it can still cause lots of heartache. Often it is accurate, but a lot of time is spent on explaining *voodoo math.* Analysts and investors are always skeptical of it, especially in today's fraud-wary environment; sometimes they simply can't understand it. (See also: *cooking the books, black-box accounting* and *cookie jar accounting.*)

> USE: "The cost-of-goods formulas and data were so complex that everyone but the CFO referred to them as *voodoo math*, and no one really trusted their accuracy."

Vulture capitalist—A derogatory term to describe a venture capitalist.

> USE: "When the VC firm announced that they were closing the company to sell the assets one day after the acquisition, we knew we had been had by the *vulture capitalist.*"

Weeny window—A tiny window, often borderline usable, on a cell phone or other small electronic gadget.

Word of Mouse—Rumors, gossip, or any news spread through email.

> USE: "I always liked word of mouth vs. *word of mouse* compliments, as email didn't seem to convey all the emotion."

You won't find that pony in my stable—Refers to a stock an investor chooses not to purchase.

> USE: "ZLM has had a few good years, but I think their run is over and the company needs new management. *You won't find that pony in my stable* now."

CHAPTER
5

Employees and Operations

80 percent guy—This is the person that gets 85 percent results with 50 percent money or resources. He's likely practical, thrifty, and efficient. Sometimes in business, it's easy to get caught up in planning an initiative trying to get 100 percent results, perfectly. Oftentimes, however, especially if you apply the 80/20 rule, it would be better to go fast and get almost the same result, while spending a lot less energy or resources.

90-day witching hour—A frustrating situation in which "outliers," the not-so-hot performers or inadequately performing ventures, have stretched an executive's or owner's patience almost to the breaking point. Whatever it is they're doing, it just isn't good enough. Anyone or any initiative can have a *90-day witching hour,* wherein management may be given 90 days to get it right, or give up or possibly get out. (See also: *bad actor.*)

> **USE**: "It was my *90-day witching hour* and I knew that if my tamale production team didn't reach our efficiency goals soon, my career was in jeopardy."

Above the line—In its broadest sense, refers to a person who makes any major contribution to a business endeavor. Originally it described a person performing a major role or making a substantial contribution to the production of a movie, TV program or TV commercial. It could refer to the writer, director, producer or other key talent. Can now apply to any "heavy hitter" in a business project.

> USE: "No one goes farther *above the line* in late-night TV production circles than that creative genius Lorne Michaels, the creator and producer of *Saturday Night Live*."

All hands on deck—Describes any all-out effort to resolve a problem or a situation where all employees are needed to resolve an issue or meet a challenge. It's another military-originated line, this time from the Navy. (See also: *all hands on the pump*.)

> USE: "When it was discovered that the company was going to miss third-quarter sales targets, Greg called *all hands on deck*. At the meeting of all our key supervisors and workers, he enlisted everyone's full support."

All hands on the pump—Probably derives from the old fire-fighting days when it took the use of several firemen's muscles on the handles of one huge pump to put out a fire. Sometimes the task at hand just requires lots of people working on the solution or execution for a turnaround. (See also: *all hands on deck*.)

All hat, **no cattle**—Someone who acts like a big shot but has no substance or power or clout; also, someone who acts rich but has no assets. This type of person wants everyone to believe they are talented and can really do the job, but it soon becomes obvious that they can't. As they say in Texas "good ol' boy" business circles: "It's easy to get a hat but much harder to get a herd of cattle." (See also: *empty shirt.*)

> **USE**: "Joe, the new CEO, drops celebrity names like he knows everybody in New York, but he proved to be *all hat, no cattle* when it came to getting us any PR with all his friends in New York."

All the arrows on the back (or in the quiver)—All the tools or resources needed to accomplish the necessary results—not to be confused with "*arrows in the back*" (see separate entry). For Native American Indians, the quivers on their backs needed to be full of arrows for hunting or fighting.

> **USE:** "Sam questioned whether he would have *all the arrows on his back*, but his partners assured him that the company's lawyers, CPAs and emergency funds would be at his disposal when the liability lawsuits flooded the courts."

Apology bonus—Extra money given to employees being laid off, especially those who were just hired, like recent graduates or employees who left another viable job to join the firm.

Bad actor—An "outlier" or not-so-hot performer. As the boss, you need to focus on this staff member's key performance indicators (*KPIs*). Yes, the *bad actor* may push you toward a *90-day witching hour*. *Bad actors* may act like they're with you or know what they're doing, but you generally know better. Of course, it can also describe a troublemaker or anyone who is always causing problems. (See also: *90-day witching hour* and *KPIs*.)

> **USE:** "I hope Billy Bob is not a *bad actor*. I need all his management skills, not just an act with weak results."

Bad boy clause—An agreement, usually in an employment contract, with financial penalties for an employee who leaves the company and then hires others away. Such an agreement can include forfeiture of bonuses or take aways in retirement accounts.

> **USE:** "I would have taken Brendan and Pete with me when I left, but I have a *bad boy clause* in my contract."

Bad num—A bad or inaccurate number, usually in a business plan or other document. The number is either wrong or distrusted in some way.

> USE: "Theresa's model included many *bad nums,* so she was told to study her data for errors."

Badge—Similar to branding; in the case of an employee, giving them an imaginary *badge* makes them official: they now work for the company.

> USE: "Kathi said we should *badge* him before he got away, as he was the perfect candidate for the sales manger's position."

Balloon juice—Describes the constant rhetoric and bragging from an employee who is stuck on himself.

> USE: "Noah has a lot to say, but it's mostly just *balloon juice.*"

Batting average—Borrowed from baseball terminology. Connotes the success rate of an individual. For a baseball player, .300 (or 30 percent) is good. If you want to hold on to your job, you'd better be doing better than that.

> USE: "Rich's *batting average* is amazing. He's done wonders for our company."

Beehive—Aimless actions and lots of swarming activity, but probably no real progress; tends to cause temporary paralysis.

> USE: "The place was a *beehive,* but there were lots of unproductive, unfocused employees. They had the worst production month in over a year."

Bend over, here it comes again (BOHICA)—Used to describe the cynicism with which people greet new corporate pronouncements; feeling shafted by management again, as expected.

> USE: "CEO Smith is about to announce another round of increases on employee-paid shares for their medical insurance premiums. Well, BOHICA!"

Don't get too far in front of your skis?
Sounds like a lesson for the slopes, right?
Wrong, see page 196.

Big Chief tablet and a No. 2 pencil—The preferred materials of someone who is not very computer literate; refers to someone who is living in the past, when using a Big Chief tablet and a No. 2 pencil was used in grade school to learn their ABCs. It can also be used to describe someone who isn't up to professional standards.

> USE: "Everyone else in the office scurried around with their PDAs and laptops, but Jack was better off at his desk with a *Big Chief tablet and a No. 2 pencil.*"

Boy scout—A person who is always trying to save others, do good deeds or be otherwise honorable. Most companies have *boy scouts* on their management team. I suppose I should include *girl scouts*, as well, to be politically correct. Being referred to as a *boy scout* isn't necessarily complimentary in a business context, as always being a savior may not be well accepted by management. Being a *boy scout* can also be bad if it means making excuses for another employee's bad performance; or if it causes him to hold back on the implementation of new initiatives. (See also: *girl scout.*)

> USE: "We could always count on David as the *boy scout* on the team, because he could be completely trusted. He wasn't necessarily good at meeting heady goals or clinching bargain deals, though."

Brick shy of a load—A derogatory term for a person whose ignorance or stupidity is showing; someone who doesn't seem to have his or her act together. This indicates that a crucial element in the thinking process is absent. He doesn't have a full load of bricks so he can't build anything. (See also: *rode the short bus, elevator doesn't go to top floor, can't walk and chew gum at the same time, through the eyes—there aren't many bulbs there, one card shy of a full deck, the light is on but nobody's home, can short of a six-pack, not the sharpest knife in the drawer,* and *hamster died.*)

> USE: "Pete's new idea was 'half-baked,' as were all of his presentations, so we often wondered if he was a *brick shy of a load.*"

Can short of a six-pack—(See: *rode the short bus, elevator doesn't go to top floor, can't walk and chew gum at the same time, brick shy of a load, through the eyes—there aren't many bulbs there, the light is on but nobody's home, not the sharpest knife in the drawer* and *hamster died.*)

Can't walk and chew gum at the same time—Another description of. . . what else can I say, just a real dummy! (See also: *rode the short bus, elevator doesn't go to top floor, can't walk and chew gum at the same time, through the eyes—there aren't many bulbs there, brick shy of a load, the light is on but nobody's home, can short of a six-pack, not the sharpest knife in the drawer,* and *hamster died.*)

> USE: "I don't know how she even got this job; she *can't walk and chew gum at the same time,* much less work."

Cappuccino cowboy—A nickname for an employee who just has to have a cup of Starbucks on the way to work everyday; generally someone who lives in the suburbs and commutes to the city to work.

> USE: "Amanda just had to go by Starbucks every morning even if it made her late, she is such a *cappuccino cowgirl.*"

Career ending move (CEM)—A very, very big mistake or tragic decision. With this, a person loses the job and perhaps a career. (See also: *CLM.*)

> **USE:** "When the HR director heard of Tom's felony, she knew it was a *CEM.*"

Career limiting move (CLM)—A potentially dangerous mistake. Certainly such a mistake will limit advancement at least for a few years. (Also see: *CEM.*)

> **USE:** "If Pete doesn't accomplish the goal of meeting the product launch date, it will definitely be a *CLM.*"

Carrot and stick—Refers to offering a reward and threatening a penalty at the same time as a form of negotiation or motivation. A carrot is a treat or reward, and obviously a stick stirs memories of the switch when we were young.

> **USE:** "One management strategy is the old *carrot-and-stick* approach, in which a reward is offered yet a threat of a demotion is understood."

Catch and release—This is what happens to new employees of a struggling company, and usually applies to new young employees that were recently hired when the company was flush with cash.

> **USE**: "We had a bunch of bright, new, minds, many fresh out of college, but things went south and now we're instituting a *catch and release* policy."

Census reductions—Layoffs.

Champagne tastes, beer pocketbook—It's also heard as "champagne tastes on a beer budget." It means having tastes or preferences for expensive things and services, but little money to pay for them; a taste for the high life in someone with low funds.

> **USE**: "Her modest income belied her *champagne tastes*; she longed for a BMW, but her *beer pocketbook* could only afford a Chevy."

Clear all the cats in the alley—Alley cats are usually wild pests. This term refers to people who have similar characteristics. The term was coined by Alan Greenberg, chairman of Bear Stearns, to describe employees who need to be culled from the team. In singular form, it is used to describe one outlier: someone who is disruptive or isn't a team player.

> **USE**: "In our last meeting, it was announced that new policies affecting outliers should *clear all the cats in the alley*."

Close, but no cigar—(See: *good try, but no cigar.*)

Coaster—A negative term used to describe an employee who just isn't productive enough and/or has no ambition. I use it as part of one of my favorite sayings, which I use to autograph my books at speaking assignments: Coasting will only get you to one place, the bottom of the hill.

> **USE**: "Mary was a *coaster*, always late to work, never meeting deadlines, and she always had an excuse for her poor performance."

Coming up or going down—Used to refer to an employee who is either sinking under or resurfacing (as if almost drowning) from a flood of major problems. His job may be on the line, and he may feel like he's drowning or being rescued. (See also: *drinking from a fire hose.*)

> USE: "Shipping Supervisor Johnny B. Good was so beleaguered by job pressures that he could feel as if he were *going down*, gasping for air one moment, and *coming up* the next moment, exhaling a sigh of relief."

Cover your ass (CYA)—Preemptive defense tactics designed to make sure no colleague or superior can blame you if something goes wrong.

> USE: "When Anna wrote our new hiring procedures, she *covered her ass* by sharing credit for her work with other executives, just in case some rejected job applicant successfully sued us for discrimination. By not claiming full credit, she would not get the sole blame."

Creepback—When employees who are let go end up being hired as consultants for the same company.

> USE: "When Adam and three other programmers were laid off in the spring, no one would have guessed that by summer all of them would be back, working on the network as consultants, charging 150 percent of what they made as employees. The *creepback* effect made us miss our expense budget by even more."

Cubicle lizard—Someone who appears to almost live in their cubicle. They are always at work, their cubicle is littered with their personal belongs, and may even include a microwave and fridge.

> USE: "Hey Bob, clean this place up. What is that, an ironing board under there? You're such a *cubicle lizard.*"

CYA—(See: *cover your ass.*)

Desk potato—Someone who just stays at their desk, often doing silly things, but not generating any significant work product. I am sure you can see the correlation to a couch potato.

> USE: "James, if you don't change your *desk potato* habits, we're going to have to let you go."

Dirty fingernail person—Usually a person with a great deal of experience, perhaps one who grew up in a business or who started at the bottom and worked his way to the top or near the top. (See also: *scars on my body, MBWA,* and *arrows in the back.*)

> USE: "A reliable *dirty fingernail person* has loads of self confidence, solves problems efficiently or finds the right person to do the job, but never toots his or her own horn too loudly."

Doctor's appointment—Code for "off-premise job interview."

> USE: "I need to run, I have an, ahem, *doctor's appointment.*"

Dog trick—Refers to a problem with employees who like to play dead. It can also be used in reference to a manager who will be judged by his ability to stop the employees from doing the *dog trick.*

> USE: "Ted said it was the last time Patty would be allowed to play dead and not meet a deadline without being written up. He wondered what she was doing in her cubicle, since she darn sure wasn't producing any work. She was doing the old *dog trick.*"

Do you read me?—Borrowed from the language of the United States Military. Similar to "comprende?" An off-handed way of asking, "Do you understand?" Carries a tone of authority, and if you're hearing this, you probably haven't been listening.

> USE: "I need those reports by tonight; *do you read me* on that?"

Duck and weave—Usually an employee's strategy for avoiding accountability, reporting or meetings. He or she generally cannot be counted on to deliver results.

> USE: "Ted was always *ducking and weaving,* and everyone knew not to count on him for the weekly reports."

Elevator doesn't go to the top floor—Limited mentality. (See also: *can't chew gum and walk at the same time, rode the short bus, through the eyes—there aren't many bulbs there, brick shy of a load, can short of a six-pack* and *sharpest knife in the drawer.*)

Energy drainer—Someone who worries all the time, and has no energy left for productive things. (See also: *toxic worrier.*)

> USE: "Dave is an *energy drainer.* He worries so much about his job security that he never gets anything done."

Farm Team—A term from baseball. In baseball potential players are brought in and trained, and then the best ones selected to play. In business, it refers to a company that hires employees, teaches them specialized skills, but has poor retention. As soon as the employees are fully trained, due to poor management of them, they leave to go to work for competitors, ready to be productive. The company with the bad practices just farms the people, growing them, only to be gone.

> USE: "the company had rampant turnover in their specialists, and they were spending heavily to train them, but they were really just a farm team for their competitors."

Fat is in the fire—Something has occurred which is likely to cause a dispute or some sort of disciplinary action. We all know what happens when the steaks on the grill ooze too much fat onto the hot coals; the flames flare up.

> USE: "Well, the *fat is in the fire* now, because Sarah Jane just accused the boss of sexual harassment."

Fence-mending—Making up. After a particularly heated dialogue or disagreement with a co-worker, if you don't do your *fence-mending,* you might get stuck with burnt bridges. To *mend* your *fences* is to resolve the past and make amends. Repairing a fence makes it good again.

> USE: "After their argument, James and Sharon *mended fences.* It was the best thing to do to keep the project moving forward on pace."

Flame out—The sudden end of a bright career brought on by setting unrealistic goals.

> USE: "Though Pete's brilliant performance had exceeded expectations for months, no one was really surprised when he *flamed out* on that last ambitious project."

Flight risk—A valuable employee known to be considering leaving, or who is being pursued by a head hunter, or an executive who is about to be caught for accounting or other impropriety.

Food chain—Used to describe the hierarchy of workers with executives at the top and hourly workers at the bottom.

> **USE**: "I'd never want to be in the hot-tar roofing business. Those laborers are at the bottom of the *food chain*."

Fresh off the boat—A derogatory term for a new immigrant who hasn't adapted to the local culture (often most noticeable in poor driving skills). It can also refer to any person in a new position.

> **USE**: "It was obvious Tim was *fresh off the boat*, he didn't have a clue how the conveyor worked."

Gadget trance—The state of an employee who is fixated on having the latest gadgets, and constantly discusses this fascination with fellow employees.

Girl scout—Female version of *boy scout*. (See also: *boy scout.*)

> **USE**: "Everyone felt she was the *girl scout* of the department because she always volunteered the most time, helped her co-workers, got along with everyone and never complained."

Good try, but no cigar—Old backhanded praise for trying hard but not quite succeeding. Once upon a time a good cigar was a common gift for an accomplishment. If you came close to hitting the goal, you might get a pat on the back but no bonus or cigar.

> **USE**: "We missed our annual sales goal by just $20,000, but the increase from $275,000 last year to $280,000 wasn't thrilling enough. '*Good try, but no cigar,*' the boss said."

Groom or broom—I like this one. It's quite simple really, and applies to any weak employee. You either have to *groom* them and get them productive, or *broom* them out the door.

> **USE**: "After seeing John's dismal numbers, they knew that if he wasn't properly *groomed* at next week's training session, he'd have to be *broomed* out with the dust bunnies."

Hammock pay—Compensation for someone who isn't working, such as someone who receives severance, or even retires on a fat pension. The picture is that of an executive swinging in a hammock, holding a drink and waiting for the next check to arrive.

> USE: "After so many years with the company, Evan was happy to finally relax and let the *hammock pay* roll in."

Hamster died—When the hamster dies, the wheel stops turning. With the wheel not turning, things just aren't the same. (See also: *rode the short bus, elevator doesn't go to top floor, can't walk and chew gum at the same time, through the eyes—there aren't many bulbs there, the light is on but nobody's home, brick shy of a load, can short off a six-pack* and *not the sharpest knife in the drawer.*)

> USE: "We knew that Ken couldn't complete such a difficult task; his *hamster died* a long time ago."

Head up his/her ass (HUHA)—A discreet notation, often put on a memo, to alert others that ideas, data, or opinions are flawed. It implies that the information source doesn't know what he or she is talking about.

Helicopter manager—A boss who is always hovering overhead, likely micromanaging.

> USE: "My boss has already stopped by my desk six times today to ask about this project. He's such a *helicopter manager.*"

Helicopter skills—The ability to rise up and see things from a higher perspective as needed; ability to see the big picture and then zoom back down to handle a detail or an area that is in need of change. (See also: *30,000 feet above.*)

> USE: "Mike made such a great manager because of his *helicopter skills,* which allowed him to see things from a much better perspective than the other managers."

HUHA—(See: *head up his/her ass.*)

Jesus Christ syndrome—A desire or compulsion to find the perfect employee or manager for a tough job. It usually becomes a problem when hiring, transferring or promoting, where speed is required and patience for delays is thin. If you wait to find the *Jesus Christ* candidate, you'll never find anyone. (See also: *looking for Jesus.*)

> **USE:** "Stoney was in a rush to find the perfect candidate for the critical sales position, but after searching for two months, he still hadn't found anyone. Our sales manager accused him of having the *Jesus Christ syndrome* and told him to fill the position within a week."

Johnny Lunchbox—An employee who is not willing to front money out of his pocket for company expenses (travel, etc.) because he doesn't trust the company to reimburse him, or simply doesn't have the funds (likely due to his mismanagement).

> **USE:** "Old *Johnny Lunchbox* over there in the HR department was sure a cynic. He didn't believe in expense reports, and wasn't willing to spend any money and then have to wait for reimbursement, so I had to pay for our clients' lunches every time we took them out."

Jump out of the airplane—Refers to someone who is no longer participating; mentally or physically AWOL. Sometimes people threaten to *jump out of the airplane* to frighten or intimidate others; sometimes they are just done.

> **USE:** "Rick wasn't pulling his weight on the project, and we all realized that he had already *jumped out of the airplane*."

Just came (in) on a potato truck—Derogatory reference indicating that someone isn't bright enough to do the job, usually because he is young and inexperienced. The implication is that he was raised on a farm and simply not exposed to the best training. We know it's pejorative as folks from farms can be as bright as anyone. (See also: *just fell off the turnip truck.*)

> **USE:** "At the end of the work day it's standard for everyone to shut down his/her computer, but the new employee didn't because he *just came in on the potato truck* and hadn't been yet notified of this procedure."

Just fell off the turnip truck—(See: *just came on/in a potato truck.*)

Kevork—To kill or assist in killing an idea. Named for Dr. Kevorkian, of assisted suicide fame.

> **USE**: "It was clear that Nancy's plan was going nowhere, so James stepped in to *Kevork* it."

Lackey—This is someone who will do anything to please his or her boss. Usually given menial tasks.

> **USE**: "She needed the job so badly, she was willing to be her boss's *lackey* by getting his coffee and newspaper and taking care of all of his personal errands."

Let the dead bury their dead—Indicates an impatience to move ahead, without being dragged down by those mulling over their losses. We should always focus on the present and future rather than linger too long on the past, but we need to allow some time to consider or weep over failures in order to learn from them.

> **USE**: "I always say '*Let the dead bury their dead*,' but we had to allow time for consoling our engineering associates on their design failures before we could move on to a brighter future with innovative cars."

Looking for Jesus—Looking for perfection. (See also: *Jesus Christ syndrome.*)

> **USE**: "Why haven't you found a better insurance agent for the employees yet? Are you still *looking for Jesus* while they're suffering with inferior health benefits?"

Lose virginity—Embrace change, try new things, get your "feet wet." Often employees are encouraged to try new tasks or learn new skills. Obviously, many people are hesitant to do it. Once they lose virginity, they become experienced and hopefully more valuable. (See also: *losing your virginity.*)

> **USE**: "It's good to *lose virginity* by taking that first training step toward the big leap into a new career."

Marching orders—Orders to an employee, much like in the military. It can be as simple as an assignment, but more likely it's a bit more important and may involve some controversy or difficult task, like firing someone or replacing a vendor.

> **USE:** "Cory was unhappy to get his new *marching orders*; he really liked his team and didn't want to be the one to fire three people."

McJob—A negative term for low-wage workers or employees in the service industry.

> **USE:** "Bob didn't bother finishing high school and didn't seem to have much motivation, so his parents feared he would never get anything beyond a *McJob*."

Nails in the 2x4—Maximum effort to get stubborn or unfocused employees to pay attention or follow orders. When hitting them in the head with a 2x4 board doesn't do the trick, nails have to be placed in the 2x4.

> **USE:** "We tried termination threats, cash incentives, even free champagne dinners and stern meetings. But none of those ploys convinced our workers to adopt good safety practices. Maybe *nails in the 2x4* could spur them to do it."

Nibbled by ducks—An experience, like being yelled at by your boss, that is unpleasant but not life threatening. Being nibbled may be a recurring action.

> USE: "The boss pestered me all month about Pete not hitting his sales goals, but the sales team delivered their goal despite his underperformance, and all those comments were just *nibbles by a duck*."

Nonstarter—An initiative or idea that will never get going, just like a racehorse that never leaves the gate. Usually a bad idea, it is something that is just not going to happen. It can also be a person who does not exert initiative. (See also: *stillborn*, and *it will never fly*.)

> USE: "Selling beer at Billy Graham Crusades is a *nonstarter* if there ever was one."

Old China hand—A nickname for someone who has been in the company for a long time. An *Old China hand* is probably someone you can learn a lot from. They are especially good for answering questions, as they've probably heard them all before.

> USE: "Pete has been here for more than 50 years and knows everything about everything, which qualifies him to be an *old China hand*."

One card shy of a full deck—(See: *rode the short bus, elevator doesn't go to top floor, can't walk and chew gum at the same time, brick shy of a load, through the eyes—there aren't many bulbs there, the light is on but nobody's home, can short of a six-pack, not the sharpest knife in the drawer,* and *hamster died.*)

One percenter—My good friend David Disiere uses this saying to describe those who "run" the world (or who at least hope to someday). The *one percenters* are ambitious, competitive, innovative, capable and all about accountability (their own and others'). They have another unique characteristic: they don't feel entitled to anything and are willing to earn it and deliver 100 percent without complaining about adversities. They focus on their performance not their compensation. Nothing aggravates me more than an employee who tells me they will do more if I will pay them more, then use their compensation as an excuse for poor performance. Maybe I am just too much from the "old school," but I think top performers are always noticed and rewarded by management.

> **USE:** "David said that Kevin was clearly one of the *one percenters*: He wasn't afraid to take risks, was decisive and had a good track record of delivering both ambitious goals and impressive results."

Want a free copy of Green Weenies and Due Diligence?
Visit **www.greenweenies.com** now!

Outlier—Someone who is different and/or performs unsatisfactorily compared to others. This refers to the fact that they are far away from the mainstream of the group.

> **USE:** "Pete was definitely an *outlier*—his sales were always less than the average and he constantly complained. It was time for him to go."

Parachute in—Describes an action to rescue or bring in additional resources to help with an initiative. It's reminiscent of a military action with the same goal.

> USE: "The CEO ordered that we *parachute in* out brightest process engineers to address the continuing quality issues in the Smithfield production plant."

Cool beans, are they left over from dinner?
See page 75 to find out for sure.

Pink slip party—An informal gathering of employees who were recently laid off.

> USE: "The union was quick to tell us to ask for more wages, but they didn't attend the *pink slip party* when 50 percent of the employees were laid off."

Plug and play—A newly acquired company that requires almost no integration; it's highly compatible with the existing company, including its operating, HR and computer systems.

> USE: "Todd was relieved to see that the recently acquired company was going to be a *plug and play* deal, with hardly any hassle and quick integration."

Premature accumulation—A negative term describing a company, investor or CEO who makes ill-fated acquisitions before their time, or just too many, too fast. (See also: *acquisitive binge*.)

> USE: "Our CEO would sometimes practically gorge himself on new investments, proving that he suffered from *premature accumulation*."

Promote to customer—A sarcastic way to refer to someone that has been laid off. After they no longer work for the company, they can or will be a customer.

> USE: "Kacee was *promoted to a customer* last Thursday, when she got her pink slip."

Public hanging—The firing or admonishment of an executive or other employee in a public situation; a way of letting all remaining employees know that they could suffer the same fate if things don't change. It's the opposite of a private action. It can also be used to make sure that everyone knows that a punishment was doled out or that someone was held responsible.

> USE: "The president dismissed his Commerce Secretary in a *public hanging* when the steel tariffs backfired and China imposed huge penalties on our goods."

Pucker them—Also referred to as the pucker factor. It's used in business to refer to employees (or managers) that aren't performing up to standard, and by "poking" or putting pressure on them they tend to pucker up.

> USE: "Bill said he would see to that all the production managers were puckered up at the next meeting, since not one had hit their goals for the first quarter."

Rent before we buy—If firing or laying off workers is extremely difficult at a company, they often like to *rent before they buy* by taking people on as consultants for a few months (or years) before they offer a permanent position. Some companies also rent first to size people up, or to minimize benefits and other full time employee costs.

Want to make it into the boardroom to use these phrases?
Read Ron's first book: ***Salvage Millions from Your Small Business***.

Rest of the trees start to fall—Refers to employees that may leave after something adverse happens at a company. Perhaps a boss left or was fired, and now the company is concerned that many of the subordinates will follow.

> USE: "When Jeff left to go to IBM, we knew we had better get to work fast before the *rest of the trees started to fall* and his employees defected to IBM as well."

Riding to Abilene—(Or any undesirable location that is applicable.) This is a term used by employees when their extravagant or eccentric leader wants them to go in a direction they don't necessarily want to go. It can be used to demonstrate a kind of backhanded respect or be a show of blind faith in the wisdom of the leader. This is appended with "in the trunk" or "with no A/C" when the direction is particularly uncomfortable. When the leader asks the group's opinion of the current suggestion, the response could be "We are *riding to Abilene* with you on this one." I am from Texas, and most folks here know that the *ride to Abilene* is terrible. It's flat as a board with nothing to see or do on the way.

> **USE:** "Ted said there was no way he was *riding to Abilene*, as the proposed initiative was destined to failure and he wanted no part of that accountability."

Rode the short bus—You get the idea here don't you, or did you *ride the short bus*? Another derogatory term implying that someone is mentally slow. The big school buses carry lots of "normal" kids, while the short buses pick up the few kids who need special attention. Please don't shoot the messenger, I just wrote these as they are used. (See also: *can't walk and chew gum at the same time, elevator doesn't go to top floor, through the eyes—there aren't many bulbs there, brick shy of a load, hamster died, can short of a six-pack* and *sharpest knife in the drawer.*)

> USE: "When Mike claimed that he forgot about the most important meeting of the year, the word was out that he *rode the short bus*."

Scarlet letter—From Nathaniel Hawthorne's novel by the same name, it has come to describe a symbol of shame. In business, it describes a badge of failure with which one must live.

> USE: "Chad was the pace-setter this year, but he still wears a *scarlet letter* from his awful performance last year."

Screwdriver shop—A manufacturing business where the final product isn't manufactured at all, but is simply assembled from components purchased elsewhere.

> USE: "All of our widgets get shipped to a *screwdriver shop*, where they're put together with other widgets and then boxed up."

Scut puppy—The office *gopher*. This person handles everything from getting break room supplies to booking airfares. Although it can be viewed negatively, the smartest *scut puppies* are indispensable, and leverage their contacts within the company to move up the career ladder. (See also: *gopher.*)

> USE: "Andy didn't mind handling all the mundane details of running the office; he knew he wouldn't be a *scut puppy* forever, and he was making important acquaintances along the way."

Scuttlebutt—The chit-chat and rumors that you hear around the office. May involve business or personal rumors. If you want the *scuttlebutt*, keep your ear to the *grapevine*. (See also: *grapevine.*)

> USE: "The *scuttlebutt* around the office is that Mike's about to be let go."

Sharpest knife in the drawer—Sharpest implies smart. If someone is not the sharpest knife in the drawer, the implication is that the employee must be dull and most of the rest of the knives are superior. (See also: *can't walk and chew gum at the same time, rode the short bus, elevator doesn't go to top floor, through the eyes—there aren't many bulbs there, the light is on, but nobody is home, hamster died, can short of a six-pack* and *brick shy of a load.*)

> USE: "When she told us she couldn't see what was on the other side of the glass wall, we knew she wasn't the *sharpest knife in the drawer.*"

Shrink report/test—A personality or aptitude evaluation of any number of qualities, including a person's suitability for a position, his capabilities, intelligence or honesty; also referred to as a personality test. The *shrink test* is administered and graded, generating the *shrink report*. There are numerous versions out there, all developed by psychiatrists and psychologists, or "shrinks," in slang. Such tests are used as hiring tools and to analyze, for instance, the way members of a management team work together.

> USE: "The *shrink report* said that the COO was very risk adverse, while the CEO had a lower aversion to risk, so the two balanced each other."

Sleep camel—An employee, often a techie, who works for days at a time, then sleeps for days at a time.

> USE: "Jamie put in almost 50 hours on that project in three days last week, then crashed and spent the next three days in bed. Her schedule always works out that way; she's definitely a *sleep camel.*"

Starter marriage—A college graduate's first real job, often immediately out of school. This first job tells them about the real corporate world, the one they didn't learn about in college, and gives them better focus on their real ambitions, prodding them to move on. Not unlike a first marriage, where many lessons are learned and expectations calibrated.

> USE: "Robert enjoyed his job at XYZ Corp., but he knew it was just a *starter marriage*. His work there had taught him a great deal about business, and helped him plan out his future professional goals."

Starters and runners—There are two types of business personalities, *starters and runners*. *Starters* have a low aversion to risk, don't do details well, are very competitive, and always need to be starting something else. Obviously there are varying degrees of *starters*, and many of them never really get a viable concept up and running. More often they are dreamers, constantly trying to make a quick buck. *Runners* have a very high aversion to risk, don't mind details, and don't mind just churning ahead, doing similar things day after day, and of course, doing them excellently. I have had lots of good *runners* working for me. Many likely could run their own business, but were too cautious to use their own money starting up and risk having debt. Also, because of their aversion to risk, they like to get a steady check each week. Very few people can do both, and have success at both. I have been told I can do both, but my bias is clearly starting, or helping others start.

> USE: "Julie was a *runner*; she was the most dependable manager we had ever had, and she was very thorough. We were glad she was so conservative, as we knew she would never leave to *start* her own business."

Sticky bottom—An entry level position where the chance of promotion is slim.

Strategic firing—Dismissal of an employee just before their stock vests, or some other form of expensive bonus is about to be earned.

> USE: "It was obvious that Aaron's dismissal was a *strategic firing* to prevent him from getting his upcoming bonus. 'It's like being dumped the day before Valentine's Day,' he complained."

Stress puppy—An over-eager, ambitious, high-energy employee. It can be an especially good thing in salespersons, but also in other employees at times.

> USE: "Our *stress puppy* JC was a bundle of energy, and could really produce the results when he stayed focused on the goal."

The light is on, but nobody is home—(See: *can't walk and chew gum at the same time, rode the short bus, elevator doesn't go to top floor, hamster died, brick shy of a load* and *sharpest knife in the drawer.*)

Through the eyes—there aren't many bulbs there—Are the lights on upstairs? Is there a glint of anything behind those eyes? This is another derogatory reference to describe someone who doesn't appear capable of required performance. I have heard this more than once after a manager met a new employee; although they only talked for a few minutes, the manager was unimpressed. (See also: *can't walk and chew gum at the same time, rode the short bus, elevator doesn't go to top floor, brick shy of a load, hamster died, can short of a six-pack* and *sharpest knife in the drawer.*)

> USE: "When I asked him how he could lose the contract, he just stood there without saying a word. I could see *through his eyes—there weren't many bulbs there.*"

Tourist—An employee who signs up for out-of-town training, but who really wants to use the opportunity to take a vacation. Although he may or may not attend the training, he will convert the trip into an opportunity to visit the locale.

> USE: "John was clearly just a *tourist* when he volunteered to attend that conference in New Orleans."

Toxic worrier—A derogatory description for an employee who worries about everything, no matter how trivial, and makes everything into a huge deal with lots of drama. (See also: *energy drainer.*)

> USE: "We've got to cut down on some of the drama in the office! For starters, let's stop listening to Jay; he's nothing more than a *toxic worrier*, and he's always making mountains out of molehills."

Union delegate—Used in a non-union environment to describe an employee who is a troublemaker, has a bad attitude, or just isn't a good performer. (See also: *shitdisturber* and *stirring the pot.*)

Village is empty—A shortage of qualified employees at the company. When the *village is empty*, it's hard to execute a plan and expect good results. It also refers to someone whose brain is "empty" and doesn't seem very intelligent.

> USE: "Mike liked the plan, but since that department had lost all its talent, he reported that the *village was empty*."

Walk on water—Refers to someone with an inflated ego who thinks he's perfect.

> USE: "If Jackson is half as good as he thinks he is, how come we haven't seem him *walking on water?*"

Wave a dead chicken—A weak attempt, perhaps window dressing, to resuscitate a doomed initiative by supporting it one last time.

> USE: "Matt knew everyone else was ready to kill off his plan, but he decided he'd try *waving the dead chicken* one last time, and pitched it from a different angle."

Whistling past the graveyard—An effort to keep your confidence high in the face of fear or adversity. When things are looking grim, you've got to suck it up and *whistle past the graveyard*.

> USE: "Sales are way down, but we're *whistling past the graveyard*."

Zero drag employee—An employee with no ties, no spouse, children or pets, who likely doesn't even own a home. As a bonus, such an employee can work late or early with no regrets.

> USE: "Let's get Lori to do it—she's a *zero drag employee*, so she never complains about getting extra responsibility."

Zombies—Companies or employees that continue to operate even though they are insolvent or ineffective, also known as the living dead.

> USE: "I don't know why we are all walking around here like *zombies* since it's common knowledge that the company's going out of business."

6

Business Planning, Acquisitions and Divestitures

800-pound gorilla—The most important party to a transaction. It is important to keep the *gorilla* happy. Also used to describe the dominant member of a group. Also, it refers to the biggest competitor in a given segment, the guys to beat, like Coke in the soft drink category.

> USE: "Ted is the 800-pound gorilla in our firm. Nothing happens without his blessing."

A camel is a horse designed by a committee—Good ideas usually come from individuals, not committees. That's not to downplay the value of committees, which validate and refine the good idea. A committee tends to nit pick an idea, and by consensus, can lower it to the lowest common denominator. Committees can be a good thing when they have proper leadership.

> USE: "When the new design was finally presented, it looked like a race horse that had been redesigned into a *camel by a committee*."

155

Altitude sickness—A reference to being dominated by a deal for too long, thereby becoming dazed and self-deluded as to the deal's benefits. It can render the deal participant a bad decision maker. It can also refer to poor thinking due to thin oxygen and high altitude. (See also: *breathing our own exhaust* and *ozone thinking*.)

USE: "I think we had *altitude sickness* when we did that acquisition; our brains couldn't have been functioning correctly."

Analysis-paralysis—All talk and no action; an endless report-and-meeting style of management wherein management is swamped by analytical reports and discussions to the point of being unable to make important decisions. As a result, the issue requiring a decision is paralyzed.

USE: "*Analysis-paralysis* set in during the 10th round of discussions when our investment bankers unloaded another huge cart of reports on our table. It was obvious that we weren't going to make a decision anytime soon."

Bag of snakes—An acquisition or other project or initiative that is full of venomous surprises. It is always bad when things go wrong, but this indicates something particularly harmful.

USE: "Ted was disappointed with the sales of the newly acquired company, but he was appalled to discover that there were more than 50 customers threatening to sue over injuries caused by defective products. His investment had turned into a big *bag of snakes*."

Bake-off—A tiebreaker when evaluating equally qualified competitors (such as bidders, vendors, or employees). After everything is "baked," a winner is decided. Can also refer to the "heat" endured in a tight situation when the "baking" determines the survivor. (See also: *beauty contest, boil out* and *last man standing.*)

> USE: "After reviewing the three resumes, we decided that a *bake-off* was in order, as all of the candidates appeared capable of filling the one job we had open."

Beachfront property—In acquisitions and divestures, this describes prime assets that the seller doesn't want to part with.

> USE: "We're willing to sell you almost anything but our scrap yards; those are *beachfront property.*"

Beauty contest—Similar to a *bake-off.* This everyday business situation refers to actions designed to choose a winner, which can be a new vendor, employee, product, service or other desirable addition. Candidates are expected to look their best from the start, but in the ensuing *beauty contest*, a winner is chosen. (See also: *bake-off, boil out* and *last man standing.*)

> USE: "After reviewing all the terms of the vending deal proposals from every prospect, Brian said, 'Clearly, Chatham won the *beauty contest*'."

Brightsizing—Misdirected or mishandled downsizing that gets rid of a company's smartest employees. "Dilbert" comic-strip artist Scott Adams has used this term, but he also thinks that downsizing can make the workplace more efficient. Fewer workers mean less time to waste on idiotic pursuits like vision statements, meetings and reorganizations. Adams derives grist for the "Dilbert" mill by the way managers mishandle downsizing and not just the frequently cruel manner in which layoff news is broken to employees.

> USE: "Nynex has been *brightsizing*, shedding thousands of its brightest employees since 1990. 'That is because union rules protect senior workers, but our younger employees were the ones who had taken more time to educate themselves,' says a remaining technician. 'We have actually gotten rid of our best people.'"

Burning the ships on the beach—Ensuring that once we make a decision or move forward, we cannot back out. The ancient Romans actually burned their invading ships on the beach to make sure no retreat was possible; the legions then had to win or lose it all.

> USE: "Because the deal had no escape clause, Sam knew that our *ships would be burned on the beach* after we closed the transaction."

Burping the elephant—This happens when a really big company divests a small division that is just not material to them. Hence a *burp*, which is small compared to the overall *elephant*.

> USE: "When SuperCorp, with over 70,000 employees, divested MiniCo, with only 135 employees, they were really just *burping the elephant*."

Business ecosystem—A situation when companies in the same markets work both cooperatively and competitively to introduce innovations, support new products and serve customers. Nowadays, the big three (GM, Ford and Chrysler) work together on many projects.

> USE: "It was almost too good to be true: A balanced *business ecosystem* in which Microsoft and its competitors were battling for customers, but also working together to ensure compatibility and security for their competing innovations."

Caesar touring Gaul—Describes a situation where the senior executives of an acquiring company conduct site visits in a way that gives the sense that the conquered are being lined up to see the conqueror. This is not a professional way of handling things. It only occurs in order to make the acquirer feel omnipotent. Caesar would do this in France (Gaul) to demonstrate that he was the unchallenged winner.

> USE: "We thought it was a merger, but it soon became obvious that we were being acquired when their executives showed up like *Caesar touring Gaul.*"

You better think before you tell your boss you have a **doctor's appointment** next time. See why on page 137.

Car in the ditch—A plan that has gone awry; the plan or its implementation strategy has wrecked and is *in the ditch*. The discussion now focuses on how to get the *car out of the ditch*. Before technology, the proverbial car was an ox, but its literal translation is business plan. When the car runs off into the ditch, it can be difficult to get it out. (See also: *ox in the ditch, spinning our wheels* and, for the opposite, *hands on the wheel*.)

> USE: "Our plan was in the final stage when we realized we didn't have enough manpower to process all of the raw material we bought, so we came to a screeching halt, putting the *car in the ditch* until we formulated a 'Plan B.'"

Champagne phase—This generally occurs during the early stages of an idea, intended transaction or new ownership, employment or financial relationship. In this phase, everyone clacks their glasses together in a toast and talks about how great things are going to be. The realities that follow are usually less pleasant. I like to use it when referring to either a new banking relationship or the initial meeting with a mortgage broker when buying real estate. The lender or mortgage broker says things are going to be great, offering assurances that he can do the deal often before hearing much about either the customer or the deal itself. (See also: *honeymoon.*)

> USE: "After introductions all around, the banker said he was certain he could make the loan. We entered the *champagne phase*, even though I knew he hadn't even considered the underwriting."

Do you know a term not in Green Weenies and Due Diligence?
Submit it at **www.greenweenies.com**

Checkmate—A chess term applied in business to a strategic moment when a company or executive gains a dominant or otherwise crucial edge or position over a competitor. For example, a *checkmate* marketing strategy essentially ends the competition.

> USE: "The CEO knew it was *checkmate* when he was served with the trademark-infringement lawsuit and injunction, effectively stopping all sales of the new line of kitchen appliances."

Chewing gum and wire—Describes the fragility of a given plan that has not been well devised using proven principles with low risks. It's as if the plan is held together by only *chewing gum and wire.* In a perfect world, the plan would be robust and founded on rock-solid principles with minimum risks.

> USE: "Everyone knew the hurry-up marketing plan was inadequately researched and fraught with risks. 'It's held together with *chewing gum and wire,*' Jeff said."

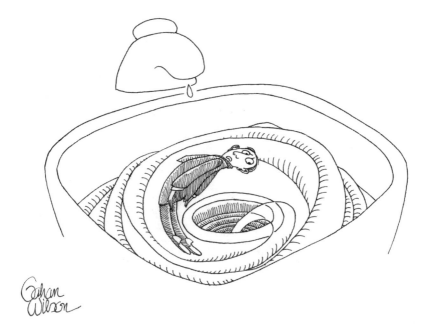

Circling the drain—Describes a business very close to total failure. Obviously the downward spiral accelerates as it gets closer and closer to the end.

> USE: "We're trying to make some changes, but there's really very little hope. We're already *circling the drain.*"

Course correction—A change in direction in a business plan to address a concern or to get the plan back on track. The best companies make such moves regularly and quickly.

> USE: "When we realized that our margins were shrinking due to salesperson abuse of cutthroat pricing options, it was time for a *course correction* to immediately begin enforcing the sales policies."

Crop failure—A business venture, division or project that has failed; not unlike a farmer's crop that either didn't come up or was destroyed by weather or pests.

> USE: "There was clearly a *crop failure* in the box division as evidenced by their dismal sales and huge losses."

Cutting bone and muscle—In a layoff situation, cutting more jobs than deemed necessary. During layoffs linked to a company turnaround, ideally only "the fat" is cut. Sometimes when deeper cuts are needed, unfortunately, some jobs critical to company performance are also eliminated. It is hard to tell where the "fat" stops and the "*bone and muscle*" start. (See also: *surgery with a butter knife.*)

> USE: "When we had cut jobs too deeply in our turnaround effort, we decided to quickly rehire our veterans as justified by the company's revival, but after *cutting bone and muscle*, we quickly lost good employees to our competitors."

Dancing on the head of a pin—Negotiating fiercely, pushing and pulling over the terms of a deal that is unlikely to please any of the parties involved. The term is commonly used by venture capitalists but can be heard in discussions by any high-powered people and/or those with big egos. Do you like the image of rivals jostling to get their way and still trying to stay on the head of the pin? It is reminiscent of seeing who gets pushed off a log first or falls into the pool while chicken fighting.

> USE: "The underwriter and the CEO were *dancing on the head of a pin* during the transaction because there simply wasn't enough money to give everyone what they wanted."

Deal fatigue—A condition common in long business negotiations wherein the principals reach a point where they feel like they do not care whether the deal is done or not. They are just mentally and physically worn out, possibly by a stalemate in the negotiations. (See also: *deals that fund [close] quickly, fund [close], those that don't, don't.*)

> USE: "After a year of negotiations and many unresolved issues concerning the merger of our two companies, *deal fatigue* had invaded both camps."

Defenestrate—A 17th century word now back in fashion meaning to drop or terminate a business operation, venture, or other activity or product. It literally means to throw someone or something out the window.

> USE: "Let's *defenestrate* this old marketing strategy and adopt a new one."

Directionally correct—Headed in the proper direction with a business venture, initiative or plan. If the required metric, such as sales, is rising, confidence rises in the belief that the program is moving in the correct direction. There can be many indicators, but sometimes it's just a gut feeling that the goal will be reached. On the other hand, if new programs to increase production are introduced, but production falls in the first week, the metrics are certainly not *directionally correct*. Watching for a *directionally correct* metric is a good early indicator of success or a problem. (See also: *you don't know what is right, but you know what is wrong.*)

> USE: "The sales department had missed several milestones and it was obvious that the trend was not *directionally correct*."

Dog—An asset that always loses money and will soon be put up for adoption. It can also be used to describe a poorly performing company.

> USE: "The CEO made it clear that if the Bloomington plant couldn't solve their labor unrest, that *dog* would be placed on the market for sale."

Don't forget what stage of the process you're in—Be cautious about what you say and how you act when moving through the negotiation, acquisition, selling, leading and other stages of a deal or new venture. Each facet of each stage may require a different approach, language or attitude. If you give up too much (or too little) now, you can kill the deal, or you can find you're *negotiating with yourself.* (See also: *ozone thinking, your baby is ugly,* and *negotiating with ourselves.*)

> USE: "We paid too much for the bargain acquisition because we *forgot what stage of the process we were in.* We talked ourselves into believing that our recently submitted offer wasn't good enough, so we proposed a sweetener before we even heard back from them on the original offer."

Drain the swamp—Often used as merger or acquisition lingo meaning to sort through all the problems and clear up the accounting questions after acquiring a troubled company. A swamp is a messy, nasty thing, and to drain one is a distasteful job. In business, one may have to drain the swamp, uncovering the *cooked books* and *cookie jar accounting,* just to clean it up and get the numbers right. Moreover, it is drained to see what is in it, whether it is fraud or losses or other hidden setbacks.

> USE: "We paid top dollar for our biggest competitor, only to discover we had to *drain the swamp* to locate the cost overruns at the source and revive profits."

Elevator pitch—A quick presentation that captures the audience's attention and conveys the basics of an idea in the time that it takes to ride in an elevator. It is a useful tool because many investors only want a quick snapshot when deciding whether to move forward. Also useful when lots of people need to hear a quick overview.

> USE: "Bob knew that he only had a few minutes until the meeting ended, so instead of his planned presentation, he gave an elevator pitch."

Fingernails on a blackboard—Something really grating or annoying. (See also: *makes my teeth itch.*)

> USE: "The way that Mike kept disrupting the meeting by tapping his pen constantly on his notebook became like *fingernails on a blackboard* to everyone else in the room."

Foreplay—Should be obvious . . . refers to games we play with each other as we circle and prepare to get down to the real business at hand. It includes posturing, play-acting, socializing and preparation. (See also: *leg sniff.*)

> USE: "As with sexual partners, some business dealings and relationships require more *foreplay* than others. When we talk with our candy vendor, JoJo James, we always have to sample the latest sugary products and listen to her rant about Wal-Mart's rock-bottom pricing demands."

Get pregnant—Getting so committed to the transaction or having so much invested in the process that the negotiators can't (or at least feel like they can't) back out of the deal. The situation is similar to getting pregnant, then wishing they had waited until later to have children; it's too late for that decision now. In successful transactions, all participants eventually become so committed that they cannot go back, no matter how much they wish things had gone differently.

> USE: "Even though there were many suitors in the beginning of merger negotiations, the proposal's original corporate sweethearts both *got pregnant*, and had to continue working to give birth to the transaction."

Green weenie—The disgusting term that started my word quest. When I first heard *"green weenie,"* I realized there was another language being spoken in the business world with mysterious words and acronyms, some funny ha-ha, some funny weird, some just wacky, some with hidden meanings and some downright offensive. Imagine what a weenie must look like when it is left in a refrigerator (which is unplugged) and forgotten for six months. A *green weenie* in business wheeling and dealing lingo is an unpleasant surprise discovered belatedly as part of a transaction or deal. If you discover at the end of your negotiations with a distributor that your would-be supplier was in bankruptcy a year ago, that's a *green weenie.* If, during your due diligence, you discover that the receivables are much older than expected or that the revenues are recognized on an accounting basis that is unacceptable to the IRS, those are *green weenies.* The image calls to mind something that would likely cause food poisoning. *Green Weenie* is also the nickname of a Pittsburgh Pirates magic charm icon used to put hexes on opposing teams.

> **USE:** "Chip learned three days before closing a merger that a huge delayed order of dealer returns was expected to arrive at the merger partner's warehouse two weeks after consummating the merger, resulting in a post-closing write-off. That *green weenie* could kill the deal."

Groundhog—An executive or other manager who is known for popping back into his/her hole without making a decision.

> USE: "Jeremy came out of his office when he heard complaints about the new incentive program, but after listening to his workers voice their discontent, he quickly became a *groundhog* and retreated back to his desk."

Hair on it—Indicates a bad or otherwise unwanted condition or situation, often one that is getting worse. Hair on certain parts of your body is fine, but on most anything else is a bad thing. The only thing worse than a *green weenie* is a *green weenie* with *hair on it*. When "hair" pops up on numbers, budgets, operations, or problems, that's bad. If it has a lot of *hair on it*, it's even worse.

> USE: "Brent knew when he saw the reports on Plant No. 7's production levels, which were 30 percent off, that his problem had a lot of *hair on it*."

Honey bucket—From *Winnie the Pooh*, who spent his whole life trying to get into a bucket of honey. In business, it can be anything we want, anything of value to us, including new groups of customers or other opportunities that have an upside. It's potentially very sweet and should be protected.

> USE: "When it opens its markets, China will be the mother of all *honey buckets* to American companies."

Horse Race—When you're trying to sell something that can only have one buyer, you always want more than one party interested. Having two or more prospects makes everyone work harder to get the prize, just like in a *horse race*—horses run faster when there is competition.

> USE: "When both Verizon and Quest sought to buy MCI, the *horse race* drove MCI share prices beyond anyone's expectations."

How does that play in Peoria?—A comedic way of asking, "What does the average person think of this?" Companies that use focus groups are always asking themselves this question. Peoria Illinois was a demographically diverse city that mirrored much of the rest of the country. Many companies used Peoria to test products there prior to a nationwide rollout.

> USE: "Anne had an idea for a new widget, but I'm not sure how well it will play in Peoria."

Ice cube in the ocean—An inadequate solution to a problem. Imagine dropping an ice cube into a bathtub of water, much less the ocean, and expecting it to cool the overall temperature. It can also refer to a tiny, unimportant market share. In any case, it's way too small and ineffective to even be a factor.

> USE: "We asked our attorney to offer $1,000 cash in upfront settlements to the 1,000-plus plaintiffs claiming our electronic dog "fences" electrocuted their pets. It was nothing more than an ice cube in the ocean; they each wanted $50,000."

Iceberg principle—Based on the premise that any problem reveals only a small portion of its true size, keeping the most important aspects hidden from immediate view.

> USE: "Always remember the iceberg principle when reviewing a manager's report on the cost overruns by his department. He'll reveal some, but not all, of the problems."

In the tent—Not only involved in a project, but actively engaged, included in negotiations and discussions, aware of the entire plan. Letting folks *in the tent* can be dangerous, as it lets them know everything you are doing, but it is often necessary in order to win support. Often there is an optimum time to let people in; for instance, after the plan has been worked out and the presentation rehearsed. (See also: *peek under the tent.*)

> **USE:** "We didn't need to let others *in the tent* because they were on a "need to know" basis."

Inbox dread—A morning condition, not unlike the morning sickness of pregnancy, where the user is overwhelmed with the amount of email in the mailbox when they first turn on their computer.

> USE: "As she neared the office, Kelly felt herself overcome with the familiar feeling of *Inbox dread*, knowing she would have several emails from disgruntled staffers."

It will never fly—A saying used to describe an idea or proposition that won't live up to its promises. Like a plane with no wings, it's got no chance of making it off the ground. (See also: *stillborn,* and *non-starter.*)

> USE: "After realizing all the holes in Rob's plan, I knew *it would never fly.*"

Just in time learning—Training in the plant on new processes or equipment, or, for executives, learning how to run a newly acquired company.

> USE: "The delays in installing the new printing press meant that Doug had to do some *just in time learning* to meet the paper's first deadline."

Keep you awake/up at night—A characterization of hard-to-resolve weaknesses in a plan or other troublesome challenges that quite literally may keep you awake at night.

> **USE**: "Jeff knew his team could hit the production goals, but maintaining quality *kept him up at night.*"

Laser gun vs. bow and arrow—A reference to capability in execution. When someone is known for using a *laser gun vs. a bow and arrow*, she or he is known for precision, accuracy and effectiveness. After all, a *laser gun* should be a better tool or weapon than a *bow and arrow*. (See also: *surgery with a butter knife.*)

> **USE**: "Since Steven always produces perfect blueprints, he was selected for the next project because it required the precision of a *laser gun vs. a bow and arrow.*"

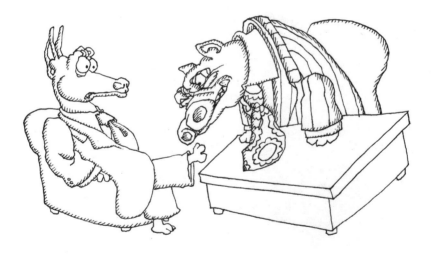

Leg sniff—The early stages of hiring an important employee when all parties are trying to determine if he will be a good fit. When dogs have just met and are trying to decide if they will get along, they sniff each other in sensitive areas. It's also used routinely in acquisitions, lending and looking for partners, as everyone wants to do a *leg sniff* early on to see if they like the players. (See also: *foreplay.*)

> **USE**: "Before he was hired, Lee Iacocca and Chrysler's directors eyed each other like dogs meeting for the first time. After the *leg sniffs*, they discovered they needed each other and could work well together."

Lens hasn't been installed—This term refers to a situation where something hasn't been examined closely, or *scrubbed*. Typically, the item is looked at from *30,000 feet*. That test may not determine if it's right, but will determine if it's wrong. If it's not eliminated as wrong, the lens will be installed and more scrutiny applied. (See also: *30,000 feet above, scrub it* and *you don't know what is right, but you know what is wrong*.)

> USE: "Steve knew there were some problems in the fulfillment department, but since the *lens hadn't been installed* yet, he couldn't explain to his manager exactly where they originated."

Long pole in the tent—The "big guy" or most important person in the deal. Typically, it refers to the largest investor or possibly first lender; the entity providing the bulk of the money for the transaction. Without the long pole, the tent falls; without the moneyman, the deal falls through. It is important to know who the long pole is, as he gets total respect and consideration and requires lots of communication from other stakeholders.

> USE: "Pete is the *long pole in the tent* and we can't make a material change in the business plan without his buy in."

Looky loo—A company or individual just wanting to browse real estate offerings despite putting up a pretense of being a serious shopper. The approach can reveal market conditions, and a *looky loo* is nosy. The term is also used for curious onlookers of traffic accidents and for hardcore window shoppers among consumers. It's hard to do transactions without some *looky loos*, unfortunately. (See also: *confirmatory v. exploratory*.)

> USE: "Real estate brokers always try to slip out the back door when they spot a *looky loo*. Browsers can sure rob a broker of valuable time that could be spent with serious shoppers."

Lot of wood to cut—A reference to a task at hand that is going to be hard, you better get *lots of hands on the pump*!

> USE: "Josh looked over the projections showing lots of growth, and commented "*lots of wood to cut*!"

Low-hanging fruit—Fruit that hangs low is easy to pick. In business, *low-hanging fruit* might include expenses that have not been reviewed or market niches that are easy to expand into. (See also: *bird nest on the ground.*)

> USE: "Following the acquisition, we found lots of *low-hanging fruit*, including travel expenses that were triple industry norms."

Macaroni defense—An approach taken by a company that does not want to be acquired, wherein the company issues a large number of bonds on the condition that they must be redeemed at a high price if the acquisition occurs. It's called *macaroni defense* because the value of the bonds swell up, like noodles, increasing in value and causing the buyer to pay much more, which acts as a deterrent to the purchase.

> USE: "The CEO made it clear that the *macaroni defense* would either thwart the buyers or put lots of extra money in the bondholders' pockets.

Makes my teeth itch—(See: *fingernails on a blackboard.*)

Upstream-downstream, you need to know before you launch the boat, right? Are you sure you need a boat? See page 246 to know for sure.

Making the soup—The process of developing a strategy or plan. There are many elements involved, with many decisions, inputs and scheduling—the ingredients and seasonings. It takes presentations, coaxing, inspiring and politicking—the stirring and tasting. (See also: *soup to nuts* and *cradle to grave.*)

> USE: "Kathi made the requisite phone calls, reserved the room, lined up the reports for copying, scheduled the presentations and arranged for refreshments to make our conference a successful one. She *made the soup*, and we were grateful to her, as it was a complex endeavor."

Management by spread sheet—A leadership style wherein all the decisions are based solely on data with no regard for personnel or operating issues.

> USE: "When Ted reduced salesperson payroll by 20 percent, he failed to consider that although 20 percent of the dollars were gone, those employees produced 30 percent of the sales. That's when he realized the error in *management by spread sheet*."

Managing up—Simply put, this is synonymous with brown nosing, where a person is managing their career up by brown nosing the bosses.

You do **eat your own dog food**, right? You might be surprised to learn that you actually do, and didn't even know it! See page 26 to find out for sure.

Manhattan Project—An expedited, urgent or top priority initiative or project requiring more staff, money, other resources and perhaps a level of secrecy. It was the code name for the U.S. government's development of the atomic bomb during World War II. When America learned that the Nazis were trying to develop the same technology, U.S. officials accelerated the work by applying more resources. In business today, a *Manhattan Project* would get similar treatment, perhaps for the same reasons: time is short and its success is a life-or-death situation.

> USE: "We knew it was going to be a *Manhattan Project* as we were simply too far behind our competitor in development. The only way to catch up was by compressing the time needed, and that was going to mean more people working 24 hours a day and greatly increased cost."

Measure with a micrometer, mark with a paint brush and cut with an ax—My all-time favorite term for someone who spends too much time over-engineering a solution, and wastes a ton of time when it is obvious that being close is all that matters (and not even very close at that). A hyper perfectionist who is ineffective due to a dysfunctional over-attention to detail that ends up eating too much time. I learned this term from Howard Nusbaum.

Negotiating with ourselves—Falsely believing that there is competition during negotiations for a sale, merger, acquisition or other deal, and acting accordingly. It's crucial to understand who your competition is, if in fact there is any. Usually a negotiator wants you to believe there's a competitor or viable alternate suitor, even if there is none. If you understand there is no viable competition, you can avoid giving unnecessary concessions. It can also be applied to personal situations. For instance, when interviewing for a job, if you feel that your proposed compensation is too high, you propose a lower salary. In fact, you are *negotiating with yourself*, as you have no firm indication that salary is an issue. Always remember which part of the negotiation you are in. When interviewing, you likely need to sell your skills and experience. (And remember, no one likes people who sell on the low price.) Later, after it's obvious that you are the *prettiest girl at the dance, stop selling* and talk about your salary. (See also: *don't forget what stage of the process you're in*.)

> **USE:** "We're upset about all the concessions we made; we were essentially *negotiating with ourselves* before we learned the other supposed contender wasn't a viable buyer since they had no cash."

No brainer—Something so simple or so obvious that anyone should know or understand it. It doesn't require a brain to know whether it's correct or not.

> **USE:** "Adding extended warranties for add-on fees was a *no-brainer*. It improved our sales, margins and customer satisfaction with no downside."

'No' usually means 'yes, if...'—Just offering a bit of sage advice here: Remember, "*no*" doesn't always mean "*no*." In business, it usually means "yes, with some caveat," so make sure you explore all exceptions, alternatives or options before you take "*no*" for an answer. In the business world a seller will almost always take a little less than he says he will, and a buyer will almost always pay a little more than he offers.

> USE: "During union negotiations, the union representatives said no to any wage reductions; however, when management offered to increase job security with the condition of lowering wages, the union conceded. Just goes to show that *no usually means yes if* the terms are right."

On a napkin—Used to describe quickly formulated down-and-dirty deals, plans, contracts or calculations; typically a preliminary proposal. It's obviously informal, only a prelude to the real thing. Many times high-level executives and negotiators do this over drinks or dinner. I've also heard attorneys use the term to say that a formal agreement isn't required by law and could just be on a napkin, but that wouldn't be very wise. (See also: *back of the envelope* and *quick and dirty*.)

> USE: "We worked out the basics for our joint marketing campaign at lunch. The key ideas were written *on a napkin*. Now we've got the big job: writing a detailed proposal in legalese."

On the Beach—Refers to a person who is in-between jobs, and so is taking it easy *on the beach*.

> USE: "Chris had made plenty of money with his last company, so he bought a new house and decided to spend some time *on the beach* before looking for his next job."

Peek under the tent/sheets—A glimpse at a deal; could also mean getting just enough detail about a deal or company to spark more interest, perhaps as a result of an *elevator pitch*. It can also involve, for instance, letting a prospective employee or lender peek so that they understand enough to move forward or maintain momentum. It can also be used as a tease. (See also: *in the tent*.)

> USE: "Our limited stock offering presentation gave them a *peek under the tent*, so we could determine their level of interest in the underwriting."

Percolate—Following a presentation or proposal, the process of interested parties examining, considering or analyzing it. Like coffee percolating or continuing to brew because it's not yet ready to drink. A proposal needs time to be absorbed so that all the ramifications, other components and strategic implications can be understood. Of course, sometimes you just need to sleep on it. (See also: *soak time.*)

> USE: "Any new deal takes some time to *percolate* through the heads of the decision makers. Sometimes proposed corporate mergers can take a year or two before consummation."

Pile of shit that stinks the least—Least objectionable of two or more undesirable options. When none of the options are good, we hope to choose the one that's least troublesome. A Hobson's choice, meaning that you are damned if you do and dammed if you don't, but one alternative might be better than the other. In business, it comes up more often than you might think. (See also: *between the devil and the deep blue sea* and *devil you know is better than the one you don't.*)

> USE: "The big fine from the district attorney was better than a full trial, so we chose it as the *pile of shit that stinks the least.*"

Pockets of resistance—Another borrowed military term, this one for a person or a group attempting to stall, block, or kill a project, initiative, or directive. Often they do so with passive resistance.

> USE: "*Pockets of resistance* were bound to pop up across the corporate hierarchy as the executive board attempted to cut the fat out of our administrative labor costs."

Pooh-pooh—To express dislike or disdain for something.

> USE: "I had a great idea but Tom *pooh-poohed* it."

Many a tense situation has been lightened by a humorous quip

Pregnant—(See: *get pregnant.*)

Pressure test—What we often do to an idea if we aren't sure it is robust. When we *pressure test* it, we determine if it is really viable by having others check the financial footings and assumptions. If we know it can withstand the pressure, we can roll it out to the entire staff with reasonably few surprises. (See also: *stress test* and *war games.*)

> USE: "If we change the commissions of our sales department, sales will increase by 20 percent in a week. Let's *pressure test* the idea by changing the compensation of only one of the sales staff and see if it works."

Probable death is better than certain death—Similar to the *pile of shit that stinks the least,* a case of following the better odds or choosing the lesser of two evils or undesirable options. Probabilities are better than certainties when all options are negative. (See also: *devil you know is better than the one you don't, pile of shit that stinks the least* and *between the devil and the deep blue sea.*)

> USE: "If opting to stay independent against superior competitors is going to doom the company for sure, and merging with one of those 'big boys' is also likely to end in failure, then *probable death is better than certain death,* so we'll opt for the merger."

Raspberry—The thumbs down. When you give something *the raspberry*, you're not approving it to go forward.

> **USE**: "The new widget had a lot of problems, so we gave it the old *raspberry*."

Ridge runner—Someone who's trying to stay out of trouble or avoid risk by postponing a decision. Staying on the proverbial ridge of an issue keeps you from falling one way or the other and being injured. Although it is good to be cautious before making a decision, good executives and managers don't wait too long. The metaphorical fall will eventually come.

> **USE**: "I was always accused of being a *ridge runner*, because I could never decide whether to buy a mutual fund or bonds, which meant I just earned sub par interest in cash accounts."

Run it up the flagpole—Test and see whether or not an idea or product will meet with approval. (See also: *balloon*.)

> **USE**: "Warren's idea looks good on paper, but we had better *run it up the flagpole*."

Sacred Cow—A company's untouchables. Even if they aren't profitable, they are the favorite projects of someone high up in the company and have very little chance of being eliminated.

> **USE**: "We're losing money on the fitness clubs, but they're David's *sacred cow*. I doubt they'll be sold."

Sand below our feet—This describes a weak plan. Things built just on sand move around and aren't stable. All plans require a strong and credible foundation. (See also: *buttoned up*.)

> **USE**: "The banker called our business plan *sand below our feet* because it wouldn't stand up to the winds of change or the storms of competition. Then he swiftly denied our loan request."

Scalability—This is the capability of a plan or process to work effectively at different volumes or rates. That is, it works now to make a profit and won't have to be changed later to continue earning a profit on a different scale. One component of any *scalable* plan is variable rather than fixed cost. In the recycling business, we pay for dismantling cars by the car instead of paying by the hour or on salary, so our costs fluctuate with volume. (See also: *cradle to grave* for full details.) Usually, technologies can make a process more *scalable*.

> USE: "By computerizing the order fill department, we achieved increased productivity, but we also got *scalability*. Now business can double, and although we will need additional order fillers, we won't need to add personnel to process paperwork."

Scientific/sophisticated wild ass guess (SWAG)—Probably not much more than an educated guess. It is certainly better than a *WAG*. (See also: *WAG*.)

> USE: "The directors were anxious to understand how big the potential market was. They wondered if it was *bigger than a breadbox or smaller than a car*. Ted had a *WAG*, but the CEO wanted to get at least a *SWAG* before he allocated any funds to research the issue."

Scrub it—The process of "poking" at the components of a plan or proposal. *Scrubbing it* cleans it and finds flaws. Soliciting others to *scrub* a plan will almost certainly make it better. (See also: *lens hasn't been installed*.)

> USE: "Mike wanted to make sure the capital investment math was well *scrubbed* prior to presentation to the board."

Sex without marriage—Prolonged merger or acquisition negotiations that end without a consummated deal.

> USE: "The office staff worked 20 hour-days for more than two weeks hoping the deal would close, but felt it was like *sex without marriage* when the deal collapsed."

Shotgun clause—A buy-sell provision used by related parties in a business venture. Investors within the partnership have the right to offer their portion to the partner at a specified price. If the partner does not buy the offered interest at this price, they must then sell their own interest to the offering party at the same specified price. I have personally used this, and it is an effective way to force a fair price for both parties so long as both parties have the capability to come up with the money. In my case, the contract required the seller to finance the purchase price with a 20 percent down payment, which assured that either party could prevail on equal footing. It could also raise the price of the offer, since the business being bought could actually make the payment. The security for the seller was the buyer's shares in the entity.

> USE: "In order to make sure we could have a fair dissolution of the partnership, we all agreed that a *shotgun clause* would be required."

Sleeping beauty—A company that is ripe for a takeover and is sleeping because it has a lot of under-performing assets. The company is typically under-priced and has great potential, and its management has not taken any defensive actions.

> USE: "Their assets were worth double the asking price, making it a true *sleeping beauty*, but the investors wanted out at any price."

Slow target—Any target, competitor, employee, department, etc. that is an easy mark because it simply doesn't perform well.

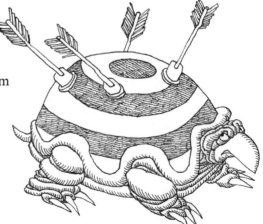

> USE: "Because he hadn't hit a sales goal in more than a year, Pete had become a *slow target* for some other aspiring employee who wanted his position."

Soup isn't made yet—Refers to an incomplete project, plan or initiative. Soups require many ingredients; this is a reference often made when ingredients are missing, or when the soup just isn't mixed or fully cooked yet.

> USE: "My boss asked me about the project and I had to tell him that the soup isn't made yet."

Soup to nuts—Meaning it has it all: usually refers to a total plan or solution, incorporating all the necessary components or ingredients from inception, through planning and execution and on to fruition and hopefully success. It can also refer to a process that provides everything necessary to complete a given task. (See also: *making the soup* and *cradle to grave.*)

> USE: "Ted's plan was brilliant and completely well thought out from soup to nuts with no further documentation needed."

Stillborn—Some lousy (and even some good) ideas or proposals don't stand a chance. Even as they're suggested, they're already dead in the water. (See also: *nonstarter* and *it will never fly.*)

> USE: "When Nelda suggested paying each employee a $1,000 bonus for meeting his or her sales goal every month, we knew her idea was stillborn, there just wasn't room in the budget."

Straw man—A preliminary draft, suggestion or proposal that's offered in order to gauge its reception; a method of testing the waters. It may be easy to change or knock down (remember, it's made from straw), but still may be a good idea. (See also: *balloon.)*

> USE: "We knew we needed a new customer service policy, so Danny was asked to prepare a straw man to start the departmental discussion that would lead to a serious proposal."

Strengths, weakness, opportunities and threats (SWOT)—Four factors or conditions analyzed when reviewing a new market, business idea, strategy, product or service. *SWOT* is a concept taught in business school.

> USE: "Our in-depth surveys and other market research covered the SWOT for the Dallas market; we're not going to be surprised by any market condition there."

Stress test—(See: *pressure test* and *war games.*)

Sucks like a Hoover—I suppose this one should be self-explanatory, but in the business world, some things just aren't any good. It can be applied to results, ideas or an initiative. In any case, if it sucks like a Hoover, it's not a good thing. I suppose it's a gratuitous compliment for Hoover that their vacuum cleaners suck so well.

> **USE:** "Cindy just laughed at Paula's silly idea, adding 'Boy, that *sucks like a Hoover.*'"

Sudden wealth syndrome—A disease where someone who suddenly becomes wealthy (having never managed wealth, and likely having earned it as a result of a windfall such as stock options), buys everything, but still isn't happy.

> **USE:** "As Tim sat by his pool admiring his new Ferrari, he realized that his new belongings didn't satisfy him the way he had expected. It was a classic case of *sudden wealth syndrome.*"

Take in strays/stray dogs—Buying companies that no one else wants. Although they can be cheap acquisitions, it's not necessarily a good strategy.

> **USE:** "Erwin had raised so much money on stock sales during his stint as CEO that the funds were inexhaustible, and he just kept *taking in stray dogs.*"

Target rich—Refers to a business environment with many viable and rewarding targets. It can be a new market with lots of customers and very little competition. It can be a company needing to cut unproductive employees and having many they can dismiss without hurting productivity.

> **USE:** "China is said to be *target rich* in nearly every consumer market sector since it has the highest populations at every level from ultra rich to ultra poor, as well as the fewest suppliers."

Three finger booger—A situation that gets completely botched up (typically unexpectedly) and is extremely difficult to get rid of or to get away from, similar to a deal with a lot of *hair on it*. It can also describe something you end up with that you didn't ask for and don't want, but can't get rid of.

> **USE:** "Mike got a new client referral, but it turned out that the client had all kinds of problems nobody expected to have to deal with, and was a general pain in the ass. His friend that referred the client said, "Man, I'm sorry, I didn't mean to send you a *three finger booger*."

Thumb expert—A nickname for one of the many new gadget freaks using Blackberrys and Treos, or any other device requiring skills on a keyboard using their thumbs. (See also: *chipmunking.*)

> **USE:** "We could see that Dave was a *thumb expert* by the way he was taking notes on his Blackberry during the meeting."

Tin Handshake—A small severance package for a departing executive who did a bad job.

> **USE:** "Bruce had been coasting for the past several months, even after repeated warnings, so all he got when they let him go was a *tin handshake.*"

TINS—Acronym for two incomes, no sex; a marriage with two Type A personalities, most likely workaholics.

> **USE**: "As they passed each other in their own driveway, each on their way to work, Mary realized that theirs had become a *TINS* marriage."

Trust slug—Offspring of a rich business person who lives off a trust. Likely has no ambition or work ethic, but doesn't need one. Paris Hilton certainly doesn't seem to mind if folks think she is a *trust slug*.

> **USE**: "Don't ask Ken for career advice! He's nothing but a *trust slug* and has never worked a day in his life!"

Turn the box upside down—Stir things up; make big changes and shake up the status quo. It can easily happen in a turn-around or management upheaval. When the box gets turned upside down and shaken, lots of things fall out. Often "shaking the box" is also mentioned, which would cause even more things to fall out.

> **USE**: "When Disney CEO Eisner fired COO Lovitz for incompetence and paid him $140 million in a severance package, the major shareholders were ready *to turn the box completely upside down* by firing Eisner and the rest of his management team."

Vetting or Vetted—Testing, researching, challenging and investigating something or someone. In the executive world, no one is hired without serious *vetting* by the HR department and the senior management team. (See also: *buttoned up*.)

> **USE**: "After the new product launch plan had been *vetted* by all the senior staff, it was ready for final deployment. The sales manager also wanted all applicants for the new marketing area thoroughly *vetted* to avoid bad hires."

White space opportunity—The kind of opportunity where no other opportunities exist, as in a blank sheet of paper. It also means starting a venture with no prior knowledge or preconceived notions.

> USE: "For mom-and-pop grocers, adopting frequent-shopper cards amounts to a *white space opportunity*; much more research is needed to figure out a way to exploit the space."

Wild ass guess (WAG)—A *wild ass guess* is just that: a guess. Not as reliable as a *SWAG*. (See also: *SWAG*.)

Won't hold water—When an idea or argument is not fully thought out and has numerous "holes."

> USE: "His plan to finance that addition by the beginning of the year *won't hold water*. He hasn't even considered the fact that the bank won't finance work on the site of an old gas station until a clean environmental survey has been obtained."

Your baby is ugly—In negotiations and transactions, this is a term disparaging the other bargaining party's preferred agenda or individuals. "Baby" is a metaphor for anything the other party is sensitive about. Calling it ugly can be tantamount to calling that party's real baby *ugly*. Such words could adversely affect negotiations, especially if you fail to remember *what stage of the deal you're in*. If in opening negotiations, for example, the buyer announces that in the event of a purchase, they won't need the current CFO (who happens to be the CEO's son), the deal could die. If the buyer had only waited until after closing the deal, the situation could have been handled more tactfully. (See also: *don't forget what stage of the process you're in*.)

> USE: "We knew better than to say *your baby is ugly*, because we wanted to resolve the major issues as smoothly as possible."

Due Diligence

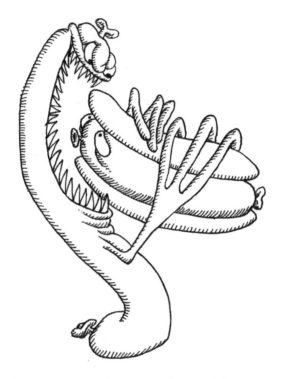

These chapters just aren't as much fun, and they certainly don't have much entertainment value. Some of these terms have been defined in countless books. I have tried to include only those that I recall using or those that are most important and likely to be needed by the reader. Oddly, some words that are used commonly in transactions and business don't seem to be defined anywhere in previous business dictionaries, such as "disclosure schedule" or "indemnification," so I have included them. Also, I haven't provided example sentences, as their meanings are usually more obvious.

7

Jargon

Abortion—A project that is disastrously *fouled up beyond repair*. (See also: *FUBAR*.)

Administrivia—Small, annoying tasks of the administrative staff that are pesky but very necessary.

Adventure travel—A visit to a newly acquired business, plant or office to meet all the new employees and review operations and facilities.

Alligator—Allocating the majority of profits from an option spread toward commissions, thereby "eating alive" the investor's share of the profit.

Arm around the shoulder—Used to describe a skill a good manager simply must have. The manager has to know when to hold, when to fold and when to scold. Sometimes it's important to just put your arm around an employee, try to empathize with them, and befriend them, if only for a moment. I am always amazed how many mangers don't have this skill; they just do it by the book, and are always harsh.

Armchair quarterback—A negative reference to someone who thinks they could do better on a task. It's easy to sit in a chair, drinking beer and eating popcorn, watching the game, shouting at the players and telling them what they did wrong. It's much harder to be in the game and always do the right thing. The implication is that an *armchair quarterback* should just shut up; he isn't as smart as he thinks. My wife insisted that I use "he" in this definition. (See also: *peanut gallery*.)

Back door—Often used to describe dealings that are unethical or dishonest, but can also mean those that are exclusive to a small audience or group of players. The back door typically isn't watched as well as the front, and sometimes things just seem to slip in and out unnoticed. A *back door* deal can also be one that is reached during the eleventh hour, the last possible minute.

Back in the saddle—Ready to try again. Just like it sounds, this refers to someone who is back up on the horse, charging ahead. Sometimes, for one reason or another, people get off the horse. It can be due to illness, disengagement, personal problems or any number of reasons. At some point, ideally, they get *back in the saddle* and move on.

Bait and switch—An unethical sales practice whereby customers are lured into a store by low-priced goods that are not actually available at the advertised price.

Bang for the buck—If you're getting *bang for your buck*, you're getting the most possible impact per dollar spent on a given task. A highly efficient company gets a lot of *bang for its buck*.

Basket case—An utterly hopeless and mixed-up person or situation. A *basket case* usually needs immediate attention, as something must have gone desperately wrong for things to have reached this point.

Bells and whistles—This term implies that there is more to the investment or other item than appearances indicate; bells and whistles on a piece of machinery distract from its actual performance. Investments can have extras added to be more appealing to investors. Preferred stock, for instance, can have floating dividends. It's also used in many other business areas. For example, with every case of Coke you buy this weekend they give away one box of popcorn. The popcorn is the *bells and whistles*.

Black-box accounting—A method of accounting that is so complex that financial statements are nearly impossible to accurately interpret. *Black-box accounting* may be used to hide unfavorable information. (See also: *voodoo math, fuzzify.*)

Bloody knees—This describes what happens to us when we have been working very hard, and are beat up and tired, much like we have been in a fight.

Boilerplate—Refers to the standard small print on nearly all contracts, sales agreements or legal documents. It is text that is reused in transaction after transaction without significant changes. Historically, a *boilerplate* was used in journalism to stamp the same text onto newspapers at printing presses across the country. Such a provision is generally more favorable to the creditor and doesn't offer much solace for a debtor. The reality is that in most consumer transactions the borrower doesn't have any choice in the matter. Obviously, on negotiated transactions and contracts, anything can be negotiated. The reality is that if most of us read the boilerplate in our loan or mortgage agreements, we wouldn't even consider signing them. But, oh well. (See also: *the big print giveth and the small print taketh away.*)

Boot camp—Borrowed from military language. A place or program where employees go for intensive training about a particular project or initiative in their company.

Bootstrapping—What an entrepreneur often does to finance a startup business from the beginning. It includes everything from long hours of work to running up credit card debt in order to make payroll. I used to open my business just long enough on Sunday to get grocery money rather than taking it out of weekly sales—truly a case of *bootstrapping*.

Bricks and mortar—A physical business presence. In this era of e-businesses, *bricks and mortar* refers to a business or a part of a business that can be seen, visited or touched. It's used in contrast to a business that has no physical presence in a given area and instead sells by utilizing the Internet or salespersons. Such a company would have no *bricks and mortar*.

Brownfield—An existing site or plant that has been updated for use rather than constructing a new plant at a raw site. It can also be a site or plant that was previously used by a related industry. For instance, a large manufacturing plant for cars might be purchased and remodeled for building lawn mowers. It's called a *brownfield* since it is already "stained," having been used before. (See also: *greenfield.*)

Buck—Slang for a million dollars or an informal reference to one dollar.

Bull—An investor who believes that any or all of the prices of securities in general will follow a continued increase in price.

Called on the carpet—Someone who is *called on the carpet* is in trouble. They have probably been called to face some sort of accusations and will need to defend or account for their actions.

Care and feeding—This is used to describe what some employees or entities need to be satisfied. For instance, if a business isn't doing well, its banker is likely to need a lot of *care and feeding* to remain happy. Employees may need extra care and feeding if they are unhappy and a competitor is trying to entice them away.

Carrot equity—If the company reaches certain financial goals, the opportunity to purchase more equity is allowed. Such an opportunity would be very desirable, like a carrot to a bunny. It should motivate the employees to hit the goal.

Cash cow—A business or part of a business that produces dramatically more cash than it consumes.

Cash sponge—A business or division that requires a lot of cash resources; should be a short-term situation. New ventures or expansion projects are typically *cash sponges.*

Channel stuffing—Artificially inflating current sales and earnings by shipping more goods than are usually (or actually) ordered. This is analogous to trying to stuff too much into a box. If a vendor ships you 200 of something when you only ordered 100, and does it to 100 other customers as well, he ships 10,000 extra pieces in a given period. Even though he may have to issue credits later, he gets to record the income in the earlier period. *Channel stuffing* is a hot issue in the current accounting climate, as are revenue recognition policies.

Chinese wall—A figurative wall separating a brokerage firm's investment banking business from its trading and retail business. It's often used in business to keep one department from having information that could compromise another party. For instance, often when companies are doing acquisitions, the sellers are reluctant to furnish sensitive information about finances, sales or employees. So there is a *Chinese wall* between the acquisition team and the operators. This prevents operators, for instance, from going out and hiring employees from the target firm. It's important that the acquisition team be able to offer such discretion to the seller or the seller won't cooperate.

Circle back—To discuss again.

Clawback provision—A provision in an executive's employment agreement that entitles the company to take back some compensation, or declare compensation not owed under certain situations, such as fraud. This has become much more prevalent in the last few years, since the Enron and Adelphia debacles.

Convergent thinking—Ability to see the similarities and make the connections between different products, information or events. (See also: *divergent thinking.*)

Cookie—A number code that a website copies onto an unknowing user's computer. It is later used to identify the user and track where he or she has been on the Internet. I suppose it's called a cookie because it's something sweet that a user leaves for the company.

Course of dealing (or course of trade)—When standard trade practices or prior business deals set the precedent for the terms of a deal or for the way business is conducted.

Cram down provision—In bankruptcy law, this provision allows the court to approve a company's reorganization plan when only one class of creditor has approved it. It is basically being *crammed down* everyone else's throat, so to speak. (See also: *crammed down.*)

Crammed down—A deal in which venture capitalists refuse to invest in a project unless the preceding investors of the company lower the value of their original investment by being diluted. If the original investors paid $2 per share for their stock, but now need cash and want to sell more equity, the new buyer may *cram down* a deal wherein their purchase is at $1. (See also: *cram down provision*.)

Credit cliff—Arises when credit deterioration could be compounded by provisions such as financial covenants or rating triggers. These can put significant pressure on the company's business or on its liquidity. For instance, if a company owes $100,000 and has a lending covenant that says it must pay off some portion (or all) of the loan if current assets fall below a minimum, a *credit cliff* is created and the company could actually fail as a result.

Crown jewels—The most valuable units of a business due to its profitability, asset value, future prospects, etc.

Dirty laundry—Also known as skeletons in the closet. *Dirty laundry* is past activities that may have been dishonest or unethical. The guilty usually try to hide their *dirty laundry* in the same closet as their skeletons. (See also: *smoking gun*.)

Divergent thinking—Ability to see the differences in products, information and events as well as the possible end results of those differences. (See also: *convergent thinking*.)

Diworsification—When the risk/return tradeoff is worsened by adding poorly performing stocks to the portfolio, which are typically in the same sector. Diversification requires that the investment be spread over different industries, sectors or types of investments, and generally improves the long-term viability of the portfolio. This word applies when that goal isn't reached, usually due to poor choices.

Doesn't amount to a hill of beans—Worth absolutely nothing. (See also: *wrapped our fish in that one*.)

Doesn't move the needle—This action doesn't impact earnings; likely a bad thing. Everyone likes to move the needle and make earnings go up. It's kind of like going faster in a car, it's more fun. (For a guy, anyway, according to my wife.) It can also apply to just about any other area of the business, or even your personal life. Moving the needle is a metaphor for a gauge, any gauge. It doesn't move your needle when you eat out and the meal is just so-so. Likewise, if adding five more workers doesn't move the needle on the assembly line (by increasing production or raising quality), then why add the five people?

Don't get too far in front of your skis—Simply put, don't get ahead of yourself. If you lean out too much, you will fall.

Dummy director—A *dummy director* acts and votes according to the wishes of another party who is not a member of the board. He is only a figurehead with no true control, but he is still liable; it might be someone who acts as a director during the formation of a corporation until the official directors are elected. It can also be a person who is put on the board by someone who doesn't want his or her true influence, motives or ownership known. (See also: *dummy shareholder*.)

Dummy shareholder—Doesn't actually own shares but has them in his name. He holds them for someone else, much like a *dummy director*. (See also: *dummy director*.)

Dutch auction—The bidding for identical items starts out at a high price and gradually becomes lower until someone places a bid. The bidding price continues to sink until all the identical items have been bid. At the end of the auction, the lowest price, which is the last bid, is what all bidders pay.

Eager beaver—An *eager beaver* is someone who is overly enthusiastic and energetic, perhaps to a fault. *Eager beavers* are generally good for morale and motivation, but sometimes they have a tendency to get on peoples' nerves. (See also: *wide eyed*.)

Eating someone's lunch—An aggressive competition in which one business takes portions of another business's market share, or outperforms them based on some metric.

Elephant—An institutional investor whose investment decisions can have a major impact on a security's market price; someone who controls a substantial amount of funds.

Elephant hunt—The soliciting of a major corporation to move into your area. It's usually very beneficial, as big business means jobs to the people of the area.

Energy—Excitement or level of involvement. Some people get excited about an initiative, product or service, and that can contribute to increased productivity. Negative *energy* can become a hindrance. Positive *energy* needs to be channeled into productive actions so it's used wisely or so that it's not wasted. It's important to always have positive *energy*; I learned this well from my mentor, Brian. It's surprising how often something that is negative can actually be approached and even described with positive *energy*. (See also: *lemons into lemonade*.)

ERP—Acronym for Enterprise Resource Platform, a powerful software solution that integrates all the functions in a company, such as accounting, production, fulfillment, sales and H/R, providing the *gauges, KPI's* and controls needed. Companies like Peoplesoft furnish the systems, which can cost tens of millions of dollars.

Eureka point—A sudden creative or innovative idea on how to solve a problem. The point of realization occurs when a break-through has finally been made, frequently after many attempts.

Face the music—We've all had to do this at one time or another. When you *face the music*, you step up and accept the consequences of your actions. When profits are way down, someone has to *face the music*. It often happens at a *prayer meeting*, or a *come to Jesus* meeting. (See also: *step up to the plate*.)

Fallen angel—A once popular high performing employee or security that loses favor and declines in value.

Finder—A person who puts together deals by locating funds for a corporation that's seeking capital, brings together funds for a merger, or finds a takeover target for a company that's seeking an acquisition.

Flip-over pill—An entitlement that is granted by a firm's management to its stockholders, which gives them the right to purchase shares of an acquiring company's stock at a bargain price in the event of a merger. The *flip-over pill* is a variation of the poison pill.

Ford-Chevy argument—An argument that is really just tit for tat; everyone has an opinion, and one is likely as good as the other.

Free ride—A gain without expense. For example, if your brother is an accountant and he does your taxes without charging you, you just got a *free ride.* You won't get many of these in business.

Friction—Anything that gets between two initiatives, people or companies. There is usually some *friction* to selling, perhaps because the price is too high. A little *friction* between a board of directors and management is a good thing; it keeps everyone on their toes.

Friction cost—The cost caused by something that creates friction, and ultimately it grows to be large enough that something is done to reduce the friction. If the *friction cost* of tardiness from production employees becomes too great, there will be a change; employees will be fired or replaced. If a business is doing poorly, it may languish there for some time, but eventually the *friction cost*, be it mental stress or cash flow issues, will trigger a solution—either the owner will turn over a new leaf and *find religion*, becoming recommitted to the business, or he will shut it down. If pricing for a product causes too much friction, and hence reduced sales, the price will be lowered or the item eliminated due to poor sales. Friction cost always brings change, perhaps it's a fire caused by the heat, or cold water to cool it down.

FTE—Acronym for "full-time equivalent." It's used to compare and understand the actual number of full-time employees and total cost per employees. Two part-time employees, who work 20 hours per week, for instance, would be counted as one *FTE.*

Fungible goods—Goods that are so similar in nature they can be interchanged; they are not separated by individual characteristics and are sold by quantity (i.e. wheat, oil, coffee beans). Items that are distinct, such as those with a serial number (computers, automobiles, etc.), are not considered fungible.

Garage sale—When you unload a lot of merchandise at a very low price, you're having a *garage sale.* This is usually an act of desperation wherein you try to move excess product that's sitting around growing mold in your warehouse or on your shelf. Selling high is nice, but it's better to sell low than to not sell at all. It's not at all different than the ones you have at home when you sell all your personal junk. Tends to attract *bottom fishers.* (See also: *bottom fishing.*)

Globasm—When a company's leader becomes fixated on expanding operations globally, he or she is said to be having a *globasm.* While *globasms* seem to be exploding all over the place these days, just remember that sometimes it's easy to lose focus.

Goldbrick shares—A stock that shows quality and worth on the surface but in reality is worth very little.

Golden handcuffs—A lucrative incentive offered to a firm's executive or other employee to keep him from moving to another company, or to buy the executive's extended cooperation after his exit.

Golden parachute—An employment agreement providing key executives of a firm with lucrative severance benefits in case control of the firm changes hands, which then jeopardizes their positions. A *golden parachute* is a benefit to management, but not usually to shareholders.

Gopher/Go-for—A low-ranking and usually young member of the office team whose job often involves running errands and *going for* things. Hence: *gopher*. (See also: *scut puppy*.)

Gorilla—A company that controls a market without having a complete monopoly.

Grapevine—The informal "hot-wire" of office gossip. If you want to know more than what you're hearing from the boss, just keep your ear to the *grapevine*. Information has a way of getting around, just like a wild grapevine. (See also: *scuttlebutt*.)

Graveyard market—A declining market that has low prices that discourage investors from selling. There is also little interest among investors to buy.

Greenfield—Opening a new operations facility or commencing new construction as opposed to buying an existing operation or facility. It's similar to a *brownfield*. It's an age-old dilemma: Do we buy existing businesses in the market we want to be in and instantly have an operating business, or a parcel of land with a building and convert it to our use (a *brownfield*), or do we build a brand new facility and open up a new business or branch there (a *greenfield*)? A *greenfield* gets its name because it starts with a virgin grassy field, while a *brownfield* has already had activity so is "stained." (See also: *brownfield*.)

Greenshoe—A provision in an underwriting agreement which permits certain investors or investment groups to purchase additional shares at the original offering price, even though the stock may be trading higher.

Gunslinger—An aggressive investor who purchases speculative securities or companies because he is a risk-taker; the goal is to get high returns. (See also: *bottom fishing*.)

Head hurt—This is what happens when we are faced with a difficult problem or perhaps some complex math; usually we're not in physical pain, but we imagine headaches when considering the task at hand.

Hired guns—Consultants, lawyers, accountants and other outside business specialists who are brought in to provide their services on a contract basis. These are the suit-wearing mercenaries of the business world.

Hitter—One who is extremely talented both inside and outside the office. This is the guy loved by the client because he always knows exactly what to say; the guy whose colleagues respect and admire him because of his tremendous skills. He also has the uncanny ability to stay at the bar until the wee hours of the night getting hammered, yet still function at 110 percent the next day.

Holding your mouth right—What it takes sometimes, to get something right—a superstitious way of explaining success. There can't possibly be another reason why something went wrong the first time, right?

Hot money—Funds that are manipulated by investors seeking high, short-term yields because the funds may be moved somewhere else at any given time.

Incubator—An organization that helps very small businesses, often startups. They offer support services, low-cost office space and flexible contracts, all of which give small businesses the opportunity to become established and grow. It comes from the real item; an *incubator* is used to hatch eggs.

Info lush—A manager or executive who always wants more data, using it to delay or stall a decision.

Ironclad—Something that is *ironclad* is guaranteed. If I make an *ironclad* promise, it's as good as gold.

It will bank—Means that the proposed idea, investment, acquisition or employee is viable.

Job enlargement—Adding tasks to a job in order to broaden the scope of the job; it is also known as horizontal growth.

Job enrichment—Adding tasks to a job that build motivation, such as planning, organizing, decision-making or other management functions that make it more challenging. It is considered vertical job growth.

John Hancock—A signature. Hopefully, the boss puts his *John Hancock* on your paycheck. If you'll mail me your copy of *Green Weenies and Due Diligence*, I will be glad to add my John Hancock to it for you.

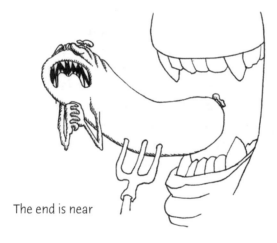

The end is near

Killing—A substantial and often quickly achieved profit. The profit may be at someone else's expense, or may just come to you because you were smart and quick. If you bought technology stocks in the early 90s, you probably made a *killing* so long as you sold before the bottom fell out.

Kitchen cabinet research—Personal opinion, determined by looking at your own approach to the issue. Example: A toothpaste company could design a new flavor by conducting extensive independent research of its flavors on customers, or they could just look in their own "cabinets" at home and form an opinion.

Kowtow—To stroke someone's ego or cater to their needs. If you're looking to impress a new client, you should *kowtow* to them. The term derives from the ancient Chinese custom of touching your forehead to the ground in a show of respect to your superiors. (See also: *yes man.*)

Kudos—Praise and congratulations for a job well done. When you've worked hard and achieved your goals, you deserve some *kudos.*

Last straw—The last problem in a series of difficulties that finally forces a manager or owner to make a change in personnel or method. If you caused the *last straw* to break, then that change might be you. From the proverb, "The last straw broke the camel's back." It's something that may seem insignificant by itself, but when put on top of an already large pile it proves to be the decisive factor.

Lead balloon—Does this sound like a good idea? Of course not. A *lead balloon* is a complete failure, a horrible idea that never had any chance of getting off the ground.

Left-brained—Refers to a person whose left lobe of the brain is dominant. It can be positive, when referring to a person who is logical and reliable; it can be negative, when referring to someone who shows off or intentionally hinders progress. *Left-brained* thinkers aren't as creative as *right-brained* thinkers but tend to be more organized, reliable and consistent. (See also: *right-brained.*)

Legacy cost—The financial expense of maintaining benefits for retirement, including health care, pensions and insurance.

Lemons into lemonade—It simply means to turn something that is bad (sour) into something good. You can *turn lemons into lemonade* by taking an opportunity after being laid off to find the job you really wanted. If sales are weak but better than the last period, you can *turn lemons into lemonade* by announcing that sales have increased over the previous period. (See also: *optics* and *energy.*)

Less than trailer load (LTL)—Loads that don't use all the space in the trailer, which means that they must be combined with shipments from other customers so that the carrier can maximize efficiency. *Less than trailer load* doesn't qualify for discounts that are offered for full loads.

Lifeline—Something thrown to a person, initiative or company. It can be new funding or new resources, or anything that allows something to stay alive.

Lightning rod—A person who instigates change, often in an energetic and explosive way. Can also be used to define someone who is a magnet for problems.

Lip service—When you pay *lip service*, your lips are moving, but you likely aren't saying much or intending to do much as a result. For the sake of solidarity, you may speak up in favor of an issue despite having reservations about it.

LTL—(See: *less than trailer load.*)

Machiavellian—Named for the infamous political philosopher Niccolo Machiavelli, known for proposing that the ends justify the means. In business, it is used to describe someone who is particularly ruthless or cutthroat in his tactics. "Chainsaw" Al Dunlap could easily be described as *Machiavellian*.

Mailbox rule—A rule relating to contracts which states that an offer is accepted when the written acceptance is mailed (physically dropped in the mailbox or handed to the mail carrier). This means acceptance occurs as soon as it leaves the hands to enter the mailbox or postal representative, as opposed to when it is received by the location to which it is mailed. This only applies if mailing the acceptance was an agreed way to accept the contract. If the contract requires an email or fax acceptance (to be more timely), then the acceptance is valid as soon as the fax or email is sent.

Management information systems (MIS)—Originally, systems and procedures set up to manage the data and functions of a company's mainframe computer system and to provide this information to management. Now it applies to any system designed to organize computer resources and records.

Mark—Borrowed from the language of the con artist, the *mark* is the target of a dishonest business practice. Can also be used in a more innocuous sense; someone could be the *mark* for advertisers.

Money left on the table—The difference between an excessively low bid and the actual value of the work. If it had been calculated more carefully, the bid could have been much higher, still been the winner, and assured more profit.

Move the needle—(See: *doesn't move the needle.*)

Nanny state—An undesirable state of the nation in which the government oversteps its boundaries in the regulation of business and other areas. Applies to business in the same way.

Nervous Nellie—An investor who isn't comfortable with investing or the risks associated with investing.

Nest egg—A portion of funds that are set aside for a certain purpose, often retirement. If I'd started thinking about this when I was 20, I'd be sipping margaritas on the beach in Mexico instead of writing this book.

New bet—This describes new money in the form of capital or equity. It usually follows a first bet (or it wouldn't be new), and of course has some risk.

On the back burner—Used to describe an idea or project that is not a major priority. It's probably not receiving much attention, if any at all. Items *on the back burner* of a stove are a little out of reach, and are likely just simmering, while more important things are prepared up front.

One night stand investment—A security that is purchased with the intent to keep it for the long term, but then is quickly sold the next day when panic sets in.

OPM—Acronym for "other people's money."

Opportunity cost—The cost of accomplishing a gain by giving up an item; the cost of choosing one option over another.

Orphan—A stock or other type of investment where security analysts don't offer much coverage, and there is not much trading activity. The item basically has no market. If no one is "working it," it becomes an *orphan*, and price usually drops. Being an *orphan*, sadly, is a bad thing.

Outside the box—The expression refers to "thinking *outside the box*," but it frequently means performance that is outside a *paradigm*; not the usual way of performing. (See also: *paradigm*.)

Overhang—Has many meanings, but I learned that it is relative to leases where a business operation is closed, but lease liability continues even after the business is no longer operating or using the facility. In this case it's called lease *overhang*. It can apply to other "leftover" obligations or "stubs." For instance, if a company is self-insured or not insured, and the boss' new Lexus is stolen with 70 payments left on it, there is an *overhang* of debt.

Ozzie and Harriet—The traditional two-parent, two-child household.

Pace-setter—Like the car in first place, the *pace-setter* is the person in the office that everyone else is chasing. In sales, they are the most successful product movers. It should be every worker's goal to be the *pace-setter*.

Painful—Something that is highly unpleasant, but not in a physical sense. For instance, one of my current peers talks and talks, but never says anything or answers a question; he just rambles and talks in circles and it's hard to even get away from him. For me it's *painful*.

Pari-passu—When two parties have equal rights to payment or ownership. Often investors want to assure that they stay *pari-passu* in the event of a write-down, so that everyone shares the loss equally.

Pay for performance—A compensation plan that pays more for higher productivity and less for lower productivity. It can range from pure commission pay for salespeople to paying by the piece in manufacturing. In the auto salvage business, when we implemented this type of plan for drivers (pay per stop) and dismantlers (pay per car), production increased more than 35 percent the first week. There have been many management books written on pay for performance; some teachers like it, others are opposed to it. Having had employees paid with and without pay for performance, I wholeheartedly support it. There are some employees, (10 percent is a swag), that will work just as hard no mater how much or how they are paid, it's just in their genes. I have to dedicate this portion of the book to the best employee I ever had, now gone, Bob Swart. Bob gave 110 percent, and was all about accountability and gave it regardless of the pay.

Payment in kind (PIK)—Bartering, or a payment made in something other than cash. (See also: *consideration*.)

PIK—(See: *payment-in-kind*.)

Pipe dream—Outlandish hopes for an unlikely event. Say you're the junior assistant branch manager's intern and you want to be CEO by next week. That, my friend, is a *pipe dream*. Originally used to describe the vivid fantasies of opium smokers.

Play devil's advocate—During the brainstorming phase of a project, someone ought to *play the devil's advocate* by anticipating the likely flaws in the plan or the arguments of potential critics. It is this person's job to predict problems within the planning of the project in order to be suitably prepared for them later. (See also: *war games*.)

Positioning—Understanding who the customers are and creating an image for a company's product or service which appeals to them.

Power lunch—Much more important than a regular lunch, so I'd leave my tie on if I were you. When you're conducting big business over turkey on rye, that's a *power lunch*. Other types of sandwiches also qualify.

Procrastination on the customer's part always constitutes an emergency on our part—The meaning is pretty obvious, but it's an important thing to keep in mind.

Puffing your chest—Refers sarcastically to a person that is proud, maybe cocky, and tries to intimidate others by blustering.

Quality circle—The segment of workers in a company who are accountable for maintaining the quality of the product.

> How about a gift that is educational
> but also makes you laugh out loud?
> ***Green Weenies and Due Diligence*** is that gift!

Quick and dirty—A less-than-perfect solution to a problem. It may not be the prettiest, most efficient or most conclusive solution, but it will work. (See also: *shake and bake, Mickey Mouse, back of the envelope* and *on a napkin*.)

Rapid prototyping—Quickly turning an idea into a model to help eliminate flaws in the design and to make improvements. It is usually a step in the final design of the product.

Refrigerator—Refers to an old computer from the 1970s. It was about the size of a refrigerator, had to be in a heavily air-conditioned space, and didn't have as much power as a single chip today.

Reverse auction—An auction where the sellers ask the buyers to bid, and keep bidding, until one gets the best deal. Priceline.com has a model like this for selling airplane and hotel tickets.

Right-brained—This is a person who uses the right lobe of the brain more than the left. It can be positive when referring to a creative and innovative person, but can be negative when referring to an emotional person or one who gets distracted easily. *Right-brained* thinkers tend to be more creative and less logical than *left-brained* thinkers; artists, musicians and writers are generally considered *right-brained*. (See also: *left-brained*.)

Ron time—Substitute anyone's name for Ron here, if you like. My employees always refer to my projected time for completion of a given task as *Ron time*, a derogatory reference to their perception that I underestimate the task at hand. I think they are wrong of course. (Well, maybe not.)

Rube Goldberg—Named for the cartoonist from the early 1900s whose drawings included comically complex machinery that, in reality, accomplished very little. Now used to describe any contrivance that is unnecessarily complicated; something that could have been far simpler and achieved the same results.

Rules of engagement—The rules or requirements that must be met before something else can happen, such as a meeting or initiative.

Seed capital or seed money—Funds used to finance the initial stages of a new venture. *Seed money* may be used to conduct research, develop the prototype for a product, or to determine if an idea is feasible or economically viable. It is the initial equity capital used to start a new business.

Shooting star—A fast growing company, or exemplary employee.

Smoking gun—Something that serves as indisputable evidence or proof, especially of a crime. Finding a *smoking gun* indicates a certainty that the gun was indeed shot. In the FTC case in which I testified against ADP, the FTC alleged that they found a *smoking gun* in board meeting minutes of an alleged improper takeover. (See also: *dirty laundry*.)

Spinning our wheels—Simply put, we're not getting anywhere. The car must be stuck in the ditch? (See also: *car in the ditch.*)

Splitting the sheets—Means splitting up, as in a divorce. In a business conversation, it likely means a partnership breaking up or one company parting ways with another company or division.

Square headed girlfriend—Metaphor for a computer; applies to that employee who works constantly and doesn't have time for a real girlfriend.

Stag—A short-term speculator.

Stem the tide—An attempt to stop a prevailing negative trend. (See also: *stop the bleeding.*)

Step up to the plate—From baseball terminology, meaning to accept responsibility for or to take active control of a situation. When things are in disarray, it's time for someone to *step up to the plate.* (See also: *face the music.*)

Sterile investment—An investment that provides neither dividends nor interest to the investor. The return is generated entirely by gains in the underlying asset.

Sticky site—A website that attracts visitors and maintains their interest by offering information or activities designed to keep them on the site. Most sites aren't that sticky; customers just click through quickly. A *sticky site* is designed to be simple, attractive and easy to use.

Stop the bleeding—(See: *stem the tide.*)

Stub debt—A remainder, much like a check stub. It can be almost any kind of remaining amount due. For instance, if a loan has a balance of $8,000, and only $6,000 is paid, the remaining $2,000 might be referred to as a *stub debt.*

Super Bowl indicator—An indicator based on the belief that a Super Bowl win for a team from the AFC division foretells a decline in the stock market for the next year, while a win from a team from the NFC division means that the stock market will be up for the coming year. As strange as it seems, it has been about 85 percent accurate.

Surgical hiring—This is a term for hiring a specialist in a given area, or persons with specific skills or experience. In most jobs, applicants are interviewed, sized up for their qualifications and then likely given some training. With *surgical hiring*, you actually solicit very specific candidates, perhaps from a competitor, and they need very little or no training. You might also *surgically hire* someone because they have the relationships with customers you want. I have seen it used with salespeople, where the product and process was very complex, or the customer relationship was part of the qualifications.

Tailspin—If your company is in a *tailspin* it's headed for disaster, just like an airplane going down.

That dog won't hunt—A term popularized by ex-President Lyndon Johnson. A Southern-flavored way of saying, "that won't work."

Things in the drawer—These are things we have that we haven't used yet. Perhaps we are holding them for a better time to present, say, during negotiations. Keeping them in the drawer keeps them hidden.

Tough crowd—Refers to the participants in a meeting; when sarcastic barbs are thrown at each other, it's a *tough crowd*.

Turkey—An investment that yields disappointing results.

Under the table—Describes illegal dealings that take place out of the view of public eye, such as bribes or kickbacks.

Viral marketing—A type of marketing that spreads on its own momentum, usually with little or no cost. It's the holy grail of marketing, since it accomplishes so much for so little. As the term indicates, it spreads much like a disease. Companies nowadays are trying to create *viral marketing* to avoid having to spend money on traditional methods. Apple uses *viral marketing* by getting young people to try its products, so that they tell their friends, who tell their friends and so on.

Viral site—A popular website. A site which hosts a huge amount of traffic and whose link is sent out by many users to friends and family.

Wallpaper—The name that is given to stocks, bonds and other securities that have become worthless. So called because their only value is as *wallpaper*.

Warm fuzzies—(See: *kudos*.)

Watchdog—A person or group who has the responsibility to scrutinize the practices of a given business or government. *Watchdogs* prevent the abuse of permissive business practices.

Watered stock—Stock issued for less than its market value. An investor may be offered stock at a discounted price as an incentive to invest.

Whipsaw—A quick movement in price followed by another quick movement in the opposite direction. In business, it's generally used to describe an adverse action, such as sales shooting way up then way down, *whipsawing* the ability to cope with other functions, such as production.

White knight—A person or company who buys a firm, thereby rescuing it from an unwanted takeover by another party.

White noise—Noise in the market place that is low level, almost transparent, but nevertheless there. Black noise, on the other hand, is louder, and will overcome your marketing message.

Window dressing—A strategy that is used by management near the end of the year or quarter in order to improve the appearance of the project or company's performance prior to presenting it to others. (See also: *cooking the books, creative accounting, gaming the numbers,* and *cookie jar accounting.*)

Winner's curse—A financial theory stating that when there are several bidders in an auction for a company, the winner will generally pay too much.

WOMBAT—A project that is a Waste of Money, Brains and Time. Also can refer to webwombat, Australia's search engine.

Yard—One billion dollars or other units of currency.

Yes man—An employee whose entire existence revolves around approving of his or her supervisor's decisions. Such employees are often subject to ridicule by other more valuable employees; can most likely be seen *kowtowing* to the boss. (See also: *wallpaper the meeting* and *kowtow.*)

Zero-sum game—A situation in which there will be a clear winner or loser; one with no room for compromise. The winner wins at the expense of the looser.

CHAPTER

8

Investments

Above par—Describes a stock or other security that sells at a price greater than face value. For example, a $900 par bond that trades at a market price of $950 is selling *above par*. (See also: *below par* and *par value*.)

Accredited investor—In an attempt to prevent risky investments, federal securities law places minimums on net worth or income when determining who can invest. The basic requirements in order to be considered an *accredited investor* are having a net worth of liquid assets exceeding $1 million or having an annual income exceeding $200,000 for the last two years.

Angel—A type of venture capital investor who usually invests smaller amounts, typically under $500,000.

Anti-dilution clause—Stipulates that in the event of any occurrence that would dilute the value of the conversion privilege (such as stock dividends, new stock issues and stock splits), every convertible security is to be adjusted to the conversion terms. For example, a bond that would normally convert into 30 shares of stock might have its terms changed to convert into 90 shares if the stock split 3 for 1.

Anti-greenmail provision—A provision in a firm's by-laws that keeps management from purchasing a large amount of stock at a premium price before the same offer is made to other shareholders. (See also: *greenmail*.)

Asset-backed security—A debt security with specific assets as collateral; it is backed by notes or receivables against any asset other than real estate.

At-risk rule—A law preventing investors from receiving tax benefits greater than the amount of money they actually invested; this is achieved by limiting tax deductions to the amount that is directly invested in an asset. For instance, you can't get a deduction for a loss of $50,000 if you only had $25,000 invested. You can only deduct what you had *at risk* in the first place. It sounds simple, but securities and tax avoidance techniques actually create situations where the write offs are much larger than the amount originally invested.

Below par—A security selling at less than face value or par value. For example, $1,200 par bond with a market price of $725 is *below par*. (See also: *par value* and *above par*.)

Blackout period—A time before the release of financial information during which specific employees of a public company are not permitted to trade in the firm's stock.

Book—A document such as a *PPM* which is circulated in order to get financing, sell stock or sell the company. (See also: *private placement memorandum*.)

Cardboard box index—Used by some investors to gauge industrial production. The output of cardboard boxes helps predict the purchases of non-durable consumer goods. When more boxes are being produced it logically follows that more goods are being manufactured to fill them. It's important to note that a manufacturing index does not necessarily mean that more consumer goods are being sold; it can simply mean that inventories are growing.

Casino finance—Any investment classified as very high risk.

Cats and dogs—Speculative investments.

Common stock—A class of capital stock carrying no preference in dividends or any distribution of assets. *Common stock* usually conveys voting rights and is often termed *capital stock* if it is the firm's only outstanding class of stock. Common stockholders are the residual owners of a corporation because they have a claim to what remains after all other parties have been paid. (See also: *conversion price, voting stock, debt exchangeable for common stock, convertible security* and *preferred stock.*)

Consolidation—This describes the *roll up*, or *consolidation* of a bunch of smaller businesses into one large company, usually a public company. Consolidations have included pawnshops, funeral homes, used and new car dealers, ambulance services and the trash industry. The theory is that by combining these smaller businesses into one large business, and installing better management tools, access to capital, best practices and other synergies that should exist, the entire company can produce more profit than the individual business did. Some times it works, sometimes it doesn't, but everyone agrees it's very hard, and the synergies can be illusive. Typically, a *roll up* or *consolidation* occurs over months or years, contrasted to a *poof offering*, which happens in the blink of an eye. (See also: *roll up* and *poof offering*)

Conversion price—The price per share that a *common stock* will be exchanged for a *convertible security* or debt. (See also: *common stock* and *convertible security.*)

Convertible security—A security that may be exchanged for another asset at the option of the holder; generally a fixed number of *common stock* shares. (See also: *conversion price* and *common stock*.)

Debt exchangeable for common stock (DECS)—Debt that may be exchanged for a pre-determined amount of equity in a company. It can serve to reward or protect investors in the event that they want debt instead of equity. I had such an investment and chose to convert my equity to debt and start getting payments, as the company was neither performing nor paying dividends. (See also: *common stock*.)

Derivative—The value of an underlying security or asset that depends on the performance of a security, such as an option or futures contract. *Derivatives* are generally very complex.

Dilution—A decrease in the equity position of a share of stock due to more shares being issued. *Dilution* can be detrimental to the position of existing shareholders since it lessens each of their proportional claims on earnings and assets. For instance, if 100 shareholders each own one share of stock worth $1, the company has a total capitalization of $100. If the company issues 100 more shares, and sells them for 50 cents each to 100 persons, now there is $150 worth of stock, but it's divided among 200 people so the earliest investors suffer *dilution*.

Direct placement—Selling new securities directly to a limited number of large buyers rather than to the general public. Such transactions might save deal costs; more importantly, they don't interrupt the trading of public stocks by adding new shares to the market. Also allows companies to avoid dumping too many shares into the market all at once.

Drag-along right—A right that enables majority shareholders to force minority shareholders into joining in on a sale of a company. These allow them to complete a sale even in the event that a buyer wants to own 100 percent of the firm. They can effectively *drag along* smaller investors.

Earnings surprise—This occurs when the earnings reported by a company are different from the earnings that the investment community had been expecting, or when earnings are not within the range projected by the company.

EPS—Earnings Per Share. (See also: *LGAP.*)

Float—The number of shares in the hands of the public that are available for trading. (See also: *float* in Chapter 9, and *uncollected funds.*)

Follow-on offering—An issuance of stock that follows an initial public stock offering by a firm. For instance, a company might sell 500,000 shares in a public offering and then issue another 200,000 shares as a *follow-on offering.*

Full valuation—In a VC firm or other investment firm, such a statement means that the proposed price is too expensive to justify the investment.

ACME Green Weenie trap

Going private—The process of a publicly held company having its outstanding shares purchased for the purpose of obtaining complete ownership and control. Some companies that have been reduced in size do this because it costs so much to stay public. It can also occur when one or several investors buy all the stock from the public (perhaps at above market value), because they believe they can run the company better or get better returns.

Investment banker—A firm that functions as an intermediary between organizations that need additional funds and individuals and organizations with surplus funds to invest. Most people have dealt with at least one type of *investment banker*: A mortgage broker, who helps homebuyers identify sources for home loans.

Junior debt or security—A class of debt that is lower in status to another class of debt issued by the same party. *Junior debt* is riskier for an investor, but it pays a higher rate of interest than safer kinds of debt.

Lob in a call—In a brokerage house, to call someone.

Lockup period—The time during which employees and other early investors are not permitted to sell their stock in a newly listed company.

Market capitalization—The total value of all of a firm's outstanding shares. Calculated by multiplying the current market price per share by the total number of shares that are outstanding.

Negotiable—An item that can be assigned or transferred. A *negotiable* security is a security that can be sold and transferred.

Option—A written agreement that gives one party an exclusive right for a specific period of time; a purchase *option* gives the party the right to purchase at a specific price during a specified time.

PE Fund—Private equity fund.

Poof offering—A type of public offering where individually owned businesses suddenly combine their ownership into a new public company. In 1992, I met with several other auto recyclers about such an offering, which is very difficult to complete, and I quickly determined that it was not feasible due to a lack of consistent accounting practices. It's called a *poof offering* because on one day you have four private businesses and the next day, following the public offering, *poof!* You have one new public company. (See also: *roll up* and *consolidation*.)

Poop and scoop—Market manipulation whereby a small group of informed people attempt to lower the cost of a stock by distributing falsely negative information (*poop* on the reputation), then purchase the stock at bargain prices (*scoop* up the cheaper stock). This is highly illegal and occurs mostly on the Internet. (See also: *pump and dump*.)

Preemptive right—A stockholder's right to maintain a constant percentage of a firm's outstanding stock; the stockholders always have the opportunity to purchase shares in a new stock issue proportionally to the percentage of outstanding shares they already have. If a stockholder owned 20 out of 100 shares and 200 new shares were released, he would have a *preemptive right* to buy 40 more shares, thereby keeping his holding at 20 percent.

Preferred stock—A class of ownership in a corporation which entitles the holder to a stated dividend, which must be paid prior to paying dividends to *common stock* holders. *Preferred stock* usually does not have voting rights. (See also: *common stock* and *prior preferred*.)

Price-earnings ratio (P/E ratio)—A statistic from a common stock analysis in which the current price of a stock is divided by the current or projected earnings per share of the issuing firm.

Prior preferred—A class of *preferred stock* that has preference over one or more other classes of *preferred stock* of the same issuer. (See also: *preferred stock*.)

Private placement memorandum (PPM)—The documentation providing information on a new security issue. It is similar to a prospectus but less extensive. This document outlines the business plan and other items of interest to prospective buyers, so it documents the transaction and can create expectation while making representations. Anyone issuing one should be very careful not to make false statements, as they can be grounds for litigation. Such litigation is more common that you might think, as many businesses raising money with a *PPM* fail. Generally speaking, all securities sales have to be registered with the SEC, although there are fewer regulations governing the rules for small offerings of $1 million or less. (See also: *book.*)

Publicly traded company—A company whose stock is freely traded in the public markets, whether over the counter or on an exchange such as the New York Stock Exchange.

Pump and dump—Opposite of the *poop and scoop* strategy. Market manipulation in which thinly traded stocks are accumulated, promoted and then subsequently sold at an artificially high price to unsuspecting investors. (See also: *poop and scoop.*)

Quiet period—The period of time during which an issue of security is in registration and cannot be promoted by the issuer. The *quiet period* starts during the filing period and ends 25 days after the security begins trading. The *SEC* wants potential buyers to make a decision based solely on the prospectus, so all other sources of information should stay "quiet."

Real estate investment trust (REIT)—A company that purchases and manages real estate and/or real estate loans. Income earned by a trust is generally passed through and taxed to the stockholders rather than to the *REIT*.

Red herring—The red legend stamped on a prospectus by the *SEC* stating that it hasn't been approved yet. (See also: *red herring* in chapter one.)

Regulation D—Some smaller companies are permitted by this *SEC* regulation to offer and sell securities without registering the transaction or with a reduced amount of rules regarding regulation.

Roach motel stock—Shares that are hard to sell, especially in a falling market.

Roll up—(See: *poof offering* and *consolidation.*)

Securities Exchange Commission (SEC)—The independent federal agency that was formed in 1934 in order to enforce federal securities law.

Stakeholder—Any party who has an interest, usually financial, in an organization. *Stakeholders* of a company might include stockholders, bondholders, customers, suppliers, employees and so forth. *Stakeholders* usually have something to gain or lose in their investment whether it is monetary or not.

VC fund—(See: Venture capital firm)

Venture capital—A pool of risk capital from which allocations are made available to small new companies with good growth prospects but insufficient funds. Large investors typically contribute to *venture capital.*

Venture capital firm—A firm that specializes in making funds available to companies. Some specialize in startups, others in turnarounds, and some in specific industries.

Vulture fund—An investment money pool that is used to purchase distressed financial assets at bargain prices.

Vulture investor—An investor who attempts to make a profit by buying the debt in companies that are bankrupt or have impaired credit.

Voting rights—The type of voting and the amount of control that owners of a class of stock have.

Voting stock—Stock that gives the holder the right to vote in the election of directors, the appointment of auditors and in other matters arising at the annual meeting. Most *common stock* is *voting stock*. (See also *common stock*.)

Warrant—A security that permits its owner to purchase a specific number of stock shares at a predetermined price. For instance, a *warrant* may give an investor the right to purchase five shares of XYZ common stock at a price of $25 per share until September 3, 2007. *Warrants* usually originate as part of a new issue, but after issuance they trade separately. *Warrants* generally have limited lives. Their values are much more volatile than the values of the underlying stock. Thus, investment in *warrants* is not for the timid. *Warrants* are frequently offered to investors as additional incentive to buy the underlying stock.

Widow-and-orphan stock—A conservative investment with little possibility for large gains or losses or volatile swings in value. It's appropriately named since widows and orphans can't afford to lose any money, and this type investment has very low risk.

Accounting

Accounts receivable turnover—The number of times a firm converts its credit sales into cash during an accounting period. A high number of turnovers indicates that a firm is effectively extending credit and successfully collecting payments. The *accounts receivable turnover* rate is calculated by dividing the average amount of receivables by the annual credit sales.

Accretive—Adding to the *whole,* making it greater than the sum of the parts. When making one change gives a benefit to a project and also improves some other existing part, which in turn gives added benefits to the whole. (See also: *synergy.*)

Accrual accounting—This method of accounting recognizes expenses when they are incurred and revenue when it is earned, rather than when the payments are made or received. (See also: *cash basis accounting.*)

Accrued expense—An expense that has been incurred but has not yet been paid.

Accrued interest—Accumulated interest that is owed on a debt but has not yet been paid.

Accumulated depreciation—The total depreciation of an asset since the date of its acquisition. For instance, if a forklift was purchased five years ago for $15,000 and it's being depreciated for five years, it will generate $3,000 per year in depreciation. In three years, it will have generated $9,000 in accumulated depreciation and will have a net book value of $6,000. The depreciation is intended to resemble the speed with which the asset will deteriorate; in this case, the indicated market value of this forklift should be about $6,000. Of course, depending on how it is maintained and the resale values for such equipment, it may be worth less or more. (See also: *book value, depreciation,* and *capital gain.*)

Acid-test ratio—(See: *quick ratio.*)

Green Weenies and Due Diligence makes a perfect gift for that business prospect you know!

Additional paid-in capital—After buying the stock, the additional investments that stockholders make in the venture that are greater than the stock's stated or par value.

Aging—Arranging the contents of an account in chronological order. This term is heard mostly in inventory and accounts receivable. For example, in accounts receivable, all invoices that are outstanding would be in their own list, then subtotaled based on the date they were initiated. By this *aging*, one can see when each of the accounts receivable is due by the date (i.e. within 30 days, within 60 days, and within 90 days). It provides a better understanding of the value of the accounts receivable. Inventory, of course, is always more valuable when it has a low amount of days in stock. As it stays in stock longer and longer, its probability of sale (and value) declines. (See also: *tainting.*)

Amortization—Decreasing a debt or intangible asset by paying the principle and interest in installments. An *amortization* schedule for a debt is calculated to determine how much of each payment goes toward the principle and interest. For an intangible asset, the amount is deducted as an expense to compensate its cost or to minimize the value of the asset over a period of time.

Amortize—Gradually and systematically deducting a specified amount of money within a specific time period. For instance, an accountant *amortizes* the cost of a long-term intangible asset by deducting a part of that cost against income in each period. The term can really be used to describe almost anything intangible that is used up, paid down, etc. over a given period of time.

Appreciation—The increase in the value of an asset over a period of time.

Asset—A valuable item or resource. (See also: *net worth.*)

Audited statement—A financial statement prepared according to *generally accepted accounting standards* (*GAAP*), which are utilized by all accountants. (See also: *GAAP.*)

Beginning inventory—The value at cost of the inventory in stock at the beginning of a given period.

Bifurcation—In finance, it means branching or dividing into two parts. It can be used for almost anything, however, that is divided into two pieces.

Blue Sky laws—Laws that dictate the requirements for performance or registration on the purchase and sale of securities; can be different in each state. Stems from the idea that these requirements protect investors against unscrupulous individuals who would try to sell them "a piece of the *blue sky*," that is, something with no value.

Book value—The net dollar value of an asset as it appears on a firm's balance sheet. For example, a building purchased for $1,100,000 but depreciated by $500,000 has a *book value* of $600,000. *Book value* is an accounting concept that frequently doesn't coincide with an asset's market value. (See also: *accumulated depreciation.*)

Calendar year—A period lasting from January to December. (See also: *fiscal year.*)

Cap ex—Short for capital expenses, those larger assets that are to be depreciated rather than expensed. It is used generally in budget planning when determining the *cap ex* for the coming year. Capital expenses are a use of cash that does not show up on the P & L. (See also: *EBITDA.*)

Capital gain—The amount generated from the sale of a capital asset that exceeds the cost basis. (See also: *accumulated depreciation.*)

Did you eat all your **peas and carrots** at dinner as a child?
Even then they were important, and they still are,
see page 44 for more information.

Capital gains tax—Tax on gains that are made by selling capital assets such as bonds and stocks.

Capitalization—The amounts and types of long-term financing in a firm such as retained earnings, long-term debt, common stock and preferred stock. A firm that has *capitalization* with little or no long-term debt is considered conservatively financed.

Capitalization rate—Converts an income stream into a present value lump sum. For example, a *capitalization rate* of 20 percent and an annual income stream of $3,000 provide a present value of $3,000/0.2 or $15,000.

Cash and equivalents—The sum of all cash and short-term assets that can easily be converted into cash, such as stocks and bonds.

Cash basis accounting—A method of accounting in which the receipt and payment of cash are the basis for documenting transactions, rather than recognizing expenses as they are incurred and revenue as it is earned. Corporations don't use this type of accounting; individuals typically use it for tax purposes. Also, small businesses that don't have material amounts of inventory, A/P, or A/R may qualify for cash basis accounting. Once a business starts with one method (cash basis vs. accrual basis), it can't change without getting permission from the IRS. (See also: *accrual accounting.*)

Cash flow—The amount of net cash that is generated by an investment or a business during a specific period. One measure of *cash flow* is earnings before interest, taxes, depreciation and amortization (EBITDA).

Cash ratio—A type of current ratio that compares a firm's cash and cash equivalents to its current liabilities. A firm's *cash ratio* proves its liquidity. The higher the *cash ratio*, the better.

Chattel—*Personal property*; tangible property other than real estate. (See also: *personal property.*)

Clearinghouse—A system where banks exchange checks that are drawn on each other in order to secure amounts owed. It can also be a place where two parties meet to physically exchange items and settle accounts.

Closet accountant—A term used to describe someone that is acting like they are an accountant, thought they don't have training in that field. It's likely derogatory, inferring that the person has been "staying in the closet", with their accounting competency, which of course is just a snide reference to their lack of accounting expertise.

COGS—(See: *cost of goods sold.*)

Consumer price index (CPI)—A measure of the difference between the relative cost of living now and the relative cost of living in a base period (currently 1982-84).

Contingent liability—The liability that arises from the "co-signing" or guaranty of any financial obligation such as a lease, loan or financial performance contract for another party.

Contributed capital—Funds or property transferred to a company by its stockholders. The contribution may be made in return for stock, in which case the payment is recorded as paid-in capital.

Cost of Living Adjustments (COLA)—Increases in pay that usually correspond to the rate of inflation. The average rate of inflation in the U.S. economy is about 3 percent. Many employees expect these increases from their employers in addition to merit raises.

Cost of goods sold (COGS)—The combined costs of buying raw material, producing finished goods and marketing the goods during a specific accounting period. For instance, if a firm buys a raw material, then manufacturers it into a finished product at a total cost of $50, the product has a *COGS* of $50 and a $50 gross margin when sold for $100.00. Basically, the cost of making a product. (See also: *operating ratio* and *regression analysis*.)

Current assets—Cash or other assets which are either highly liquid or can easily be converted into cash without losing considerable value over the next 12 months. For example, inventory is considered a *current asset* but equipment is not.

Current liabilities—Debts which must be paid within the next 12 months, including expenses incurred but not paid, current maturities of long-term debt, accounts payable, short-term loans from financial institutions and dividends declared but not paid.

Current ratio—Not the same as *"quick ratio."* A company's ability to pay its debts (divide current assets by current liabilities). The rule of thumb is a ratio of two to one, but bankers will accept a lower ratio if it is within or above industry standards. Ratios that are lower than one are a concern, because they need to increase. Ratios that are too high signal that there are unused resources and can be a sign of inadequately managing capital. It's sometimes referred to as the Working Capital Ratio. (See also: *liquidity ratio.*)

Debt coverage ratio—This is a ratio that a banker uses to determine if a borrower (or proposed borrower) can make the payments on a loan. They take the business operating income, add back depreciation, and that amount should be at least 120 percent of the annualized loan payments. Example: If the business has $50,000 in ordinary *operating income*, which includes $5,000 in depreciation expense, and the requested loan for $500,000 will have payments of $6,000 per month, the *debt coverage ratio* is 76 percent. ($55,000 divided by $72,000) The largest loan payment this business could afford, and still have the required 120 percent coverage, is $3,819. Some banks want more than 120 percent, depending on other items, such as *debt to equity ratio*, and of course, the customer's credit history. With very few exceptions, the bank's underwriting standard relies on actual past income, not proforma income.

Debt-to-equity ratio—This figure shows how much is provided in funds by creditors and how much in funds by owners. A firm's *debt-to-equity* ratio is calculated by dividing debt by owner's equity. Depending on the application, it may include only long-term debt or all debt outstanding. Both items appear on the balance sheet. A low *debt-to-equity ratio (below two to one)*, indicating conservative financing and low risk, results in fewer losses in large amounts or results in large gains in earnings. A high *debt-to-equity ratio (above two to one)*, indicating a history of large losses or aggressive financing, results in very volatile earnings. Put simply, the banks like to loan two dollars for every one dollar of equity in the company, but no more.

Delta—The difference in two numbers and how they change, relative to each other. For instance, the difference in 20,000 and 50,000 is 30,000, so that is the *delta*. If the base number changes to 25,000, and the same *delta* remains unchanged, the relative number changes to 55,000. It's used to determine whether progress is being made or not.

Depreciation—When an asset loses value over time. In accounting, it's the act of deducting or expensing the cost of an asset over a period of time, which is not necessarily the same as its *economic lifetime*. (See also: *accumulated depreciation* and *economic life*.)

Discounted cash flow—Calculation of the current value of money that will be received in the future. Because money has a time value, there is a cost applied to waiting for a payment. If one could make 10 percent on an investment today, then the value of a payment of $100 received in one year would have to be discounted by the rate of 10 percent for one year. Thus today, $90.91 is what the $100 would be worth in one year. To put it in perspective for you: Which would you rather have, $1 today or $1 in five years? (See also: *time value of money*.)

Green Weenie scared
of the dog

Discretionary earnings—What a business makes prior to interest expense and income, income taxes, depreciation and amortization, non-operating and non-recurring expenses; commonly known as *EBITDA*. (See also: *earnings before interest, taxes, depreciation and amortization*.)

Dividend (stock)—A portion of a company's net profits that are distributed by the company to a class of its stockholders. The *dividend* is paid at a fixed amount for each share of stock that is held.

Earned interest—The interest that has been earned, generally daily. It may have been paid, or it may be accrued if it has not been paid.

Earnings before interest and taxes (EBIT)—(See: *operating income*.)

Earnings before interest, taxes, depreciation, and amortization (EBITDA)—This is one popular measure of the amount of cash that's generated from the operation of a company. Critics contend that *EBITDA* can be a misleading financial tool, in part because companies have lots of discretion in determining the dollar amount of the components used in its calculation. Financial analysts frequently use *EBITDA* to evaluate the ability of a company to fulfill its debt obligations. *EBITDA* is also used as a measure of profitability in assessing the value of a company and to compare a company's financial performance with other firms. In addition, *EBITDA* does not consider the funds that a company may require for capital investments (*cap ex*). Depending on the asset class and the strength of the borrower, lenders generally want at least 120 percent debt coverage, meaning that annual *EDITDA* should be at least 120 percent of the annual debt payments. (See also: *cap ex*.)

Earnings multiple—(See: *price-earnings ratio*.)

EBIT—(See: *earnings before interest and taxes*.)

EBITDA—(See: *earnings before interest, taxes, depreciation* and *amortization*.)

Economic life—This is the time during which an asset (fixture or improvement) is profitable or useful. This does not necessarily line up with the period over which an asset is depreciated; if you buy a 50-year-old metal building, for example, the IRS may require you to depreciate over 30 years even though its economic life is apt to be much less. (See also: *depreciation.*)

Ending inventory—The goods that still remain for sale at the end of an accounting period.

Exchange rate—The value of one currency expressed in terms of another currency as a ratio. What the rate of one principle unit of currency, from its origin, is worth in another country. For example, if the U.S. dollar buys 1.60 Canadian dollars, the *exchange rate* is 1.6 to 1.

Extraordinary item/loss/gain—Caused by an unusual event or transaction. For instance, if a company sells its only building, this would be considered an *extraordinary item,* as it's not likely to sell another one in the foreseeable future. If sold for less than book value, they have an *extraordinary loss.* If sold for more than book value, it's an *extraordinary gain.*

FASB—(See: *Financial Accounting Standards Board.*)

FASB Goodwill—The amount that's above the fair net book value (adjusted for assumed debt) which is paid for an acquisition. It's called *blue sky* because you can't see it; it's intangible, like the blue sky. *Goodwill* is an asset on the balance sheet of the acquiring firm and the value must be reduced if the value is impaired. (See also: *blue sky,* as opposed to *Blue Sky laws,* and *intangible asset*).

FIFO—(See: *first-in, first-out.*)

Financial Accounting Standards Board (FASB)—An independent accounting organization that determines the standards for financial accounting and reporting. The rules set by *FASB* influence the numbers that companies show to financial analysts and stockholders. Lately, the *FASB* has been wrestling with the rules for expensing stock options. (See also: *GAAP.*)

First-in, first-out (FIFO)—An accounting procedure for identifying the order of items sold or used and estimating their value. With *FIFO*, the oldest items in inventory are assumed to have been sold first.

Fiscal year—A year that starts in any month other than January. Some companies choose to base their business years on something other than a *calendar year*. (See also: *calendar year.*)

Fixed asset—Cannot easily be converted to cash that could be used in the daily business operations.

Fixed cost—A cost that doesn't change regardless of variations in output. It can describe, for instance, rent payments on real estate. (See also: *variable cost.*)

Free cash flow—The cash flow that remains after taking all other cash flows into account, such as working-capital expenditures, fixed-asset acquisitions and asset sales. Obviously more is better.

Generally accepted accounting principles (GAAP)—Standard accounting practices and procedures. They are established by the Financial Accounting Standards Board. (See also: *Financial Accounting Standards Board (FASB), pro forma earnings, audited statement* and *LGAP.*)

Gain—The amount received in a transaction that is in excess of the book value. For instance, a receipt of $7,500 from the sale of an asset with a book value of $2,500 results in a gain of $5,000. Depending on how long the asset was held, and other factors, the gain (or loss) could be a long (or short) term capital gain (or loss).

Going concern statement—An auditor's statement of concern regarding the ability of the company being audited to maintain operations. A *going concern statement* indicates that there is substantial risk for equity investors. Such a statement can be issued because the company is losing large amounts of money, or perhaps because it has impending debt which it is unlikely to meet.

Gross margin—(See: *gross profit margin.*)

Gross profit—The amount of a sales dollar left after the product's cost and certain costs directly related to production, raw materials, storing and inbound shipping of raw materials are deducted. From the gross margin are deducted general and administrative expenses, leaving net profit.

Gross profit margin—Calculated by dividing gross profit by *net sales*; expressed as a percentage. In other words, it is the revenues that remain after all direct production costs are paid. (See also: *cost of goods sold* for an example and *net sales.*)

Gross sales—Total sales for a period not including any discounts or returns. It drives me crazy when I hear people refer to gross or net sales as "income." (See also: *net sales.*)

Hard assets—Generally those tangible assets that are easy to identify: furniture and fixtures, equipment, inventory, vehicles, tools, real estate, etc. They can be touched or seen, unlike conceptual assets such as goodwill.

Green Weenie all cut up

Income—Income can be defined many ways, most are defined here. One thing income is not is the sales of the company (gross sales or net sales). It drives me crazy when people talk about how much money they take in (sales) as their income. I suppose they do that because they don't know any better, or because it always makes their company sound bigger than it is. (See also: *Operating income, EBITDA* or *EBIT.*)

Intangible asset—An asset that doesn't have physical characteristics but represents value to the company such as goodwill, trade name, etc. (See also: *blue sky* and *FASB goodwill.*)

Intellectual property—Unique innovations or ideas that are not tangible parts of the business; these may be protected by patents, trademarks, and copyrights. It also refers to the skills and creative processes that have developed in a business that can't be quantified. It may be a sales and marketing team with skills in putting together an effective and successful marketing plan for new products. That marketing skill can be thought of as part of a company's *intellectual property*. Although that can't be patented, it should be protected.

Internal rate of return (IRR)—The discount rate on an investment that equates the present value of the investment's cash outflows with the present value of the investment's cash inflows. For instance, if you spend $50,000 on a given investment, the *IRR* percent would be the annualized rate of return of the profit. It's not just the annual rate of return per year multiplied by the number of years. If you loan $50,000 and get no interest the first year, but you get $20,000 in interest or return in the second year, you actually got about $10,000 each year, so the *IRR* is approximately 20 percent. It's actually somewhat less since you got zero in the first year. It's a fairly complex calculation, one that I can't do, which is why I keep my friend Joe Mannes around. Well heck, maybe I should admit that I just don't know how to make the calculations. Also defined as the discount rate at which the present value of expected cash inflows from a project equals the present value of expected cash outflows.

Lady Godiva accounting principles (LGAP)—A theoretical set of accounting principles under which corporations must fully disclose all information, including information that doesn't often get reported to investors under *GAAP. LGAP* includes disclosure of all off-balance sheet items, the way in which goodwill accounting rules impact *EPS*, the impact on *EPS* of stock options issued in lieu of salaries and how pension expense are accounted for. In the legend, Lady Godiva rode naked on horseback through the streets; this type of full disclosure strips the corporation of all its "clothing," leaving nothing hidden. (See also: *generally accepted accounting principle, EPSs.*)

Last-in, first-out (LIFO)—An accounting method for identifying the order that items are used or sold. With *last-in, first-out*, the most recent inventory is assumed to be sold first.

Liability—An obligation to pay an amount in money, goods or services to another party. The balance sheet lists the *liabilities*. A *liability* is a company's responsibility. (See also: *net worth.*)

LIFO—(See: *last-in, first-out.*)

Liquidity ratio—A measure of a company's ability to meet its short-term obligations, which is computed by comparing financial variables. (See also: *current ratio* and *quick ratio.*)

Long-term debt—The portion of debt that will be due after the next 12 months. A five-year loan will have long-term principal due on the last 48 months of the 60-month loan.

Lower of cost or market—A method for determining an asset's value. It is either the original cost or the current replacement cost, whichever is lower. Please note this is not the same as book value.

Material—An accounting and investing term used to describe something that could have a meaningful effect on a company's performance. It's variable, since a $100,000 default on a small bank could cause it to fail, while such a loss at a big bank wouldn't even be a rounding error, much less have a *material* effect.

Net Profit—(See: *gross profit.*)

Net quick assets—Current assets that can be easily converted into cash minus current liabilities.

Net sales—Gross sales minus returns, allowances, discounts and credits. (See also: *gross sales, gross profit margin* and *operating ratio.*)

Net worth—Total *assets* minus total *liabilities*. (See also: *asset, liability.*)

Nonrecurring charge—An expense that is not expected to be encountered again in the foreseeable future. (See also: *extraordinary item.*)

Off the books—Transactions that occur only in cash or barter. People who conduct business *off the books* are usually trying to avoid taxation, and in most cases it is illegal. So if your daughter isn't reporting the profits from her lemonade stand, she's running *off the books*, and I'm sure the IRS will be around any day now.

Operating expense—Incurred as a necessary part of operating a business; includes salaries, taxes, insurance, utilities, etc. (See also: *operating ratio.*)

Operating income—Revenues derived from daily operations, which are in excess of expenses, excluding income tax. *Operating income* represents income from normal business activities. Unusual nonrecurring items, such as gains from selling a subsidiary or losses from closing a plant, are not included in calculating *operating income*.

Operating ratio—*Operating expense* divided by *net sales*. (See also: *COGS, net sales, operating expense.*)

Ordinary income—Income that does not qualify for special tax treatment. Examples are wages, dividends and interest.

Paid in capital—Capital received from investors in exchange for stock that's not a result of operations. This appears on the balance sheet. It includes funds and property contributed to a firm by its stockholders.

Par value—The dollar value of a security as stated on the certificate, or the minimum contribution that is made by investors in order to purchase a share of common stock when it's issued. For instance, if the founder of a company contributes $2,000 for 20,000 shares of stock in the company, the cost for each share is 10 cents; however, future shares might be sold at a different value. (See also: *above par* and *below par*.)

Parallel economy—A black market. An unregulated, informal underground marketplace.

Passive activity—An activity from which one could potentially profit without physically participating, or an activity in a business or trade in which the taxpayer does not participate significantly. For instance, if you have a full-time job but also own a rental house, the rental house is likely a *passive activity*.

Passive income (loss)—A special category of income (loss) that is derived from activities in which one isn't directly involved, such as limited partnerships, real estate and other forms of tax advantaged investments.

Personal property—Property that is not real estate and that is not permanently affixed to the land. It is tangible and so it can be moved. (See also: *chattel*.)

Prepaid expense—An expenditure that will provide future benefits because it's paid in full, rather than financed. Often, it is a recurring expense. For instance, you might pay your insurance for a year all at once. You have now *prepaid* an *expense*.

Privately held company—A firm whose shares are held within a small circle of owners and do not trade publicly.

Pro forma earnings—Income that is not necessarily calculated in accordance with *generally accepted accounting principles*. For example, a company might report *pro forma* earnings that exclude depreciation expense and one-time expenses such as restructuring costs. (See also: *generally accepted accounting principles.*)

Pro forma financial statement—A financial statement based on projected or restated amounts.

Profit center—A segment of a business for which profits, costs and revenue are calculated separately. The manager of the segment is responsible for, and judged on, the performance of that segment.

Quick ratio—Cash plus marketable securities plus receivables divided by *current liabilities*. The rule of thumb here is a ratio of one to one. Anything less than one means there aren't enough liquid assets necessary in order to pay short-term debt without converting short-term assets. (See also: *acid-test ratio* and *liquidity ratio.*)

Green Weenie sprung a leak

R & D—Research and development expense.

Recapitalization—Restructuring a company's mixture of debt and equity when the debt is too high. Usually the aim is to make a company's capital structure more stable.

Regression analysis—Predicting the value of one variable by looking at the value of other variables. We used a form of regression analysis to predict future *COGS* by looking at the past ratios and turns. (See also: *cost of goods sold.*)

Reserve—Funds from the retained earnings earmarked to be used in the future for things such as payment of potential bad debts.

Residual value—The price at which a fixed asset is expected to be sold by the end of its use by the purchaser. It is important to be able to predict this with some accuracy. For instance, if you lease a new car that cost $50,000 and the *residual value* is projected to be $40,000 after 24 months of use, then the lease payment is calculated on the $10,000 in reduced value, plus interest divided by 24 months. If the value turns out to be less, the lessor can lose lots of money.

Restructuring—When a firm dramatically rearranges its *assets* and/ or *liabilities*. There's usually a one-time charge against earnings for *restructuring*.

Retained earnings—The accumulated net income retained to reinvest in the business instead of paying it out in dividends to stockholders. *Retained earnings* are a part of the owners' equity section of a firm's balance sheet.

Return on equity (ROE)—A measure of net income that a firm is able to earn as a percentage of stockholders' equity. *Return on equity* is net income (after taxes) divided by owners' equity.

Return on investment (ROI)—A measure of the net income that a firm's management can earn plus its total assets. *Return on investment* is net profits (after taxes) divided by net assets.

Return on sales—The portion of each dollar of sales that a firm converts to income, stated as a percentage.

Right side of the balance sheet—Refers to the liability side of the balance sheet.

Robbing Peter to pay Paul—Moving money or resources from one entity or project to another, which results in no net gain for your business.

Run rate—How the financial performance of a company would look if one were to extrapolate the current results over a certain period of time. For instance, taking the last two months' income and multiplying it by six would give you annual projected income based on the most recent *run rate*.

Short-term debt—That portion of debt that will be due in the next twelve months.

Shrinkage—The amount of inventory documented minus the amount of inventory actually present. It's a nice way of describing what is probably theft.

Simple interest—Interest that's charged against the principal only, as opposed to compound interest (which is where the interest is charged against the remaining principal and accrued interest). For instance, if 6 percent annual interest is charged on $100, the interest is $6, calculated as *simple interest*. However, if the interest is calculated (compounded) daily and added back to the principal, the principal increases on Day Two (by the amount of interest earned on Day One) and then the interested is calculated on the new total amount, so on and so on. The yield is higher when interest is compounded instead of using a *simple* method.

Sources and uses of funds statement—It describes the sources of cash (sales, loans, etc.) and the uses of cash (expenses, buying new equipment, repaying loans). (See also: *statement of cash flows.*)

Statement of cash flows—A financial statement that lists how a firm obtained funds and how they were spent within a period of time. (See also: *sources and uses of funds statement.*)

Stock sale—This is the sale of a business in its entirety; all assets, liabilities and stock are transferred to the buyer. The buyer buys the stock in the company, not just the assets. It's an important distinction. When you buy just assets, you get just assets. When you buy stock you get all the underlying value contributors (or detractors), including liabilities and contingent liabilities. A stock purchase can be dangerous, especially if the company has more liabilities than you expected. Most small business sales are asset sales, and the seller retains the stock. At that point in time, in theory, the stock has no value left for the seller, as the underlying asset is gone, but the seller retains the contingent liabilities associated with the company, which although emptied of assets, is still a taxable and legal entity.

Straight-line depreciation—A method of recording depreciation. During each period of an asset's life, the original cost minus the estimated salvage value of an asset is written off in equal amounts. Example: If an asset cost $15,000, and its estimated value at the end of the period it will depreciated at, say, five years, is $2,000, then $13,000 would be depreciated equally over five years, at $2,600 per year.

Tainting—An accounting term in conjunction with accounts receivable, in which the value of receivables is questioned because of high levels of returns, excess delinquencies or other misuse or fraud. Often it is used to describe a portion of the receivables in a current *aging* group, which might be considered delinquent when the same customer has amounts in, say, the 90-day *aging*. If the customer has unpaid invoices in the 90 day column, the items in the 30 day period are tainted as they are probably less likely to be collected. (See also: *aging.*)

Tangible asset—An asset such as a building or piece of equipment that has physical properties; it can be moved, it's not an idea or concept.

Time value of money—The concept that a specific sum of money is more valuable the sooner it is received. (See also: *discounted cash flow*.)

Turnaround—The process of improving from a period of losses or low profits into a more profitable period.

Turnover—The number of times an asset is replaced during a financial period. It generally refers to the number of times inventory is replaced annually. For example, an inventory turnover of five indicates that the firm's inventory has been turned into sales and then replaced five times. *Turnovers* can be inventoried in different ways: in dollars, at cost or retail, or by physical count.

Uncollected funds—A deposit or a portion of a deposit that has not yet been collected by a financial institution. Financial institutions typically don't permit customers to write checks against *uncollected funds*. For instance, when you give someone a check, they deposit it. Until your bank actually sends cash, they have *uncollected funds*. Banks are moving on almost instantly transferring funds. The difference in time between the time they get the check and the actual cash is removed from your account is called a *float*. (See also: *float*.)

Undercapitalized—Of, relating to, or being a firm that doesn't have the sufficient equity to support its assets.

Underperforming asset—An asset that earns a lower rate of return than it would be capable of earning if properly used.

Unrealized loss—Comparing the original cost of an asset to the reduced value of the asset that is being held. An *unrealized loss* is generally realized by closing out the position before it can be recognized for tax purposes. For instance, if you buy a car for $10,000 and put 100,000 miles on it in two years, it's likely worth less than book value. If its fair market value is less than book value, you have an *unrealized loss*.

Green Weenie—Heaven bound

Upstream-downstream—Used to describe a method for verifying inventory accuracy. Items in inventory are verified in the warehouse via a physical inventory. Those same items are checked against written, or more often computerized, records to see if they have corresponding records. This is the *upstream* side. Conversely, items in the computer are physically verified in the warehouse. This is the *downstream* side. The order of *upstream* or *downstream* isn't important. Usually a small sample is done, and if it checks out, further verification may not be needed. But if there are discrepancies, a larger sample is tested. It's amazing, but if the sample is a reasonable size and there is a 10 percent error, the entire inventory likely has errors of about 10 percent. This was a useful tool in the auto recycling business with literally hundreds of thousands of SKUs and a potentially large margin of error in stocking, returns, damaged parts, etc.

Variable cost—The costs of production that vary directly in proportion to the number of units that are produced. *Variable costs* usually include labor expenses and raw material costs, because generally these must be increased in order to increase output. Firms for which *variable costs* represent a high proportion of total costs are generally less likely to experience large fluctuations in earnings, because when sales and revenues change, costs also change by nearly the same amount. *Variable costs* are better than *fixed costs*. (See also: *fixed cost*.)

Vested—In the area of retirement or profit sharing, it means fully earned. It conveys how long an employee must work before the profit sharing or company-matching funds that he accrues will totally belong to him. If an employee leaves a company before that date, any funds that are not *vested* are forfeited. It can also mean a level of personal commitment or investment.

Working capital—The amount of current *assets* that is in excess of current *liabilities*. (See also: *asset* and *liability*.)

Write-off—Lowering the value of an asset on a firm's financial statement, usually to zero. Usually it's *written off* because it is no longer worth anything. Often, the company has discontinued operations or eliminated a line, and *written off* the related assets.

Yield—The return on an investment as a percentage.

Zilch—Zero. Nothing. Nada. If you're making *zilch*, you're either doing something wrong, or you're in the wrong business. Again, I suppose it's not a technical accounting term, but what are the CFOs going to do, shoot me?

10

Debt and Banking

Acceleration Clause—Allows the holder of a note or other timed instrument like a loan to declare all payments due in full, usually upon a particular occurrence (such as default in a payment, or violating a lending covenant).

Balloon payment—The final payment owed on a note or loan; usually a large lump sum.

Bank examiner—A government employee who examines a bank's loans and other facets of the operation to ensure adherence to the standards set by the government agency.

Basis point—A unit for measuring an interest rate yield that is equal to 1 percent of yield; 1/100th of 1 percent; 150 *basis points* is 1½ percent.

Borrowing base—The assets that a business can readily use as collateral against a loan. These assets primarily include accounts receivable, equipment, vehicles and inventory.

Borrowing base certificate—A form that a borrower prepares for the lender at regular intervals that gives the status of the collateral. The frequency with which this form is prepared is generally stated in the loan documents. The lender may require this form at the end of each week, month or quarter. The form can be as simple as a list of assets that are included in the borrowing base (accounts receivable, inventory, etc.) and the balances of those accounts. Usually, the assets are not used at 100 percent of their value for a borrowing base. For example, inventory may be given only 50 percent value and receivables are given 75 percent for the current and 30-day items. The older receivables are calculated at zero.

Bridge loan—A short-term loan that is obtained until permanent financing is arranged—also called a swing loan. It bridges the gap where no financing is available. (See also: *interim financing.*)

Call—Demand from a lending institution that a loan be paid sooner than the original terms specified. Also an option that allows its holder to purchase a specific asset at a predetermined price until a certain date. (See also: *call date* and *call protection.*)

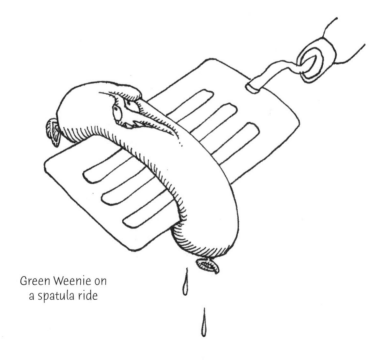

Green Weenie on
a spatula ride

Call date—The date that a note or other investment can be *called* or payment can be demanded in full. (See also: *call.*)

Call protection—A caveat, typically negotiated in a private placement or agreement, which protects the buyer of the security from a *call* for a specified period (which may be for the term of the contract). (See also: *call.*)

Classified loan—(See: *non-performing asset.*)

Clean price—A note's (or bond's) quoted price without accrued interest.

Commitment—A form issued by a lender to a prospective borrower that states the terms of the funding they are willing to provide and the conditions that are required of the borrower. (See also: *term sheet.*)

Commitment fee—A lender charges this to a borrower for the lender's expense in due diligence and paperwork in order to qualify a loan. The fee may be non-refundable or may be refunded at the time of closing.

Compensating balances—An account that a lender requires a borrower to maintain as collateral against a loan that is made; could also be to compensate or offset other expenses the bank incurs on behalf of the customer. For example, the borrower may have a $200,000 certificate of deposit or money market account at a bank as collateral for a $200,000 line of credit that the bank extended to the borrower, or they may not charge you additional checking account fees if you maintain at least $10,000 in an account.

Conduit financing or conduit lender—A lender using *match rate funds* to extend a fixed rate, long-term loan, typically on real estate. The lender relies on the cash flow from the collateral to pay off the note while holding the title to the property as collateral. (See also: *securitization lender.*)

Conforming loan—A conventional mortgage that is under the limit set by FHA or VHA. This conforms to the loan amounts and mortgage guidelines (underwriting standards) that are used by Fannie Mae and/ or Freddie Mac home mortgage lenders.

Cost of capital—The overall percentage cost of financing a firm's assets or rate of return that management expects to pay on all borrowed and equity funds. Different classes of assets may have different costs; this is the aggregate. Very large corporations, such as Ford Motor Company, manage all the debt at a high level and don't allow any other debt to be assumed elsewhere in the company. By doing so, they get the benefit of large volumes with debt rated by third parties and they sell bonds, commercial paper, or other instruments with really low rates.

Sex without marriage? That's for sure taboo, but maybe it's not what you think? See page 180.

Covenant—Basically, a promise in a contract. A clause that's written into a loan agreement to protect the lender's claim by maintaining the borrower's financial status from the time the loan agreement was made. *Covenants* state what the borrower may do and must do to satisfy the terms of the loan. For instance, the borrower may not be permitted to issue more debt by using certain assets as collateral. (See also: *cure, cross default, positive covenant, negative covenant* and *subordinated debt.*)

Coverage ratio—A corporation's measured ability to cover a particular expense. Generally, a high coverage ratio indicates a higher probability that the expense will be covered. (See also: *earnings before interest, debt coverage ratio* and *depreciation and amortization.*)

Credit line—(See: *line of credit.*)

Credit rating—Assessment of an individual's or a corporation's worth for the consideration of granting credit. It is based on their history of repaying loans in addition to their available assets and the extent of their liabilities. It's also known as a credit score, which is objectively considered by agencies that grant or deny credit. Loosely speaking, a personal score below 600 is not very good and scores above 700 are very good. There are three credit bureaus and each uses a slightly different method to calculate the score. The methodology is secret, at least at its core, but the components are known. When applying for a mortgage, the lender will pull a tri-bureau score, which is the average of all three bureaus.

Creeping call option—This is an option that creeps along and changes as it gets closer to the call date. For instance, in order to offer a debtor an incentive to pay off a debt early, one could offer him a creeping call option wherein a $2,000 note which has a maturity of two years could be paid off with a 50 percent discount as long as it's paid within the first twelve months, otherwise the payoff increases by 4 percent per month until maturity, at which time 100 percent of it is due.

Cross default—A provision in a loan agreement which states that a borrower will be in default if he defaults on another obligation. The other obligation can be one with the same lender or any other obligation. Other things can trigger defaults, and hence a cross default occurs, such as a violation of a *covenant* or a legal judgment or filing of some predetermined size. (See also: *covenant.*)

Cure—To fix a problem much like curing an ailment. *Cure* a default means to solve the problem by making a past-due payment or resolving a violation of *covenant*. (See also: *covenant.*)

D&B—Report on the credit-worthiness of a business prepared by the information firm Dun & Bradstreet. It normally contains more information on a company than what general credit reporting agencies obtain.

In the cuts—Banking jargon for being overdrawn. As a customer, you don't want to be in the cuts, and if you must be, hopefully you will have a good enough relationship with your banker that he pays your checks even if it overdraws your account. I see lots of small business people who don't understand why the banker cares, since they charge such large fees. Of course, the first reason is that if he pays your checks, he makes you a loan. But my lifelong banker friend Gary Noel said it the best: "Of all the customers *in the cuts*, not all went bankrupt, but all the customers that went bankrupt were *in the cuts.*"

Inter-creditor agreement—In general, it defines the rules of engagement between lenders of "like" classes (i.e., two senior secured lenders in a syndicated deal) and between lenders of "unlike" classes (i.e., senior secured lender and junior secured lender). For lenders in "like" classes, the agreement typically defines things such as which parties contribute to which *tranches* of debt, how priorities will be handled in event of default and what percentage of debt has to vote to amend the agreement in order to handle forbearance. In "unlike" classes, the agreement typically defines issues such as priority on liens and time restrictions for the second lien holder (in the event of default) before the senior lender has to act to protect its position. (See also: *tranche.*)

Interim financing—The temporary financing that supports a transaction up to the point that permanent financing can be arranged. It's very similar to a *bridge loan*. (See also: *bridge loan.*)

Kiting—A scheme wherein someone deposits a check in one bank, and before it clears, takes the cash out of the same account to take to a third bank. He immediately makes a deposit in the second bank from the third bank where the cash got deposited. It creates "phantom funds" until one of the checks bounces or other problems cause one of the other accounts gets overdrawn, at which point all the checks start bouncing and the *kiting* becomes evident.

Letter of credit—A promise in the form of a letter from a bank which guarantees that a buyer's payment to a seller will be received on time and will be in the correct amount. In other words, the credit of a borrower is substituted by the credit of a third party.

Leveraged buyout (LBO)—Financing most or all of the debt in an acquisition by using the target company's asset value to secure the loan.

LIBOR—(See: *London InterBank Offered Rate.*)

Line of credit—A credit arrangement in which a financial institution agrees to lend money to a customer up to a specified limit. A *line of credit*, which is usually arranged before the funds are actually needed, gives flexibility to the customer to ensure the ability to meet short-term cash needs if necessary. (See: *rest the credit line.*)

Loan syndication—The process of involving numerous lenders to provide various portions of a loan.

Loan to own—A term used to describe a type of loan or lender, where the lender doesn't really care if he gets paid off, and in fact makes the loan knowing he will end up owning the collateral. It's a lot like a pawnshop.

Loan to value—(See: *LTV.*)

London InterBank Offered Rate (LIBOR)—The basic short-term rate of interest in the Eurodollar market and the rate to which many Eurodollar loans and deposits are connected. The *LIBOR* is similar in concept to that of the prime rate in the United States except that it is not subject to as much individual bank management. The *LIBOR* rate is always lower than the U.S. prime rate, but loans are just priced at more points over *LIBOR* so it's really an equivalent. Many large debtors borrow based on *LIBOR*.

LTV—Acronym for "loan to value." It's typically part of a lender's underwriting policy. It's the ratio of the loan amount relative to the value of the property. The value is almost always defined as the lesser of cost or market. Cost is easy to understand, market (value) is determined by an appraisal. Lenders will generally loan 80 percent on owner occupied real estate. If a property cost $500,000, and it's owner occupied, the maximum loan is $400,000. On investment property, the limit is more like 70 to 75 percent. Such percentages are part of a lender's underwriting policy.

Match rate funds—An interest rate on a loan that matches the approximate interest rate for of the source of funds. For instance, a conduit lender (or intermediary) might agree to pay a depositor 4 percent for their money, fixed for 10 years, and loan it at 4.25 percent interest to a borrower. The borrower must pay a steep penalty to pay off the loan early, because the intermediary has guaranteed the fixed rate to the depositor for 10 years. (See also: *securitization lender.*)

Maturity—The date on which payment of a financial obligation is due.

Min-max—Used in a stock offering, usually a private placement. It refers to the minimum amount that will be considered to break escrow (*min*) and the most that will be taken (*max*). When an offering gets past its max, it is oversubscribed (meaning that there are more buyers for stock than the number of shares available for sale). Both of my private placements were oversubscribed. If the minimum amount is not received, the monies in escrow are typically returned to the investors and the offering fails to fund.

Mortgage banker—A banker who makes real estate loans that are subsequently sold to another party.

Negative covenant—A loan *covenant* that prevents certain activities unless all parties agree upon them. (See also: *covenant.*)

Green Weenie bursting point

Non-performing asset—An asset that produces no income. For example, a loan on which the borrower is not making payments is often described as a *non-performing asset*. Such a loan is likely to be classified by the bank examiners. A customer who has a loan classified is out of luck for new loans. (See also: *OAEM.*)

OAEM—(See: *Other Assets Especially Mentioned*).

Off balance sheet financing—An accounting technique that prevents an obligated debt from showing as a liability on the company's balance sheet. There are rules outlining how such items are treated and disclosed, but lots of "tricks" still allow it to happen. A lease, if not properly treated, can be off balance sheet financing.

Orderly liquidation value (OLV)—One of the methods used to value assets that are being purchased or sold. Typically, this type of liquidation would be conducted slowly and methodically in order to maximize the value received for the assets, rather than making a quick sale to a low-ball buyer.

Other Assets Especially Mentioned (OAEM)—A term used by bank examiners to describe a loan that is on a watch for weakness and may be troubled. If it doesn't improve its performance, it will likely become a *classified loan*. OAEM is the first of three categories in which examiners place a troubled loan, this being the least likely to fail but still troubled. The second category, a bit weaker, is called substandard. Following substandard is doubtful or classified. The first two groups generally require a reserve to be set aside in an amount equal to 1 to 25 percent of the outstanding loan amount. As a customer, you should make sure your loans never fall in any of these categories. A classified loan generally requires 100 percent reserve, unless there is strong evidence that there may be some recovery of assets that would limit a total write-off. (See also: *classified loan* and *non-performing asset.*)

Permanent financing—The long-term financing that supports a long-term asset.

Personal guaranty—When a borrower (or some other party) guarantees the debts of a company. On almost all small business loans, a *personal guaranty* is required for loans and leases. Larger private businesses don't usually give *personal guaranties*, and public companies rarely do. (See also: *recourse* and *unsecured creditor.*)

Points—The amount paid on a mortgage closing in order to receive a reduced interest rate on a note; *points* are typically stated as a percentage of the loan amount. One percent of the loan amount would be one *point*. These amounts are paid up front, as fees are. They increase the yield to the lender while they increase the effective interest rate to the borrower. Frequently, some or all points are split between third parties. For example, a mortgage broker might get a portion of the fee while others who were involved in the transaction may also receive a portion of the points.

Positive covenant—A provision in a loan agreement that requires a specified action by the borrower. For instance, a *positive covenant* may mandate that the borrower maintain a specific level of working capital. (See also: *covenant.*)

Preferred creditor—A creditor who has priority for payment over one or more other classes of creditors.

Prime rate—The interest rate that commercial banks charge their prime customers or their customers with the best credit worthiness (usually the large corporations). Many transactions are priced at a certain number of points (or portion of points) over prime. (See also: *sub prime loan.*)

Promissory Note—A promise to pay. A written, dated, and signed instrument, by two parties, which contains an unconditional promise that was made by the debtor to pay a stated sum of money to a payee on demand or at a specified future date.

Recourse—Having an alternative for recovery. If a mortgage is purchased with *recourse* and if the seller defaults, the buyer of the mortgage can force the seller to purchase the mortgage back from him. *Recourse* could include a *personal guarantee*. (See also: *personal guaranty.*)

Recourse loan—A loan in which the lender can claim more than collateral to repay himself in case the loan goes into default. A *recourse loan* places the personal assets of the borrower at risk.

Red lining—The practice by financial institutions of discriminating against potential borrowers who live in certain geographical areas or census tracts by failing to make loans available in those areas; originally discrimination based on race.

Rest the credit line—A banker expects a credit line to "rest" occasionally, meaning it will be paid to zero, usually for at least 30 days consecutively in a year. Credit lines are usually needed by businesses with fluctuations in supply or demand, such as seasonal businesses. If a credit line stays drawn up to the limit all the time, a line is likely not needed; permanent working capital, which is a loan with amortizing monthly payments, is needed instead.

Reverse mortgage—A special type of loan that converts one's home equity into cash. Senior citizens generally use the money that is obtained through a reverse mortgage. For instance, if they have a home that is paid for, they would get a loan against it and begin making payments. The mortgage is designed to provide them income through their expected life span. After their death, the home is sold to pay off any remaining balance.

Rule 101—As in school, with the basic starter course, the rule is: "You can't be mad at me because you owe me money and I want it." It's one of my favorite rules, and I call it *"Ron's Rule 101."* Just substitute your name to make it yours. Customers who owe me money can have any number of attitudes, starting with contrition, but anger at me for wanting the money isn't one of them.

Scrip—Private currency that is issued in the form of an IOU by a corporation or individual. Airline frequent traveler miles are corporate *scrip* issued by the airlines.

Secured creditor—A creditor who has a claim that is collateralized by specific assets.

Securitization lender—A *securitization lender* buys or warehouses loans, then packages them to sell as securities or derivatives. Such loans would likely fund with *match rate funds*. (See also: *conduit lender* and *match rate funds*.)

Securitized—Consolidated mortgage loans that are sold to investors for them to resell to the public as securities. They are typically match rate funded and, as such, carry big penalties for early payoff.

Senior debt—A bond or other form of debt that takes priority for repayment in bankruptcy

Sight letter of credit—A letter of credit which is payable when it is shown along with other necessary documents. For instance, if you ship goods to Taiwan, the buyer's bank or agent is required to pay your sight draft when it arrives with no regard for whether the goods have been received.

Sub prime loan—A loan offered at a rate above prime to those who don't qualify for *prime rate* loans. Most small business loans are priced at one-half to two points over prime, and aren't actually considered *sub prime*. The designation is actually reserved for much weaker debtors, such as loans on mobile homes, where the rate is many points over prime. Credit cards can be 20 points over prime. (See also: *prime rate*.)

Subordinated debt—A loan (or security) that ranks at a lower status than other loans (or securities) as far as claims on assets or earnings. In small businesses, if the company owes the owner money and the debt is on the balance sheet, the lender may require that it be *subordinated* to the bank debt; this way the owner isn't allowed to pay himself back without paying back the bank first. If the owner does pay himself back first, he likely violates a *covenant*, and the entire loan could become due. Under these circumstances, a lender is likely to view the subordinated debt as equity, which improves the customer's ratios, increasing his debt capacity. (See also: *covenant*.)

Subordination—Making a primary lien become regarded as secondary or junior to another lien. This may be done to induce a lender to make a loan against a business property that already has a lien on it. The owner would agree to *subordinate* his lien in order to give the bank primary position in case of default.

Term sheet—A sheet of paper with the proposed terms of some transaction. Banks issue them to customers when their loan has been approved. (See also: *commitment*.)

Tranche—Levels or installments of investments; new companies will usually experience several *tranches* as their business grows. Bonds or other investments are also organized into *tranches* (slices) by similar maturity dates or similar securitized collateral. For instance, if some investors pay $2 per share and are entitled to some type of distribution, and other investors pay $3 per share with some rights, they are in different *tranches*. I actually like a simpler explanation, using trench as a proxy for tranche: Picture two trenches. In one trench are all the shareholders who paid $1 per share, and who get certain rights. In the other trench, another set of shareholders who paid a different price or have different privileges. (See also: *inter-creditor agreement.*)

Underwrite—To assume the risk of securities' sale by purchasing the securities from the issuer to resell to the public. Say a loan underwriter *underwrites* an offering of IBM stock; they actually agree to buy the shares from IBM and are responsible for payment before they are sold to the public. They incur very little risk and charge large fees for this service. The term is used in many other instances, and for small businesses, the most common definition is to underwrite the customer's loan. This requires the bank to make sure the loan meets its underwriting standard. For instance, some banks have an underwriting rule that says they don't finance commercial real estate unless it's owner occupied. They can choose to override that policy by seeking the concurrence of other required parties. Underwriting also includes analyzing the financial statements and cash flows of the company. You should understand the underwriting policies of your lender, so you can strive to meet them, or find another lender. The standards don't vary too much from bank to bank.

Unsecured creditor—A creditor who has no claim on assets and has no collateral other than the good intentions of a borrower to pay the loan back. Large private and public companies secure their debts with assets but don't generally *personally guarantee* the companies' debt. Specific assets are pledged. (See also: *personal guaranty.*)

Legal, Real Estate, Insurance and Contracts

Acknowledgement—When a person signs a document, this notarized statement or declaration proves that the person signing is who he claims to be.

Addendum—This is not the same as an *amendment*. It is a written statement that adds to a contract or clarifies a term; it may be a list of assets that are included in a business transaction where the term "Business Assets" is stated in the contract and "Business Assets" is defined in "*Addendum* X." (See also: *amendment*.)

AKA—Acronym for "also known as."

Amendment—This not the same as an *addendum*. It alters or changes a contract or agreement, usually as a statement of correction. (See also: *addendum*.)

Arbitration—A neutral third party makes the decision in a dispute. This is not like mediation, wherein a mediator makes suggestions/recommendations; in *arbitration* the decision is legally binding and can be enforced by the court if the parties agree.

Audit committee—A subcommittee of the board of directors of a corporation that selects a company's external auditors.

Bare—Operating while uninsured or underinsured.

Blue laws—Statues or ordinances that prohibit commercial activity on Sundays; refer to any strict statutes or ordinances in areas where the residents support the belief in Sunday being the "day of rest."

Bona fide purchaser—Someone who is both capable of buying and who intends to make a purchase. Sometimes a shill, or dummy buyer, comes forward, who may just be snooping for information, perhaps from a competitor.

Bought it out—Selection of a vendor or subcontractor.

Builder's risk insurance—Insurance that protects a builder and his customer against losses during the period of construction before the job is finished and permanent insurance is put in place. It could also cover stolen materials, etc. It's typically much cheaper than permanent insurance.

Bylaws—Business conduct that is governed by stockholder approved rules.

Chairman—The highest-ranking executive in a corporation. In large corporations the *chairman* is not ordinarily involved in day-to-day operational activities, although it is likely that he was the *chief executive officer* before attaining the position. In some corporations, the *chairman* also serves as the president and the *chief executive officer*. The *chairman* leads the board of directors in setting broad corporate goals. (See also: *chief executive officer.*)

Chief executive officer (CEO)—The person who is responsible to a company's board of directors for carrying out its policies. The *CEO* is the highest-ranking executive who manages the firm on a daily basis. (See also: *chairman.*)

Clayton Act—In 1914, it amended the Sherman Antitrust Act. The *Clayton Act* outlaws the selling of the same product to different people at different prices; allowances, discounts, etc. are legal only if offered to everyone on an equal basis.

Closely held company—A firm where shares of common stock are owned by few individuals, usually family members, which are generally unavailable to outsiders.

Codicil—A change that is made to a will legally.

Commingled—Generally refers to assets or funds that are combined or mixed together. When business and personal assets are *commingled*, it weakens the protection of liability that is afforded to corporations and other businesses. (See also: *pierce the corporate veil.*)

Concurrent conditions—Conditions that are to occur at the same time in a contract or agreement which are mutually dependent on the other. No single party is obligated until these conditions are fulfilled at the same time. It's similar to *quid pro quo*. (See also: *quid pro quo.*)

Conforming goods—Goods that meet the terms of the contract.

Consideration—Usually a money payment, although it could be compensation in some other form. Generally, a contract is not enforceable unless *consideration* is made or promised. Anything of value that is exchanged which results in a signature on a contract is *consideration*. (See also: *PIK.*)

Contingent commission—These "commissions" are better known to our attorney general as "kickbacks." He discovered that there were lots of ways insurers were paying monies back to the agents and brokers. In some instances, the customer thinks the broker has gotten him the proper coverage at the best price, when in fact, counting all these commissions, the customer may have overpaid. One of these methods, a *contingent commission*, gives a commission back to the broker if the losses come in at less than estimated for the customer or pool of customers. Other methods include steering of business to insurers or other vendors and services that promise to pay for the services of other broker owned units, or units owned by others that pay a commission for the basis, based on some formula unknown to the customer. The best way to avoid this, based on my experience, is to have your agent or broker give you a written statement that he receives no commissions or payments of any monies from any other source relative to your policy, now or in the future, including but not limited to *contingent commissions*, other than the fees as agreed in writing. Also, the agent or broker should disclose any related third parties that are receiving any portion of the business, such as reinsurance, or non-related third parties that pay for steering business their way. These agents and brokers are skilled at such, and you will have to read any disclosure from them very carefully.

Conveyance—The actual transfer of a title, which occurs upon signing a transfer of title form or other such document.

Covenant not to compete (or non-compete clause)—A contractual agreement that forbids any activity that would take business away from the company; the agreement must not require any unreasonable duration or geographic area. These agreements are most commonly found in employment agreements and in contracts for the sale of businesses and partnership agreements.

D&O coverage—(See: *directors' and officers' liability insurance*.)

DBA—Stands for "*doing business as.*" It is generally a trade name registered with the appropriate state agency, usually a local county recorder's office or Secretary of State Office.

Destination contract—A contract between a buyer and seller in which the obligation of the seller is not fulfilled until the goods are delivered and accepted by the buyer. In this case, the seller is liable for any loss during the shipment of the goods, so the buyer doesn't have to pay for goods that are lost or destroyed in transit.

Diligence—This means being prudent, careful and responsible. In contracts and business dealings, it means taking prudent and reasonable actions to verify information and meet requirements. Buyers always use diligence when reviewing an acquisition target's assets, liabilities, officers, and other items or issues that could have a *material* effect on the company. (See also: *material.*)

Director—A member of a firm's board of directors, which is a group of people who control a corporation. A director may also hold a management position within the firm.

Directors' and officers' liability insurance (D&O)—A type of insurance that protects a firm's directors and officers against lawsuits, mainly suits that are initiated by unhappy shareholders of the firm. *D&O insurance* has become more expensive and more difficult to obtain due to the increasing number of lawsuits in recent years. Companies find it very difficult to recruit outside directors unless the candidates have their own liability insurance.

Disclaimer—Statement that attempts to limit liability or applies caveats or conditions to something to free a business owner or corporation from responsibilities.

Disclosure—Submitting facts and details concerning a situation or business operation.

Disclosure schedule—A list of items that are disclosed. It can be taxes owed, a list of vehicles, legal claims or real estate owned. A purchase contract outlines what is to be disclosed on the schedules. It sounds easy, but it can be a lot of work and becomes a representation (*rep*) that the buyer relies on. Failure to disclose or false disclosure can be a source of serious damages against the seller. (See also: *reps and warrants.*)

Dispute over a contract

Due diligence—In contracts, it's the effort to verify information and to research the validity of documentation and material facts. It's a required standard of care that a professional is expected to maintain. Essentially, buyers review, audit, sample, and verify that the assets and liabilities as shown are accurate. Obviously, they are interested in finding items that aren't listed or recorded accurately. If they find something bad that they didn't expect, it's a *green weenie*!

Durable power of attorney—A legal document that transfers authority to someone, allowing him to conduct legal affairs on behalf of someone else.

Duty of care (or due care)—Exercising reasonable judgment and acting as a reasonable and prudent person would. It is the responsibility of a person who does business. In legal terms, a person who does not exercise *due care* can be guilty of negligence (referred to as the tort of negligence). (See also: *tort*.)

Earnest money—Amount of money that is paid to bind an agreement or offer. Depending on the agreed terms, the *earnest money* can go toward the purchase price, or it can be refunded if the purchase is not made; sometimes it's forfeited if the purchase isn't made.

Employee Retirement Income Security Act (ERISA)—Passed in 1974. It's a federal law requiring employers that offer this benefit to protect the retirement income of pension fund participants. The act sets minimum standards for eligibility, performance, investment selection, funding, and vesting of pension plans in the private sector but doesn't require an employer to offer a pension plan.

Employee stock ownership plan (ESOP)—A qualified retirement plan in which employees can receive common stock shares of the company for which they work. The company receives an investment tax credit for offering employees a *vested* interest in the company, plus it provides employees with an incentive to help increase profits. (See also: *vested*.)

Endowment insurance—A type of insurance that has an investment aspect in case the insured outlives the term of the policy. If he does, a value will be paid to him; but if he does not, the face value will be paid to his beneficiaries.

Environmental impact statement (EIS)—A statement that's required by federal law describing the effects that any actions (construction, demolition, renovation, etc.) may have on the environment and any alternative actions that can be followed because of the effects.

ERISA—(See: *Employee Retirement Income Security Act.*)

Escalator clause (also escalation clause)—A *clause* in a contract that passes cost increases on to another party, such as a labor contract that increases wages in conjunction with increases in the *cost of living*. It can also refer to a clause that increases compensation when levels of volume or performance increase. (See also: *cost of living adjustments*.)

ESOP—(See: *employee stock ownership plan.)*

Exclusivity clause—Tenants frequently ask for these when they want to be the only restaurant or nail salon, for instance, in a strip center or other real estate project. Also, in acquisitions and divestitures, buyers or sellers frequently ask for exclusivity clauses so they know they are the only person working on the proposed transaction. This prevents an "auction." It can be problematic for sellers, as they want lots of prospects considering the purchase.

FKA—Acronym for "formerly known as."

Forbearance agreement—It's much like a standstill agreement. A lender agrees to take no action, such as foreclosure, in return for something from the debtor, likely a fee. (See also: *standstill agreement.)*

Force majeure—A clause included in contracts to remove the liability of unforeseen and natural disasters that interrupt normal activities which could prevent parties to the contract from completing their responsibilities. In French, it's literally translated as "great force."

Foreign corporation—A corporation that does business in one state but is incorporated in a different state.

General partnership—A partnership where each partner is liable for all of the firm's debts. In addition, all of the partners are obligated to one another. (See also: *limited partnership* and *joint and several.)*

Going hard money—Proceeding with a binding financial commitment to a real estate transaction. Typically, money going hard is held in escrow, and when the required actions or diligence is complete, it goes hard.

Graduated lease—When rent is increased at predetermined intervals throughout the duration of the lease.

Grantor—A seller of real estate or a seller of stocks. (See also: *revocable trust.*)

Gross domestic product (GDP)—The total value of final goods and services in the economy during a given period (usually one year); indication of the strength of the economy.

Gross lease—Including insurance and taxes, the costs of maintaining the leased asset are paid by the lessor (landlord). (See also: *net lease, NNN* and *triple net.*)

Indemnify—To reimburse a loss or to guarantee protection from previous business conducted. In most business sales contracts, the buyer of the business requires the seller to *indemnify* the buyer from any loss that is due to certain activities (such as lawsuits, warranty claims, or other losses) that are a result of activities of the business when it was owned by the seller. (See also: *indemnity.*)

Indemnity—An amount paid to reimburse a loss or damages or to defend someone from damages. When one party offers *indemnity* to another party, they agree to defend that party and pay any damages resulting from the covered claim. Often, when a company sells out, the seller can't know all the repercussions that might come later, so the seller *indemnifies* the buyer for future claims which may arise later or those which were not disclosed. (See also: *indemnify.*)

Irrevocable—Can't be revoked, changed, or cancelled; not *callable.* (See also: *call.*)

Irrevocable trust—A trust that can't be changed at all once it is set up.

It's easier to get forgiveness than to ask for permission—This is so true. It's especially true when dealing with big companies or the government. Of course, you never want to break a law, but if it's "iffy," this saying applies. There is no upside to saying yes, only downside, so in order to cover their backsides, many employees in government or private companies just say no. They typically have no upside in granting permission, only downside.

> Do you know how much a **ton of money** weighs, or how much money it is? Amaze your friends with answers to such questions (yeah, sure), see page 59.

Joint and several—A loan term, meaning that both or either party is responsible in the event of a default. It really gives the lender 200 percent debt coverage assuming both parties are capable of repaying the loan.

Joint tenancy with right of survivorship (JTWROS)—Asset ownership for two or more persons in which each owner holds an equal share and may give away or sell that share without the permission of the other owner(s). Each person's share can be bequeathed to someone of his choosing in the event of his death.

Joint venture—A business that is undertaken by two or more people or companies, allowing them to share the risk and to benefit from the expertise of more than one person.

JTWROS—(See: *Joint tenancy with right of survivorship.*)

Lien—A claim against property (real estate or personal property) that gives the claimant an interest in the property until a debt is paid or duty is performed.

Limited liability—The liability of a firm's owners, which is an amount that is no greater than the amount of capital that they have invested in the business.

Limited liability company (LLC)—A hybrid form of a business which gives the company the *limited liability* that a corporation has, as well as the tax benefits of a partnership.

Limited partnership—A partnership in which some of the partners have a *limited liability* to the firm's creditors; the drawback is that the *limited partner* can't be involved in controlling the partnership.

Living document—A document that's intended to be revised continually in order to keep it updated.

Living trust—A trust that is created for the trustor and is administered by another party during the trustor's lifetime.

LOI—(See: *letter of intent.*)

Net lease—*Net leases* are quoted at a rate that requires the tenant to pay for taxes, insurance, and maintenance (the three Ns, net of taxes, net of insurance, net of maintenance). Generally speaking, the owner is not responsible for anything other than structural repairs. (See also: *gross lease.*)

NNN—(See: *net lease, triple net lease,* and *gross lease.*)

Non Solicitation clause—Typically found in purchase contracts, employment contracts or NDAs. This type of clause prohibits a party from soliciting employees or customers from another company. For instance, if a company is thinking about selling to a competitor, they wouldn't want the competitor as part of diligence to obtain contact information on its top salespeople, and then be able to attempt hiring them. In employment contracts, it limits a departing employee from taking others with him to his new job, or to a new company being formed.

Novation—Occurs when a new contract is substituted for an old one and the old one is terminated. This is typically utilized when there is a new party being substituted.

Operating lease—A *short-term lease* (such as that of a cable television connection box on a monthly basis) in which the lessee makes rental payments but the lessor retains ownership. An *operating lease* contrasts with a *capital lease* in which the lessee actually becomes the owner.

PEO—Acronym for *Professional Employer Organization.* This is a company that provides employees to another company. The employees include all HR personnel such as those who work in payroll, benefits management, training, and recruiting. The *PEO* acts as the employer. It's similar to an arrangement in which employees are leased. A *PEO* usually appeals to a small or mid-size company that does not want or can't afford an HR manager and full staff or simply doesn't want the associated responsibilities.

Pierce the corporate veil—Shareholders of a corporation usually have *limited liability*; however, if corporation assets are *commingled* or when there's gross negligence, that protection can be removed by the court. When this happens, the shareholders are responsible for paying the corporation's debts. (See also: *commingled.*)

Proprietor—The owner of a one-person business, also know as a sole *proprietor.*

Proxy—The written authority to act or speak in place of another party.

Punch list—A list of deficiencies which must be addressed to fulfill contractual obligations before *retainage* can be released or payment made. (See also: *retainage.)*

Quid pro quo—An equal exchange which one person or firm makes with another. It also is an express promise to do something, in exchange for something in return. (See also: *concurrent conditions.*)

Green Weenie meeting

Quorum—The minimum number of people necessary for action, usually in a board meeting. This number is defined in a partnership agreement, corporate bylaws, charter, etc. It is used less formally to mean that there is enough of a group to make a decision.

Retainage—Holding a percentage (typically 10 percent) of a periodic contract payment with the understanding that that portion will be paid out at the end of the contract, when all final *punch list* items and contract formalities are completed. (See also: *punch list.*)

Revocable trust—A trust that may be terminated or altered by the *grantor* or a trust that is created to terminate automatically on a specific date. (See also: *grantor.*)

S Box—(See: Sarbanes-Oxley Act)

S corporation—A closely held corporation that meets certain IRS requirements and has the benefit of being taxed as a partnership, yet maintains the *limited liability* of a corporation. Profits from an *S Corporation* flow through to the shareholders and are taxed at the shareholder level as opposed to a C Corporation, which taxes its earnings, then distributes profits which are taxed again at the shareholder level. *S Corps* are typically used only for small businesses, and have limits on the number of shareholders allowed. (See also: *limited liability.*)

Safe harbor—A regulation protecting individuals or corporations from the legal consequences of a certain action.

Sarbanes-Oxley Act—Legislation that regulates certain corporate financial activities and improves the accuracy of financial statements. Among other things, the act doesn't permit company loans to directors and officers that are for personal reasons. It requires that a firm's chief executive officer and chief financial officer certify financial statements. It protects employee whistle-blowers and increases criminal penalties for securities law violations. It also requires disclosure of off-balance-sheet financing and calls for improving the accuracy of *pro forma* financial statements.

See-through—Used in real estate, it refers to a completely unoccupied building—one that was built but never had any tenants, so you can see in one window and out the other on the opposite side of the building. In the bust days of the late 1980s, Dallas and Houston had many high-rise *see-through* office buildings.

Self-directed IRA—An individual retirement account that permits the owner to have wide latitude to choose types of assets and to control the investments within the account.

Severally and jointly—(See: *joint and several.*)

Shipment contract—A contract between a seller and buyer in which the seller's obligation is fulfilled as soon as the goods are shipped as long as an acceptable form of shipment was used. The terms in such a contract can have a direct effect on when payment is tendered as well.

Simplified employee pension plan (SEP)—A special type of joint Keogh plan, which is an individual retirement account created by employers for employees which permits contributions from each party. The *SEP* was developed in order to give small business a retirement plan option that's easier to establish and administer than traditional pension plans.

Spousal IRA—An individual retirement account that is in the name of a nonworking spouse.

Standstill agreement—Just what it sounds like. It's an agreement to do nothing. It can be with a lender who is not foreclosing, or it could be with a company who has agreed to standstill and not take an action until the agreed upon time or event occurs. (See also: *forbearance agreement.*)

Subrogation—A legal term used primarily in insurance. This is where one carrier pays a claim but then attempts to collect from another party whom they believe is at fault. For instance, a home insurer might pay a fire loss but when the fire marshal's report says that a defective water heater started the fire and that heater had been recalled by the manufacturer, the insurer will go after the water heater manufacturer for the loss. It can also be used where any party seeks damages from a third party.

Tort—Causing harm or injury to another person other than through a breach of contract; failing to act in a reasonable manner or failure to exercise *due care*. (See also: *due care.*)

Tortious interference—A third party's intentional and willful attempt to interfere with and/or break a contract between two parties, causing damage to the relationship between those parties.

Triggering event—A certain milestone or event in a qualified plan that a participant must experience to be eligible to receive a distribution. In business, it's an *event* that might *trigger* either a bonus or a default.

Triple net lease (net-net-net lease)—A lease in which the tenant pays for certain expenses which are traditionally the obligation of the landlord, such as maintenance, property taxes, and insurance. (See also: *NNN, gross lease,* and *net lease.*)

Trustee—An appointed institution or person that manages assets for the benefit of another.

Without recourse—Having no alternative for recovery against the other party in a transaction. If a mortgage is sold *without recourse* and the seller defaults, the buyer of the mortgage can't force the seller to purchase the mortgage back; therefore, the buyer is limited to any rights as the holder of the mortgage.

12

Business Planning, Acquisitions and Divestitures

Acquisitive binge—Something done by an out-of-control CEO, acquiring too many companies faster than they can be integrated into existing operation. (See also: *premature accumulation.*)

Allocation—How items are designated or assigned for tracking purposes. In the sale of a business, each of the assets is *allocated* a price. In other words, the sales price of the business is itemized and a price is applied to each asset or category of assets. The IRS requires an *allocation* of the purchase price upon the sale. The way the sales price is allocated will generally affect the buyer's and seller's taxes. It's always preferable, and usually mandated at closing, that both parties agree to and sign the allocation statement. For instance, if you buy a business for $50,000, the buyer and seller might assign a value of $8,000 to the forklift and $42,000 to inventory (the only other asset). If the seller has a net book value of $6,000 on the forklift, he will likely owe long-term capital gains taxes on $2,000 worth of income since it was sold for more than book value. Buyers and sellers typically have different goals in such allocations, so it can be more contentious than one might think.

Asset sale—The sale of a business in which the seller transfers the title of all assets (not shares of stock in the company) to the buyer. This type of sale is different from a *stock sale* in that the liabilities (known or unknown) of the corporation are generally not transferred. (See also: *stock sale.*)

Asset stripper or stripping—This person determines whether the value of a company is worth more purchased as a whole or divided into separate assets to be sold off. This usually occurs in order to fulfill debt agreements. By *stripping*, one selects assets to sell from an acquired company in order to raise money to pay off some of the debt that was incurred by financing the acquisition.

Basket—In acquisitions, items are divided and then placed into these. It typically refers to liability items. For example, all environmental liabilities might be placed in one *basket* while all inventory reductions or other charges might be placed in another *basket* unless those items exceed X amount of dollars, in which case, they get charged back to the seller. A *basket* is similar to a file folder you set up for one type of email.

Bear hug—When a company is under consideration for an acquisition, this type of buyout offer is so advantageous that the stockholders of the company being considered want to accept it, because the price is much higher than the market price and is paid in cash.

Benchmark—When companies study other companies, which are usually in the same industry, to obtain performance standards by which they can compare and measure their own performance. This is helpful in setting guidelines, objectives, and goals. Benchmarks are also used internally, and are a great tool of measuring improvement.

Blue sky—An intangible value of a business which is aside from the tangible assets; it's what someone is willing to pay for its reputation or goodwill in addition to the other items, because any item is worth what someone is willing to pay for it. In a transaction of the sale of a business, this added value is determined by the seller at his discretion and can't be allocated a price by an accountant because it can't be compared to any other asset. Each business has its own unique added value which equals the difference between what a company's stock is worth and what a seller feels that it's worth. For instance, if the net value of the assets is $50,000 but the seller wants $100,000 for the business including those assets, the seller is asking $50,000 for the *blue sky*. It's called *blue sky* since it goes on forever, can't be touched or held and can be valued very subjectively. (See also: *FASB goodwill* and *intangible asset*.)

Bridge—In planning, it's an explanation, usually visual with charts, supported by data, showing how you get from one point to another. For instance, if you were projecting sales to increase from $100,000 to $150,000, the graph would show each of the product lines that contribute to the sales increase. If you are projecting big expense reductions in headcount, the *bridge* might show how much would be cut in dollars for each month, plus an actual list of names to be laid off. The *bridge* allows and forces accountability and instills confidence in the plan. (See also: *bridge loan*.)

Business broker—Locates buyers for sellers and sellers for buyers. Generally *business brokers* are paid finding fees (flat amounts) by the buyers and/or commissions (percentage of the transaction price) by the sellers for assisting in the closing of the transaction between the buyer and seller, coordinating negotiations and coordinating the communications.

Caveat emptor—This connotes that the seller is not liable and will not take responsibility, so the buyer takes on the potential liabilities. Latin for "let the buyer beware."

Caveat venditor—The seller can be liable. Latin for "let the seller beware."

Character-building project—A project that is almost certainly going to fail, but is assigned to someone who is being punished, or needs a tough job in order to learn the ropes.

Clustering—Similar companies (or companies that target a similar customer demographic) that are located in close proximity to one other.

Confirmatory vs. exploratory—Used in acquisitions or divestitures where buyers are *looky-loos*, and there is a need to understand how serious they are before giving them sensitive information. If they are just *exploring*, they may not be given much information, but if they become serious and perhaps even tender a term sheet, they would be *confirmatory* (meaning they want to confirm the assets or other information). If all goes well, they are likely to close on terms similar to those outlined on the term sheet. In almost all cases, both *exploratory and confirmatory*, the following step would be to sign a NDA (non-disclosure agreement). (See also: *looky loo*.)

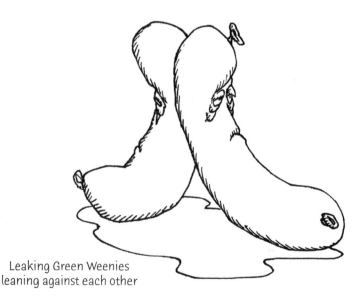

Leaking Green Weenies
leaning against each other

Core competencies—Key technologies, skills, or other competitive qualities that form the foundation of a company's business activities. (See also: *stick to your knitting.*)

Cost/benefit—An analysis that compares the *cost* of doing something relative to the *benefit*. If the cost is high and the benefit is low, it doesn't get done. Manufacturers use this routinely. For example, I had to analyze whether getting Gahan Wilson to create the art for this book would make it better, and if making it better would generate more sales, and, if so, how much those sales would be. Also, I had to analyze how many illustrations I should put in the book. Not enough and the book doesn't sell well, just enough and it's a good trade off. I am sure Gahan would have been willing to draw as many as I would pay for, but unless that generates more sales, it wouldn't make financial sense (although we are all hungry to see more of his work). Eventually, too much art would have cost too much, and there would have been a diminishing return for me.

CSI—(See *customer service/satisfaction index*)

Customer service/satisfaction index (CSI)—Statistical measurement of products and services and the degree to which they currently fulfill customer expectations and needs.

Data room—In acquisitions or divestitures, where there are buyers coming to look at the company and they all need common data, the seller creates a *data room*. Here they place all documents, legal, financial, and otherwise, for the prospective buyer to review. The seller then only has to produce one set of documents, and can also control who sees them, when, and which ones do (or don't!) get copied.

Divestiture—Sale, liquidation, or spin-off of a division, assets or a subsidiary.

Earn-out—Provision in an acquisition agreement. The acquiring company agrees to make additional payments to the seller or specified employees if certain performance-based goals are reached; may be related to the balance sheet, earnings statement, or cash flow. It can also be applied to an employee who has to earn some additional compensation in order to get the total amount of earnings they want.

Exit strategy—The method that a venture capitalist or business owner intends to use to release himself from an investment that he made; also an executive's plan for how and when he will leave the business.

Fishing expedition—An informal, inquisitive, exploratory action to evaluate the potential of an undeveloped project.

Golden crumbs—Tiny market niches ignored by the big companies.

> Did you get **de-horsed** the last time you bought a car? How is that possible, you don't even own a horse? Or do you? See page 96 to know for sure.

Hardball—Serious and aggressive competition, borrowed from baseball terminology. If you want to be successful, be prepared to play *hardball.*

Integration—The difficult task of merging two companies and/or absorbing a new acquisition. Many have failed at successful *integration,* and the process always seems to take more time and money than planned. Of course, as part of the merger of two companies, many similar management and sales positions can be eliminated, causing stress for almost everyone. It's just the opposite of *plug and play.* (See also: *plug and play.*)

Jettisoning—To discard something unwanted or burdensome, usually a division, plant, or product line.

Letter of intent—A written statement outlining key points or terms in the possible business acquisition. This document includes explanations about any real estate to be transferred, whether it is a stock sale or an asset sale, terms of seller financing, the purchase price, the down payment amount, what if any liabilities will be assumed, any key employees to be retained, etc. (See also: *LOI.*)

Live within our means—Describes what all companies must do to survive. Expenses must match revenues. For Donald Trump, living within his means might mean always being chauffeured in a limousine, while for most business owners, limousines simply aren't allowed because that would be living beyond their means. It's frequently used in a turnaround where deep cuts are needed in order for the owners to live *within their means.*

Niche—Specific area in which one may excel or a specific market one may target that is best for a particular firm. For instance, a *niche* might be working on just import cars vs. all cars or maybe even Toyotas only.

Operating metrics—Basic company and staff performance measures, synonymous with *KPIs*. The term has nothing to do with the Metric Measuring System and everything to do with common sense methods to gauge costs, output, efficiency, productivity, etc. The key ratings are similar, but the formulas can be customized for every company. My first book, *How to Salvage Millions from Your Small Business*, detailed the need to use them. Most mom-and-pop operators don't use many; they rely on their hands-on management and intuition. However, in order to grow, and especially to operate multiple locations, their use is critical. (See also: *gauge, KPIs* and *driving without a dashboard.*)

Paradigm—The general concept or belief about how things are or should be, the set of rules or procedures that are usually followed, an understood state that has certain expected parameters for operating, or conventional thinking which is most common. A *paradigm* can be thought of as the unwritten rules for a situation. To break out of the *paradigm* is to be *outside the box*. We all know some *paradigm*. For instance, in the auto recycling business, for years the *paradigm* was to bring a car in and remove parts off of it as they were sold. The new *paradigm*, which evolved in the late 1980s, was to bring car in and pull off all those parts that likely would sell, stocking them ready for customers to pick up. Today, computers go one step further; they use demand planning, comparing factors such as how many parts are in stock, how many were sold in a previous period, how many times they were requested and we did or didn't have them in stock, how long we have had them in stock or had them in stock before they sold, and how much they sold for. This lets us predict whether we need to remove the part and even tells us how much to ask for it. (See also: *paradigm shift* and *outside the box*.)

Paradigm shift—When technology or social values change, sometimes the unwritten rules for a situation will change also. (See also: *paradigm*.)

Path forward—The next steps or assignments, usually as a result of planning meetings.

Perquisites—Perks; an expense in addition to wages or salary from the company that is at the sole discretion of the owner.

Proration—The division of a cost or of a benefit between the buyer and seller. It is usually related to the time value it has to each. Property taxes would be prorated based on the date of closing with the seller paying the amount for the portion of the year that he owned the property and the buyer pays only the portion for the rest of the year.

Vicious cycle

Recycled meeting—A meeting to discuss the last meeting and the path forward.

Re-investable earnings—Earnings that are good enough to service debt and provide owners with a profit; the earnings left over are *re-investable* and can be used to grow the business.

Reps and warrants—Representations and warranties; these are promises that are made in a contract. When the contract is executed there are representations that are factual statements, and warrantees or guarantees are made ensuring that the statements are true. This can, and usually does, apply to both parties. (See also: *disclosure schedule.*)

Ring fence—The action a company takes to quarantine a newly acquired company until it no longer poses a risk to the acquirer's existing business.

Segue—(Pronounced seg-way.) A path to a similar subject or logical transition into that subject.

Surgical infusion—An infusion of money in the form of capital or debt which is designated for a very specific use, and only that use.

Synergy—When a merger occurs (between companies, departments or people) and the potential for profits of the new entity is greater than the potential for profits that the individual parts had before the merger. Also, when something has an *accretive* effect, it has *synergy. Synergies* are often touted but are very elusive. (See also: *accretive.*)

Transparency—When information is disclosed fully, accurately, and in a timely manner. The term implies that the information is available for all to see.

War games—Describes the process of testing and troubleshooting an initiative. Someone plays the *devil's advocate* to challenge the thinking and math driving the plan. (See also: *play devil's advocate, pressure test* and *stress test.*)

Index

We Want To Hear From You!

Do you have "things in the drawer" for us?

How about a free copy of the book, or credit in the next edition?

Do you know some clever or classic expressions we've missed? Help us make future editions even better. We want to hear from you!

Go to **www.greenweenies.com** and give us proposed entries for the next edition! Each month we will select the top submissions and list them on our web site.

Send us your proposed Green Weenie. If your submission is selected it will be listed along with your name on our web site and may be included in the next edition.

YOUR CHOICE . . .

Get a free copy of
Green Weenies and Due Diligence
—or your name in the next edition!

For every 20 new terms, (with definitions) that we can consider for use in the next edition, we will send you a **FREE autographed copy!** If they haven't already been submitted by others and we can use them, you will get a free book or if you prefer, we will list you in acknowledgments for new terms in the next edition!

Legal Disclaimer All terms or suggestions sent to *Green Weenies* and Due Diligence via the Web site, e-mail, post, fax and any other method become the property of Ron Sturgeon or *Green Weenies and Due Diligence* and can be reproduced without prior permission.

The Works of Gahan Wilson

How to be a Guilty Parent by Glenn Collins; illustrations by Gahan Wilson — 1983

Is Nothing Sacred? — 1982

Playboy's Gahan Wilson — 1980

Animals, Animals, Animals: A Collection of Great Animal Cartoons; Edited by George Booth, Gahan Wilson, and Ron Wolin — 1979

Nuts — 1979

". . . and Then We'll Get Him!" — 1978

Upside-down Man by Russell Baker; illustrations by Gahan Wilson — 1977

First World Fantasy Awars; edited by Gahan Wilson — 1977

Harry and the Sea Serpent — 1976

Granny's Fish Story by Phyllis Lefarge; illustrations by Gahan Wilson — 1975

Bang Bang Family — 1974

Catch Your Breath: A Book of Shivery Poems; illustrations by Gahan Wilson — 1973

Harry the Fat Bear Spy — 1973

Playboy's Gahan Wilson — 1973

The Future of Hooper Toote by Felice Holman; illustrations by Gahan Wilson — 1972

Matthew Looney and the Space Pirates by Jerome Beatty Jr.; illustrations by Gahan Wilson — 1972

I Paint What I See — 1971

Good Luck Spider and Other Bad Luck Stories; illustrations by Gahan Wilson — 1970

Matthew Looney In the Outback by Jerome Beatty Jr.; illustrations by Gahan Wilson — 1969

The Man in the Cannibal Pot — 1967

Soda-Pop Stretcher by Bob Fulton; illustrations by Gahan Wilson — 1963

Matthew Looney's Voyage to the Earth by Jerome Beatty Jr.; illustrations Gahan Wilson — 1961

Green Weenies and Due Diligence
Makes a great corporate (or personal) gift!

Are you tired of giving fruit baskets during the holidays,
or handing out pens and coffee cups to prospects?
A corporate gift should meet several tests:

1. **It should have permanent value.** If your customers are like me, they get so many fruit baskets and food gifts that they give most of them away.

   How about a gift that is treasured, passed around and reminds your customers of you?

2. **It should be personalized and impressive.**

   How about a gift with your firm's name on the cover of a professional hardbound book, with dust cover? We can also put your company information on the dust cover flaps!

3. **It should cost less than typical gifts, but appear to cost as much or more.**

   How about a gift with a high perceived value, but a much lower cost than your other typical gifts?

4. **It should be educational, and entertaining.**

   How about a gift that is educational but also makes you laugh out loud?

5. **The premium gift abridged edition is G-rated with over 200 pages of entertaining and educational material.**

Green Weenies and Due Diligence abridged, G-Rated, Premium Gift Edition does all of these things! Over 200 pages of terms, with illustrations by Gahan Wilson will entertain and educate. And likely for a cost MUCH less than the gifts you typically give! Give them to customers, employees, prospects, even vendors! Any sophisticated business associate will love this gift! We also offer the unabridged edition (the book you currently have), with over 300 pages and full index as a premium gift. Whether you choose the G-rated abridged edition or the unabridged version, recipients will appreciate you and your firm!

We are now taking orders for *Green Weenies and Due Diligence,* and want to personalize it with your firm's name on the cover, and can even include your company information on the cover flaps! We can personalize it however you like, so you can use it year round or for other occasions! You will be surprised at the low cost on quantity orders.

Email orders@greenweenies.com for more
information, orders and credit terms.

Your customers will love this gift;
it promises to be the best one you've ever given!

Visit **www.*greenweenies*.com** for the latest Green Weenie, and to register for a free weekly Green Weenie with a fabulous Gahan Wilson illustration via email.

Don't forget to tell your friends about
Green Weenies and Due Diligence!

About the Author

Ron Sturgeon is a successful entrepreneur and the author of *How to Salvage Millions From Your Small Business*. After finding a following in the U.S., the book—which is now in its second printing—has been licensed and printed in Korea, China, and the Czech Republic.

Ron, whose rags-to-riches story began in the auto salvage business right out of high school, is a sought-after speaker and consultant for small business owners. In 2004, he was the keynote speaker at three international conventions, including two in Australia. His unique story of personal development and success is inspiring, and his motto is "mission possible." He especially likes speaking to students and other developing small business owners, sharing tips to his success, and challenging them to  be whatever they want to be. In addition, he has expanded his expertise to real estate development and is a noted collector of fine automobiles and antique toy cars.

Sturgeon seems an unlikely candidate to write *Green Weenies and Due Diligence*, or even know the terms. His dad died when he was a senior in high school, and left to fend for himself with only a high school education, he went on to build one of the largest operations in his industry, the auto salvage business, which he sold to Ford Motor Company in 1999. He later founded and sold another business to a large public company, while building a small real estate empire, starting a small business consulting practice, and completed two in-house over subscribed stock offerings. Throughout the last six years, he patiently gathered the terms found in the book.

Ron and his wife, Kathi, live in Texas with their three beloved Cavalier King Charles Spaniels. To learn more about him, visit www.rdsinvestments.com.

About the Artist

Gahan Wilson's work has appeared in everything from *Playboy* and *The New Yorker* magazines to children's books. Now, the inimitable artist enters the business realm with *Green Weenies and Due Diligence*, his first opportunity to bring his bizarre sense of humor into the boardroom. Wilson's all-new cartoons only confirm that the business world is, indeed, a logically illogical land—and that's something Wilson knows a thing or two about. During the past 25 years, he has mastered the art of macabre humor and, in addition to his collections of cartoons and illustrations, has written two mystery novels and a number of horror short stories.

self portrait

> "I very much enjoyed both doing the drawings for
> this book and finding out that business people are
> just as weird as cartoonists!"
> — Gahan Wilson

Want to know how to get even more out of ~~your~~ business?
Any!

Pick up your copy of

How to Salvage Millions from Your Small Business,

also by Ron Sturgeon

co-author D.L. Fitzpatrick.

Tells How to Supercharge Your Business with Savvy Tips

How to Salvage Millions From Your Small Business is a book by two highly successful auto salvage operators. Both men recently sold their businesses to a Fortune 500 auto manufacturer. The book shares their secrets to achieving significant success in an industry not often considered for such accomplishment.

Author Ron Sturgeon says, "This book is not theory. It is a practical 'how-to' guide by men who have actually done it and want to tell other business owners how to also." Co-author D.L. Fitzpatrick joins Sturgeon by sharing his insights and experience learned from three generations of a family-run business that he also sold to the automotive giant.

The book will help any small business person learn the fundamentals required to achieve financial rewards. Twelve chapters cover topics ranging from gathering metrics, bench-marking against internal operations and competitors, how to use networking and personal electronic organizers to improve productivity, and how to work with bankers.

Especially valuable are 160 practical tips, plus an action item section prodding readers into action. The book brings fresh first-hand insights to those small business owners who want a down-to-earth, easy-to-read book packed with simple implementable ideas.

See the following page for ordering information

Order Form

ONLINE ORDERS:	www.GreenWeenies.com
FAX ORDERS:	817–838–8477
TELEPHONE ORDERS:	817–999–0980 (have your credit card ready.)
E-MAIL ORDERS:	orders@GreenWeenies.com
POSTAL ORDERS:	5940 Eden Fort Worth, Texas 76117

Products

TITLE	PRICE	QUANTITY	SUBTOTAL
Green Weenies and Due Diligence	$28.95	_____	_____
Also available as a Premium Gift Please inquire about quantity, pricing and customized covers.			
How to Salvage Millions from Your Small Business	$14.95	_____	_____
	Sales Tax*		_____
	Shipping & Handling**		_____
	TOTAL		_____

*Sales Tax: Please add 8.25% tax for products shipped to Texas addresses.

**Shipping and Handling: (US) Add $4 for first product and $1 for each additional product.
Call for international pricing

Shipping

Name: _____

Address: _____

City, State Zip: _____

Telephone: _____

E-mail address: _____

Payment

❏ Check enclosed   ❏ VISA   ❏ MasterCard

Card Number _____

Exp. Date _____

Security Code _____

Signature _____

Name on card _____

Billing Address _____